Twelve Years

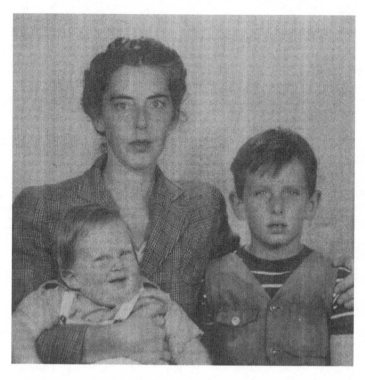

Alma's passport picture with Joel and Stefan, 1948

TWELVE YEARS

An American Boyhood in East Germany

JOEL AGEE

The University of Chicago Press
Chicago and London

The University of Chicago Press, Chicago 60637
The University of Chicago Press, Ltd., London
Copyright © 1975, 1980, 1981 by Joel Agee
All rights reserved. Originally published 1981 by Farrar, Straus and Giroux
University of Chicago Press edition 2000
Printed in the United States of America
05 04 03 02 01 00   6 5 4 3 2 1

Photographs courtesy of Joel Agee

Portions of this book first appeared in *Harper's*, *Marxist Perspectives*, and *The New Yorker*

Library of Congress Cataloging-in-Publication Data

Agee, Joel.
    Twelve years : an American boyhood in East Germany / Joel Agee.
        p. cm.
    ISBN 0-226-01050-3 (alk. paper)
    1. Agee, Joel—Childhood and youth. 2. Americans—Germany (East)—
Biography. 3. Americans—Germany (East)—Social life and customs.
I. Title.

DD78.A52 A33 2000
943'.10875'092—dc21
[B]

                                                                    99-086396

∞The paper used in this publication meets the minimum requirements of
the American National Standard for Information Sciences—Permanence of
Paper for Printed Library Materials, ANSI Z39.48-1992.

For Gina, my daughter

I wish to acknowledge the help of the Virginia Center for the Creative Arts in providing a place to work under ideal conditions. I owe thanks as well to the PEN American Center for granting me a loan at a time of pressing financial need; to William Maxwell for his generous encouragement, and for his assistance in editing an early version of this material; to my wife, Susan, and to my friends Joseph Caldwell, Bob Karwowski, Joyce Milton, and Ed Terrien for reading the manuscript with care and offering many helpful suggestions. And I am especially grateful to Michael di Capua, my editor, for the unstinting gift of his time and skill.

J.A.

Everything in this book is true, but not everything is precisely factual. While none of the events described are fictitious, I have taken liberties of fiction to disguise the identity of most characters outside my immediate family: I have changed names, I have transposed heads, bodies, attitudes. Place names have occasionally been altered for the same reason. Here and there, I chose to imagine the nuance of a gesture or look or utterance rather than bore the reader with repeated complaints about my spotty recollection. By far the greater part of my story, though, is faithful to the facts and their chronology. Foremost among my intentions, throughout the book, was finding the right word, the right phrase and image, to render as honestly as I could the essential atmosphere, conflicts, and hopes of those twelve years as I remember them.

The four of us—Joel, Alma, Stefan,
and Bodo—in Ahrenshoop, 1951

1948-1955

———

Joel, ca. 1948

Stefan, ca. 1949

Alma and Bodo in Berlin,
early 1950s

Joel, ca. 1953

I went to live in East Germany with my family when I was eight years old. Because no direct connection was available, my mother, my stepfather, my brother Stefan, and I sailed from Mexico (where we had been living) to Leningrad, on a Russian freighter, the *Dmitry Donskoy*. My first, passing glimpse of Germany was from the deck of this ship, as it slowly nosed its way through the Nord-Ostsee-Kanal, guided by a short man in a black raincoat, who, to my surprise, was called a pilot.

On the bank, running alongside the ship, was a band of boys about my age, and they were shouting in Russian: "Comrades! Comrades! Give us cigarettes!" The sailors threw packs of cigarettes into the water and the boys dashed in after them. One officer wrapped a chain around a large carton of cigars, hoping to get it all the way to the shore that way, but it fell short and sank, and the boys dove for it in vain; by the time they caught up with us again we had reached the open sea. How I admired them—their independence, evinced not only by the absence of supervising adults but by their familiarity with tobacco; the way they had all that territory to themselves, that tall grass and deep water!

Stefan was two then. I see him sitting in the middle of the canvas-covered hatch, naked, pink, and fat, toying with the pale-blue tip of his button-like penis, while

Alma (Stefan and I always called our parents by their first names, Bodo and Alma) sits reading a book, her long, black hair flying in the wind. Why do I have such a hard time remembering Bodo then? It's almost as if he wasn't there. Maybe he was absent a lot, writing his novel about the men and women who fought the Nazis in Germany.

The ship's cargo was rosin—a detail I would almost certainly have forgotten if Alma, who played the viola, hadn't asked the first mate whether he could bring her a piece or two. We watched him climb into the hold and select, among crates and crates of rosin, a fist-sized, amber-colored chunk which Alma was still using to rosin her bow shortly before we left Germany twelve years later.

The first mate and Alma liked each other. They talked a lot about music, especially Beethoven. I kept hearing him pronounce that name with a rasping *h*, accompanied by a gesture that seemed to indicate the possibility of a heart sailing in the air. His English was minimal, and he had a tendency to say the opposite of what he meant. For example, when Alma, shortly after our departure, discovered that she hadn't packed any lipstick—an indispensable accoutrement—she asked the first mate whether lipstick could be bought in Leningrad. "Impossible!" he said, with a bright smile and eagerly affirmative nod.

Once Alma and Bodo and I were invited to the first mate's cabin: the radio was going to play something by Beethoven. After much painful tuning, the first mate zeroed in on the station, but the reception was bad, the music kept wafting in and disappearing. No matter: for Alma and the first mate, Beethoven was bliss, as much of him as could be heard. What did Bodo do or say? I can't remember, though I know he was there. I imagine him stroking the bristles on his cheek and smiling and blinking rapidly, bemused by Alma's enthusiasm; or paying close attention to the music, deepening the dou-

ble vertical fold between his eyes, supporting his brow
with three fingers, while his cigarette smoldered in an
ashtray; or maybe he was jealous.

Alma and I liked to lie face down on the bow, watching the ship's nose heave up and plunge down into the
turquoise waves. Sometimes dolphins swam alongside
us for hours, tumbling and leaping and, it seemed, taking enormous delight in the churning foam tossed up by
the bow. Occasionally a flying fish would soar onto the
deck and flop there, soundlessly gasping, until someone
threw it back into the sea. Once, sitting on the toilet
(right next to the motor room, it shook and jangled like a
collection tin), I saw, thanks to a deep sliding lurch of the
ship and an accidental leftward glance, a dolphin in the
precise moment of its curved leap out of the water,
framed by the porthole's perfect circle, like a heraldic
sign.

Bodo, did you play with me on that ship? Did we
talk? We must have. I don't want to betray you by a
trick of memory. Now I remember one night when you
came out of your distance to touch me, to comfort me,
to let me know that you loved me. Somehow news
reached us, in the middle of the ocean, that Egon Kisch
had died—could it have been on the radio? Or maybe
you knew it before we embarked, but didn't mention it
until that balmy evening under a full moon and a wild
star-strewn sky, so solemnly, as if it had happened just
then. Kisch with his big face and big belly was dead.
Kisch the magician with the mysteriously capacious
nostrils into which he stuffed cigarettes and pencils,
Kisch the storyteller, Kisch with the pretty poem—
"Come out, my darling, come out, my duck, come into
the garden, I'll give you a flower"—that for some reason
made women blush and laugh and pretend to be mad. I
cried, and you comforted me. You seemed surprised by
my grief, and questioned me about it. You were touched
by my answer: "Kisch was my friend," and you never
forgot it. But I remember my own surprise at how suffi-

cient these words seemed to you (since I'd come up
with them only for lack of a better explanation), and
how they seemed to seal our communion so that it
lasted until deep into the night. What did I know about
the reason for the strangely sweet sadness I felt? Did it
have to do with Kisch at all, any more than with the brave
throbbing hum of the ship's motor, the rush and swish
of the spray, my hand in my stepfather's hand, the dignity and candor of the late hour?

No matter how often I've cast out the net for memories of our fellow passengers, and of the captain and
the officers, at whose table the passengers ate, I haven't
managed to haul in more than a few impressions: the
sonorous rumble of Russian speech, and the peculiar
throatiness of the women's voices; gold stripes on the
sleeves of a broad-chested regal presence (the captain?); and this image connects, for some reason, with
hard chunks of chocolate ("Don't chew it!") placed on
the tongue to sweeten the tea as it's sipped; a couple
who lived in the cabin above us and had a habit of
pouring the contents of their chamber pot out of their
porthole and, thanks to the wind, into ours; a pasty-
faced corpulent woman walking past us on deck with a
smile and suspicious eyes; a thin, black-haired, twelve-
year-old girl who avoided me ("a real beauty," my parents said, and I thought: So *that's* what a real beauty
looks like); a bald man whose jaw cracked when he
chewed; a frail, frightened-looking German woman who
shared our cabin and irritated my parents by constantly
doing one of three things: washing her hands, eating
dietary crackers, and patting her face to forestall the
aging process.
    The crew slept and ate at the diametrically opposite
end of the ship: they had hammocks, not beds, tin
bowls instead of plates. Several men lived in a small
room, just like people in Mexico. "Are the sailors *pe-
ones?*" My parents explained that although the sailors

worked hard and had less than the officers and than we had, it was different from Mexico, where the rich took away from the poor, and the poor were much poorer and had to work much harder, and the rich were much richer than here. In fact, there were no rich people here. "But are the sailors poor?" "No, not really." That's Bodo's voice I'm remembering. The way he said, "No, not really," meant: yes and no, they are and they aren't poor, but they're not poor more than they are. It was puzzling to be answered like that (but instructive, I think now). In later years, this vagueness, this entrenchment of his (so it seemed to me) in ambivalence and ambiguity, made me angry. Can't he give me a straight answer? Why doesn't he take me seriously? But what Bodo couldn't take seriously, I believe, was logic—not in everyday life. History, politics, and philosophy—that was a different matter, there a rigorous logic held sway, there the problem facing the mind was to penetrate through the fog of opinion to the truth, which was like a mathematical theorem, like the structure of crystals he loved to read about. That simple, that clear. And indisputable.

The Baltic Sea impressed me as completely different from the Atlantic: it was gray, not blue, and much rougher. There were no dolphins, no flying fish. You could lean against the wind here. If you faced the wind and opened your mouth, it would make a howling sound, as if in a cavern.

An atmosphere of happy expectancy developed among the crew as we approached Leningrad. They seemed to be working less. The cook, of whom until then we had seen only his perfectly bald pate through a vent that led from the deck to the kitchen, surfaced with an accordion, and some of the sailors danced during their lunch breaks, either in pairs (one man impersonating the coy blushing maiden, waving a kerchief in the air, the other prancing in sidelong pursuit with his hands on his hips) or taking turns at kicking up their legs from a squatting position, or whirling, or doing cartwheels, while the onlookers roared with laughter, clapped, and cheered. Some men had their hair cut by the carpenter (who, incidentally, built Stefan and me a fine swing, which we took with us to Germany). The sailors suggested Stefan and I have our heads shaved. I said no, because I had had an unpleasant experience with baldness in Mexico when I was six, having insisted, against everyone's advice, on having my head shaved so I would resemble the street urchins whom I admired. A bald gringo, I learned, is something faintly ridiculous, and until my hair grew back I had to submit to occasional taunting cries of "*Pelón!*" But Stefan wanted very much to be bald, and the first mate assured our parents that bald children were common in Leningrad. The carpenter soaped Stefan's head, carefully applied the razor (I winced at the sight of it), and off came Stefan's red-gold locks. Now he looked like the cook. The cook took Stefan by the hand, and together, fat, bald, and blue-eyed, they posed for the first mate's camera.

More and more seagulls came squawking for food.

One day, around dawn, the first mate knocked on our cabin door and announced with an excited voice: "The Soviet Union is here!" We put bathrobes and coats over our pajamas, bundled Stefan up in a blanket, and hurried outside. A fairy-tale city had risen up out of the sea. Looking at the map today, I can't decide which of several Latvian or Estonian cities it most probably was. The houses, all white and bathed in the pink light of dawn, were built on a hill, so that they seemed to pile up one above the other, and above all the houses stood squat towers supporting what I now readily call onion-shaped domes—but then I had no words for what I saw. Some of these domes were golden, and caught fire in the rising sun; others were purple or pink, and one, if my memory doesn't deceive me, was striped in several colors.

Why do I remember Alma standing next to me on my right, wrapped in a bathrobe and carrying Stefan in her arms, her face radiant, while Bodo's presence, though known for a fact, has left only a spectral impression? Maybe because she gave words to her feelings and mine ("Oh, it's glorious! It's like a dream!") while Bodo said nothing.

When the ship dropped anchor in Leningrad, the crew had a party. Their relatives had come to greet them on the pier, and the officers allowed them to come on board so the women could dance with their husbands and sons for a while before the work of unloading began. All the passengers except us were allowed to disembark; I remember our cabinmate washing her hands for the last time after shaking my parents' hands and hugging me and Stefan goodbye. The customs officer had found Bodo's German manuscript suspicious; someone would have to read it and confirm Bodo's contention that it was an anti-Fascist novel. We went to the crew's mess hall, where the party was. Someone had brought a phonograph and some tinny-sounding waltzes and polkas. Alma went back to the cabin to fetch her New Orleans jazz records. Three or four officers stood by like parents watching their cavorting children in a sandbox, while Louis Armstrong's voice rang through the mess hall: "_Oh_, you _could_n't catch _me_ with a _auto_mo-_bile_," and the dancing sailors attempted to jitterbug with their kerchiefed womenfolk.

Fortunately, it wasn't necessary to subject Bodo's novel to a detailed analysis, which conceivably could have taken weeks. Someone trustworthy was found (perhaps one of the small group of German anti-Fascist intellectuals who spent the war years in the Soviet Union) who could vouch for Bodo's reliability.

Just a moment ago, no amount of probing and listening inward would yield more than could be told in a

sentence or two about our stay in Leningrad; but suddenly pictures emerge: a golden dome, a thin silver
spire, and my questions: "Is it real gold? Real silver?"
and my marveling at the preciousness of a whole roof
plated with gold, and at its beauty, too; the hotel where
we stayed, the vast height of its dining room, the
English-speaking family with the small belligerent boy
who kept throwing food over his shoulder at mealtimes;
the chandeliers, the widening slope of lilac-carpeted
steps down which every day a broad-shouldered,
thickly bearded priest descended in floor-length robes;
a cleaning woman calling down to a colleague from those
same steps, and my discovery that the Russian *L* is pronounced very much like the English, and unlike the
Spanish *L*; a grandiose statue of a man on a rearing horse,
and the name of the street where it stood: Nevsky Prospect; ruins, whole streets and blocks of ruins, and people
clearing ruins, stacking up bricks; a visit to a historical
museum where a miniature Lenin could be seen reading a
miniature book in a miniature house; a woman on the
street shouting directions into Bodo's ear because she
could not comprehend that some people don't speak Russian, and thought he must be deaf; the Winter Palace (the
name pleased me more than the building) and (very
vague, this one) the half-sunken *Aurora*, whose crew, the
guide told us, had started the revolution (but the ship
looked dark and ugly to me, not at all interesting); a
men's room in a park where instead of toilets there were
stinking holes over which the men squatted and conversed while they shat; people playing volleyball in that
same park; a large group of skinny-looking men in gray
uniforms—some of them very tall and others very short—
getting off several trucks at some distance from where
Alma, Bodo, Stefan, and I were strolling. These men assembled in a long row of two abreast (here's where their
unequal height became apparent) and marched off to
the rhythmic screech of a whistle. Only then did I notice the soldiers guarding them with submachine guns.

Later we learned that what we had seen was a group of German prisoners being taken to some place where they would help clear away ruins. I remember Alma saying that this was only fair and just, since these same men had helped destroy Leningrad and other cities. I don't know what Bodo's feelings were, but I can imagine that he must have thought of these guilty and unfortunate compatriots with intensely conflicting emotions.

I remember also some stories about the war told in English by a Russian woman whose face and clothes just barely subsist in my memory, like vapors, but whose words I can still hear as clearly as if they were spoken yesterday: "It was frightful. There was blood in the streets, it flowed like a river, this high. We were so hungry we ate rats and mice. Some people even ate corpses."

Then there was Irina, a young girl who was learning English in school and who developed a great fondness for us, especially for Alma. When Bodo asked Irina what she wanted to be, she said: "A Communist." Her mother and her sister had been raped and murdered before her eyes by German soldiers. From then on, her grandmother took care of her. There wasn't a day when the Germans didn't hang someone from a lamp post. Once Irina's grandmother was summoned to report to the German authorities, and was gone for many hours. Irina, terrified that she might have been hanged, sat in a corner of a courtyard, crying and crying. Two German soldiers came along, and Irina screamed louder. One of the soldiers pulled out his gun to shoot her, but when the other pushed back Irina's kerchief and pointed to her blond hair, he put away his gun.

"Do you hate Germans?" Bodo asked. No, she knew there were good Germans as well as bad, just as there were bad Russians. It wasn't like that with the Jews, who were *all* bad, and who weren't even human, even though they looked like people. "What do you mean?" Alma asked. "Why aren't Jews human?" "They have hooves, and they have little horns on their head."

"That is not true, Irina." "But it is, Alma, everyone knows that. Maybe you have no Jews in America." "Have you ever met a Jew, Irina?" "No, fortunately not! But my grandmother told me about them. They are terrible people, they steal and they murder babies, and they don't believe in God." "It's Communists who don't believe in God," Bodo said. "Oh," said Irina, faltering, "yes, but . . . I think that's different. The Communists are against the *Church*, but they want everything Christ wanted, except they want it here on earth. But the Jews—" "Irina," Alma interrupted her, "look at this foot"—and she took off her shoe. "Is it a human foot?" "Of course," said Irina. "And I," said Alma, "do you think I am a good person?" "Alma"—Irina drew Alma to her and hugged her—"of course you are good, you are my best friend, I love you!" "Look at me, Irina. I am a Jew." Irina stared at Alma and then she collapsed into her arms, but this time like a child, not like a friend, shivering and sobbing. Then we sat down on a bench, Bodo and Alma on either side of Irina, and Irina kept holding her hands over her face and crying. Then she said she had to go home, her grandmother would be worrying. Two days later, Irina came to visit us at the hotel and gravely said to Alma: "My grandmother was wrong."

Three weeks after our arrival in Leningrad, another ship took us on to Germany, to the Baltic seaport of Warnemünde, northwest of Berlin. I was asleep when the foghorn roused me, and looking through the porthole I could sense, shrouded in blackest night, the presence of the land where I would be living from now on. The silhouette of a cliff or a building glided by, voices were calling—a loud one from our ship and a fainter one from the shore. The ship's engines had stopped, but we were moving. My stepfather joined me at the porthole with tears in his eyes. He had been in exile for fifteen years.

⟨[Our first home in East Germany was—so my mother tells me—a resort for actors and film directors near Potsdam-Babelsberg. I remember a large, half-empty building with many rooms; a dining room where people bowed to one another as they came in to take their meals, and where my parents insisted more stringently on table manners than they had on the *Dmitry Donskoy* or in the hotel in Leningrad; a downward-sloping garden with mossy rocks; and a most romantic natural tunnel formed by overarching bushes. I do mean "romantic," for at that time I was steeped in the atmosphere of *A Treasury of Victorian Verse*, an old school book of Alma's, the very title of which enchanted me. In fact, just the capital *V* on the cover with embossed roses wreathed around it figured as a kind of glyph for the vaguely religious, vaguely chivalric sentiments that inhabited that splendid mystery of a word, "Victorian." And the book's brittle pages harbored, among dried flowers and grasses, a treasure, as the title promised, of phrases and rhymes and locutions that were manifestly more beautiful than the speech of common mortals, and which therefore bespoke, by their sound alone, the existence of a realm of perfect loveliness somewhere beyond the horizons of the ordinary, familiar world. It wasn't necessary to understand more than a fraction of what was said—indeed, not knowing the meaning of some words seemed to enhance their beauty. It was enough to sit in the above-mentioned tunnel of leaves— my hideaway—with the rich smell of humus in my nostrils, my back resting against a smooth cold rock, my limbs and the open book bathed in the yellow-green light that streamed through the dense roof of whispering foliage, and to intone my latest find, and listen into this well of unfathomable import and echoing enigma:

Yet cool the space within, and not uncheered
(As whoso enters shall ere long perceive)
By stealthy influx of the timid day
Mingling with night, such twilight to compose
As Numa loved . . .

I liked to copy out such gems, and sometimes wrote imitations of them, capitalizing each word in a spidery semblance of Gothic lettering. Once, having written down all six stanzas of a poem by Kipling, the temptation of adding to my readerly enjoyment the pride of authorship and the thrill of approbation proved too hard to resist. I passed off the poem to Alma as my own. Why not? *I* could believe it. There it was in my own hand-writing. The words were all within my ken, I could recite the first stanza by heart, I liked the lilt of the galloping meter; in fact, I liked and understood my poem so well I might as well have made it. It was so plausible. If Alma believed me, it would be almost completely true. I was a poet!

After reading the first stanza, Alma glanced up at me with a look of happy surprise. "That's wonderful, Joel." I stood bathed in glory. After finishing the poem, she looked at me again, and this time she didn't look so happy. There seemed to be something she didn't understand. "Did you really write this?" "Yes." "You didn't copy it out of a book?" "No." "Are you sure?" She looked a little frightened. "Yes, I'm sure." She pondered a while, and then she said: "It's a very good poem." "Thanks." It wasn't all that gratifying, being a poet. Though maybe the poem wasn't good enough. To judge by Alma's reaction, only the first stanza really worked— I kind of felt the same way. But it couldn't stand by itself, it had to be followed up by something. I'd have to find a better poem.

That very same evening, when Alma came on her usual good-night tour to Stefan's crib and my bedside, she had my poem in one hand and *A Treasury of Vic-*

torian Verse in the other. We had to go through with the business of disillusionment, both of us. She had to show me the evidence, line by line, and word for word, because I kept insisting, idiotically, fanatically, that partly, at least, I had made it. Defeated, finally, I cried. She took me in her arms and told me she loved me no matter what I did or didn't do, or what I could or couldn't do; and that she liked the poems I really made, I didn't have to cheat. "Please don't lie to me like that again, all right? Promise?" I promised. Later I thought: Cheat? Lie? The words had a stinging effect, though I knew Alma hadn't intended to hurt me.

That frightened look on Alma's face reappeared when I told her that I had befriended a little bird, and that the bird liked to sit on the rim of my breast pocket. I think the idea came from *The Secret Garden*. This time Alma failed to come up with a textual confutation. She pretended to believe me, and I did likewise, but somehow her response lacked a certain ingredient of surprise or curiosity which my bird required if it was ever to attain a satisfactory degree of verisimilitude. Alma just nodded and smiled in an indulgent sort of way, or said, "Really?" with that flickering of hidden worry and doubt in her eyes.

Stefan of course believed me, but then he would believe anything. And he was too young to be interested in anything for very long. He wanted me to throw a pillow into the room and come scampering after it, his favorite clowning act; or for us to roll a ball back and forth to each other on the floor. I wished he would grow up a little. Or that I could join the boys and girls who tossed coins against the wall below my window, arguing excitedly in the funny guttural language which, before we came to Germany, had seemed the unique appurtenance of two bristly, smoke-puffing men, Bodo and Kisch. It was strange to hear it coming from the mouths of children, strange to think that I would someday talk like that.

That day approached very soon after the invention of the bird, with the promise of a tutor. I'd read about tutors in old-fashioned books, and was surprised to learn they still existed, and excited by the prospect of actually "having" one. Several men and women were screened by Bodo, and finally a thin, blond young man was chosen to instruct me, or, as he probably saw it, to initiate me into the mysteries of *Hochdeutsch*; that is, he officiated, rather than tutored, at my daily baptismal dunking in the language, performing this function with an earnestness that bordered on solemnity, and with very nearly selfless patience. It was the first actual work I had done in my life—not an unpleasant introduction at all, as I was quickly rewarded with the experience of making myself understood in German: *Ich bin Amerikaner; ich spiele gern im Garten; kann ich bitte ein Glas Milch haben? Guten Morgen, Mahlzeit, Guten Tag.* Of this very capable man's behavior outside our sessions I remember only that he became faintly obsequious when Bodo was around, and that he once complained to Bodo that I farted during class.

One Sunday morning, he took me to his place to show me off to his family. He lived in the French sector of town, we in the Russian. To get to the French sector, you had to pass through the British and American sectors. Each sector had its own currency, its own occupying army with distinctive uniforms, and, I liked to imagine, its own peculiarly French, American, English, or Russian atmosphere—nothing very definite, since in fact there was no perceptible difference. At the tutor's house I was fed cake and hot chocolate and made to recite Goethe's "*Zauberlehrling*" before an assembly of smiling faces. Then, in the garden behind the house, I was shown one of the world's marvels: a huge mushroom, vermilion with white warts on top, and a stem with the girth of a fair-sized tree trunk—the kind you see in illustrations of *Grimm's Fairy Tales*, serving as parasols for gnomes and toads: *Amanita muscaria*, to be exact. I couldn't have been more awed and astonished if I'd been introduced to an elephant. My bird friend took flight before this cool, soft, tangibly real presence in the French sector. Moreover, my tutor confirmed my description of the mushroom's size, forcing my skeptical mother to believe me, rather than make believe she did. Skillfully taking advantage of my enthusiasm, he taught me several folk tales involving toadstools, and a nursery song that still evokes a kind of elfin wonder in me:

> *Ein Männlein steht im Walde,*
> *Ganz still und stumm,*
> *Das hat aus lauter Purpur*
> *Ein Mäntlein um.*
> *Sagt, wer mag das Männlein sein,*
> *Das da steht auf einem Bein,*
> *Mit dem purpurroten Mäntlein um?*

> *A little man stands silent*
> *And still in the wood,*
> *He wears around his shoulders*
> *A bright red hood.*
> *Pray, who may this small man be,*
> *That stands on one leg silently,*
> *Wearing round his shoulders a crimson hood?*

(But "*still und stumm,*" "*Mäntlein um,*" "*purpurrot,*" "*auf einem Bein*"—it would take some magic to translate that.)

Bodo seems to have had little to do with me at that time. At least, all I remember is a gentle embarrassed reminder about farting, and an image, probably the composite of many nearly identical moments, of him leaning over his soup and blowing steam off a spoon before testing its edge with his lips. I see him from above, for some reason, so that he looks small, as if

foreshortened by the passage of time (thirty years
now!), not at all as he must still have looked to me then,
awesome and strong. He's sipping at his spoon, neatly
and cautiously, like a timid well-bred little boy with
premature wrinkles and a widow's peak, and I feel a
pang of pity and tenderness, just as if I were his parent.

The men and women who had fled and fought the
Nazis, as Bodo had, were expected to be the leaders of
the new Germany, which would be built on the ruins of
the old (it wasn't apparent then, or expected, that the
country would be permanently divided into capitalist
and socialist Germanys). Also, Bodo was an Old Communist—a quasi-patriarchal distinction—and he was a
veteran of the Spanish Civil War and a well-known
novelist of the Socialist Realist school. I imagine he was
very busy attending banquets and taking on Party functions and meeting old comrades. He had become an important man almost overnight. We had brought with us
from Mexico fat sacks of rice and flour to help us
through the food scarcity we knew existed in Germany,
never suspecting that Bodo would be the beneficiary of
an institution he had spent half a lifetime attacking:
privilege, a distant target during the years of exile, now
softly and treacherously enveloping him, like an octo-
pus with years for tentacles and flattery for suction cups
and a dogmatic faith for the blinding shroud of ink. We
were well taken care of from the start.

It wasn't long before a house was found for us—a villa
by the edge of a lake, in the Russian sector of the little
border village of Gross-Glienicke, about a twenty-min-
ute drive from Potsdam and Berlin. I had a room to
myself now, upstairs, with a door leading out onto a
balcony and a window overlooking the garden and the
lake and the *Laube*—a wooden bungalow that served as
Bodo's studio, right by the edge of the water—and the
garage surrounded by lilacs. (Three or four years later,
when Alma bought herself a horse, we had a stable built
behind the garage.) Stefan slept in a smaller room next to

mine, and my parents' room, the largest of the three
bedrooms, also led out onto the balcony. The room
below mine would be the maid's, and the one below my
parents' bedroom was the living room. There was a tiled
bathroom upstairs, with a spacious tub, a bidet, and a
chrome ashtray, topped by a cigar-sized trough, attached to the wall next to the toilet; and a smaller bathroom downstairs, containing just a toilet, perhaps intended for servants. An intercom connected the kitchen
with the three bedrooms. If the weather was nice, we ate
on a large stone terrace in back of the house. A flagstone
path led down to the lake and to Bodo's Laube. A weeping willow stood there, the tips of its lowest branches
touching the water. From a wooden platform you could
dive into the lake. Nearer to the house stood a large dignified fir tree. It was easy to climb up it, almost to the
top, where the wind caused the trunk to sway a little too
precariously for the enjoyment of imaginary adventures.
And beneath my window was a magnolia tree that opened
its large, delicate blossoms each spring.

Several of the lakefront villas among which our house
stood had once belonged to Jews. They were lawyers,
doctors, manufacturers. When the Nazis came to power,
some of them were able to leave the country. A Herr
Wertheim, who lived in the house next to ours, was
forced to sell his property for a pittance to a member of
the local SA, in exchange for the chance to emigrate.
Others, less wary or less lucky, died in concentration
camps.

Our house had been occupied by the Emmerich family—an "Aryan" businessman, his Jewish wife, and their
two sons. The older son was said to have shown ability
as a chemist. The Nazi authorities pressured Herr Emmerich to divorce his wife, and he complied, perhaps
hoping he would be able to continue living with his
family as usual. The children, however, were beginning
to feel the cruel effects of the new race laws, so their
parents arranged to send them to England. That was in

1938. A few months later, Frau Emmerich left the village, supposedly for a vacation. She never returned. When people asked about his wife, Herr Emmerich curtly refused to discuss her. Thus no one could say whether she had fled or been taken away by the Nazis. Herr Emmerich remained in his house in Gross-Glienicke until the end of the war and then left the country—to rejoin his wife and children in England, some said.

This information filtered down to my eight-year-old's understanding from the conversation of my elders and took its place beside other facts about the evil past—mere facts, almost empty of tragic or moral meaning for me. Not that I couldn't imagine, to some extent, what it meant to be murdered, or that I didn't sometimes wonder what the father and the mother and the children had been like who had walked these floors and looked out these windows not so long ago (the only trace of them was a box full of glass rods, ampules, and retorts in the cellar); but I knew that such thoughts were just shadows of a heartbreak that, thank God, was not only past but would never return. Bodo himself said there would be peace from now on, forever.

([It was winter when we moved in, just before Christmas. In Mexico, we had decorated our artificial Christmas tree with flakes of white cotton, but on this, our first Christmas in Germany, Jochen Rennert, Bodo's newly hired chauffeur, chopped down a tree in the woods, built a stand for it, and showed us where to buy baubles and tinsel and candle holders to clip on to the branches. On Christmas Eve, Stefan and I were told to wait upstairs in my room with Helga, the maid (who had been hired on Jochen's recommendation), until Santa Claus signaled his exit by ringing a bell. Alma and Bodo, so went the story, would receive Santa Claus as he passed by on his worldwide errand of love, but for some quirky reason of his own he did not wish any children to see him or his reindeer. This story was for Stefan, of course, for I by now knew better: first of all, Santa Claus *did* on occasion appear to children, as he had to me when I was six (threatening not to give me any presents if I didn't promise to take better care of them than of the bow and arrow he had given me the year before); second, the reindeer-and-sled business was just a myth made up by grownups. How could a sled slide on ground without snow, let alone fly through the air pulled by reindeer? I had recently pointed out the illogic of this to Bodo, and surprisingly, he had said I was perfectly right, such things were impossible—surprisingly, I say, because Alma had tried to make me believe just that, the day Santa Claus came to our house, two years previously in Cuernavaca. Santa Claus had just left, and, whispering, almost voiceless with awe, I said: "Santa Claus sounded like Kisch." "Old men usu-ally sound alike," Alma said. That seemed plausible. A moment later—I had just sat down on the floor with my toys—Alma called from another room: "Joel! Come quick! Come see the reindeer!" I ran to the window where she stood. "There he goes in his sled!" Alma said. "Do you see him? Do you see the reindeer?" I pressed my cheek against the glass and trained my eyes on the vanishing point of a crowded Mexican street, ignoring the obviously irrelevant vendors, slinking dogs, women with baskets on their heads, beggars, top-spinning chil-dren, the hot air quivering over tin roofs. You had to squint with this kind of thing. (It wasn't very different, really, from trying to see the fibrous end of a cigarette up in the dark and hairy hollow of one of Kisch's nos-trils.) "Yes, I see him," I said, "I see the reindeer." How foolish. Well, now I was older. Now it was Stefan's turn to be benevolently deceived, his turn to believe in rein-deer. I drew a picture for him of a sled drawn by rein-deer with Santa Claus in it. "*Caballos*," he said. "*No, no son caballos, son reindeer!*" "*Caballos.*" "*No, no, diga reindeer, Stefan, reindeer.*" "*Caballos.*" He could be annoyingly stubborn. Then Helga said, "*Schlitten,*" with a peculiarly meaningful look, pointing at the sled. What's the use of a sled without snow? "*Kein Schnee,*" I said philosophically, gesturing toward the darkness outside, and then we exclaimed, trilingually and in one voice, "It's snowing!" and ran out onto the balcony and scooped up snow, snow, snow, more fabulous than reindeer, and held up our hands and open mouths to the thick slow-falling flakes, the first snow in Stefan's life, the first in mine, unless one counted a trip to wintry New York with Alma in the almost imponderable past, four years ago. The church bell was gonging from across the lake, and we could hear the voices of other children laughing and shouting, and in the spaces between these sounds was that hushed white falling of snow on white snow. Then Santa Claus's little bell went *kling-kling-kling-kling-kling* downstairs, and we stormed inside, tramping snow all over, held ourselves back for a moment to give the old man time to get away unseen, then hurried on toward the living room as fast as was possible, given Stefan's sideways two-feet-to-one-stair technique of descending a flight of steps—for I'd been told not to run ahead when the time came. Bodo and Alma stood smiling on the threshold of the living room, and there was a peculiar sound inside, a little like water dropped on a hot plate, and the lights were out except for a faint glow, presumably candlelight. We stepped in and saw all the candles lit on the tree and, scattered among them, eclipsing their glow with a hard ecstatic brilliance, were dozens of sparklers all burning at once, hissing explosions of thorny white light—for a moment we forgot about our presents. But then of course we remembered, and quickly proceeded to the profane satisfaction of tearing the paper off the large and small boxes that stood under the tree, Stefan's on one side, mine on the other. Stefan seemed to have gotten more big ones—except for one here, the biggest of all. Oh, no, I couldn't complain: it

was a sled! . . . I looked at Helga, who stood behind Alma
and Bodo, smiling, her eyes reflecting the soft candlelight,
and we were all smiling, and then I saw Stefan struggling
with a stuck box top and went to help him, surprised and
glad for this sudden overflow of affection for him; and
later, in the golden afterglow of that evening's ardors—
we were listening to some record and I was sharing
Alma's embrace with Stefan, and Bodo was holding my
hand (Helga had gone home by now)—I felt my heart
washed by a wave of sweetly painful contrition for
the dislike and envy I sometimes harbored against my
brother, whose age seemed to give him so many advantages.

The next day, Jochen led me to a hill where children
were sledding, on the other side of the lake. He told
them I was an American, and new here, and asked them
to speak slowly and in Hochdeutsch, and, generally, to
be nice to me. A few of the older boys ostentatiously
rejected Jochen's authority by dashing down the hill on
their sleds before he had finished talking. But the others
listened and gaped at me in disbelief.

"*Bist du wirklich 'n Ami?*" one girl asked.

I looked to Jochen for a translation into High German. "She wants to know if you're really an American,"
he said. "*Ami* means American."

"*Ja*," I said. "*Ich bin ein Ami.*"

Everyone laughed then, Jochen too, and there was a
little malice in some of the laughter, but mostly it was
friendly—so I laughed, too. With my nationality established to nearly everyone's satisfaction, the kids resumed their sledding, and, prompted and coached by
Jochen, I joined them. After a while Jochen left, re-
minding me to come home when it started getting dark.
No sooner was he out of sight than I became the center
of a vortex of peering eyes, questions, and comments.

"*Ick gloobe Jochen spinnt.* Jochen's got to be crazy,
there aren't any Amis around here."

"Maybe he's a *Russki.*"

"No, he's an Ami, just listen to the way he talks. Go ahead, boy, say it again: *Ich bin ein Ami.*"

"*Ich bin ein Ami.*"

Again there was laughter, and I heard some imitations of my Mexican-American accent. Three little girls about my age stood up for me: "Stop laughing at him, how would you feel." That only encouraged the two or three mockers to step up their taunting: "*Guck dir mal die Dinger da an,*" said one, referring to my earmuffs.

"*Typisch Ami,*" said another.

"*Lasst ihn in Ruhe,*" said one of the girls. "Leave him alone or I'll tell Jochen. Come," she said to me then, pulling me by the sleeve, "don't listen to them, they're stupid," and her friends translated by tapping their forehead with their index finger, a gesture I hadn't seen before: in Mexico they made corkscrew motions by the side of the temple. In any case, I assumed it must be as dangerous here as it was there to associate with weak people who cast aspersions on the intelligence of people with muscles; so I carefully avoided giving any sign of complicity. But no one seemed out to hurt me. When one of the big boys inspected the runners on my sled, I feared for a moment that he would take it away from me, but then he asked if he could ride it. Of course I let him, and after him all the others. It seemed I was okay now; my sled was of superior quality and I was willing to share it. When it was time to leave, the three girls who had defended me offered to pull their brand-new Ami home on his sled, an offer which I did not refuse, even though it caused them some difficulty, since they had sleds of their own to pull.

I went to that hill every day. The three girls were absent more often than not. That was unfortunate, since no one else was quite so friendly. I remained a stranger among those tough boys, mystified (to this day) by the wild combative excitement that broke out each time someone reached the foot of the hill (neither speed nor distance seemed to be the object of whatever contest it was); mystified, too, by their incomprehensible jokes, by their occasional fights, which never came to blows but were waged with insults and staring bouts and some pushing, quarrels the origin and dissolution of which were completely hidden from my understanding by the quick choppy dialect my tutor in Babelsberg had failed to teach me. It wasn't long before my value as a curiosity wore off and the bare fact of my foreignness remained as an irritant. I could feel it coming, one day, a tentatively encircling menace of looks, sneers, and distances. It occurred to me that I should leave before being made to leave, but I stayed, as if paralyzed, or fascinated. I'd been through this before, in Mexico: in the midst of a band of children playing American-style *futból*—not soccer, the usual *futból*, which I could deal with, but a violent game with arcane rules everyone but I seemed acquainted with. On top of that, I was the only gringo. The same subtle network of tentative malice, cruel half-hidden jibes sent not at me so much as into the air, as a test, as a probe, and the confirming snicker, and the ritual repetition and variation upon the joke, increasingly deliberate and momentous, until someone delivers the catalytic stroke of brutality—a humiliating kick in the behind that time, a fistful of snow stuffed down my collar now. Mercifully, just a few badly aimed snowballs were added for good measure; back in Mexico, the kids chased me, or probably, since I wasn't caught, pretended to chase me, all the way home: "Get him! Pull down his pants!"

It's strange, the way memories cluster and illuminate one another, or even blend, as if whatever agency handles the punctilious business of storing up the past had at some point lapsed into reverie and become more mindful of meaning than accuracy. In the background, behind the shouting of those Mexican boys, in place of what should be their footsteps, panting, and laughter, I seem to remember music, and it's the same music that accompanies another memory (which dates back to about the same time, my seventh year, when we were living in Mexico City), of Alma explaining to me how and why Mussolini was lynched. It's a terrible music that sounds like something living being slowly torn to death, a shrieking and blaring and rending that goes on and on. Mussolini is a fat and very bad king who has been thrown in a pond and is being stoned. Of course, Alma must have told me something akin to the facts—that Mussolini was shot and subsequently hung upside down at a gas station in Milan. But I see him bobbing up and down in the water and stones bouncing off his round red head with a sickening, dull, thudding sound, and the music envelops and fills and explodes the scene. Mussolini puts his hands on the edge of the pond, and people step on his fingers, which are pink and very slender. But most of that's drawn from another memory, a translation of it, so to speak. I was playing marbles with a band of children— some of the same children who later threatened to pull down my pants—when someone called out from a side street in great excitement: *"Un ratón! Un ratón!"* A moment later everyone was rushing to where the rat had been trapped, in a deep and wide puddle that had developed where workmen had broken up the pavement, damaged a water main, and, I guess, left in perplexity. The rat was trapped because all around the puddle was a thick forest of legs—naked legs, legs in rags, legs sheathed in pressed cotton slacks. I remember I was one of the few kids with shoes. The rat swam in slow circles, drawing a line in the water with its long, pink tail. The boys threw stones at it, big stones and little stones. Some stones splashed into the water, and some hit the rat with a thud, and often the rat would squeal when it was hit. The boys kept running off to collect stones and stuff their pockets with them, but there were always enough boys around the puddle to keep the rat inside. One of the richer boys had a slingshot, and he was a smart shot and got a lot of applause. He was using marbles, an impressive gesture because they were worth something, and he hit the rat with terrible accuracy and force, you could see its little head snap back, and for a moment it seemed, and I hoped, that it was dead. But then it started swimming again. It was bleeding from the mouth and one eye was smashed, everyone pointed that out. The rat came up to the sidewalk where I was standing, rose on its hind legs, and curled its incredibly delicate pink fingers around the edge of the curb; its mouth was open, I could see its pink tongue, its whiskers, the smashed eye; and the other, myopically blinking eye seemed to be looking up at our faces. Someone took me firmly by the elbow, and only then did I realize that I had bent over a little and started reaching out to the rat. It was an older boy who stopped me, almost a man. He shook his head and went *ts-ts-ts* in a big-brotherly way, and then he put his hand on my shoulder, filling me with a kind of astonished pride. "Rats are poisonous," he said, "you mustn't touch them. They kill babies." Then he stretched out his leg and carefully stepped on the rat's fingertips with the tip of his sandal. The rat fell back into the water and started swimming in circles again. The big boy took his hand off my shoulder, pulled a stone out of his pocket, and handed it to me. "Throw it," he said. I threw it, and missed. "Try again." I kept throwing and missing, and the boy kept giving me stones. Finally I hit the rat in the side; there was a cheer. I looked up at the boy, he was smiling but he didn't look at me. He didn't hand me any more stones either, he kept them for himself. A woman called from a window above us, she was waving an arm: "Step aside! Step aside! I'm going to pour hot water on it!" Everyone moved away. Now was the rat's chance to escape. But it didn't know. The woman heaved a large potful of steaming water into the puddle. It came down with a huge hiss and splash. Most of it missed the rat, but some of it didn't. The rat screamed. Still, it kept swimming in circles. Later the rat was let out of the puddle. By now it could hardly walk.

People were kicking it. A truck came along, plowing aside the crowd of shouting and laughing people—some adults had joined in by then—and the truck ran over the rat, *bump* with a front wheel, *bump* with a back wheel. The driver leaned out of the window to make sure he didn't miss. Everyone cheered and applauded, including the woman in the window. Now the rat's belly was split open, its guts were oozing out. A boy took the rat by the tail and started swinging it around. Everyone started moving away fast then. I ran home to tell Alma and Bodo about it. I remember the look of disturbance in Alma's eyes, and the look of shy gravity and sadness in Bodo's expression when I had finished my story.

After that misadventure on the hill behind the lake, Alma told me—no, promised, prophesied—that once my German was good enough and I could go to school, I would be luckier in my company, I would be popular, I would have friends. She startled me once or twice by calling me "lonely"—it hadn't occurred to me to apply such a pathos-laden word to my situation. I wasn't really unhappy, or bored: there were books, and poems, and these could be read over and over; and if something I'd read, usually a poem, inflamed me greatly, I'd lie down on the floor (the desk never seemed the right place for this) and labor at making verse of my own, strewing rejected versions around the room. I wish I still had at least one of those poems, a sort of ode, in Spanish, with which I was especially pleased: it was about an idyllic swamp where frog song, bird song, and mosquito song unite to praise the sun that has stirred everyone out of sleep. But most of my writing was in English. I was fond of archaisms like "thee" and "thou," and liked to add silent *e*'s to every other word. Sometimes surprising turns of phrase resulted from a mechanical transposing of a cliché from one language to another, for example in a poem about happy hunters galloping "o'er stock and stone," which is something happy hunters are very likely to do in German folk songs, where it's called *"Stock und Stein."* Whatever the merit of these efforts may have been, I received abundant praise for them. Bodo told me he was proud of me: he couldn't write poems, he said, only stories; and Alma read me something Jim, my American father, had written her in response to a batch of my poems she had sent him (not before assuring herself that I hadn't plagiarized someone again). Jim, too, was proud of me, and conferred the word "talent" on me like a badge of honor. At least, that's how I took it.

Another favorite pastime was drawing cowboys and Indians battling it out among mountains, rocks, and cactuses, as depicted in comics my grandfather sent from America: eagle-nosed profiles, figure-eight stetsons, feathered headdresses, guns spouting angry straight lines that ricocheted off the rocks in bizarre patterns, sometimes back to the sniper's heart. No special gift, no promise was deduced from these drawings; they were found humorous, an effect which I hadn't intended but welcomed nevertheless. Whenever these solitary amusements palled, I could always play with Stefan, or watch Jochen tinkering with the car, or venture out onto the frozen lake, keeping a safe distance from spots Jochen had designated as unsafe. There were treacherous warm currents, a child had drowned just a year ago . . .

Sometimes, when Jochen drove Bodo to work in Berlin (Bodo had been appointed chief editor of *Aufbau*, a literary magazine), I went along for the ride. I remember sitting in the back seat as our black Opel rolled through avenues of ruins, some of them overgrown with weeds and young trees. Jochen tried to describe what these streets had once looked like. Bodo said that he used to live in Hamburg but it was completely destroyed now and he didn't ever want to go back, not even if it was rebuilt. Jochen said he could well understand that. I found this talk confusing. Here were Bodo and Jochen agreeing about the sadness of ruins, yet they both had been soldiers. Why did people make war in the first place? Why would people want to kill each other? Bodo explained that he had fought the Nazis in Spain because they were evil. But Jochen wasn't evil, I objected, and he had fought with the Nazis. He was forced to, Bodo explained. And he was very young at the time and didn't know much.

I actually rather liked looking at the ruins. You could see the lineaments of the lives that had once been sheltered here: flowered wallpaper imprinted with pale rectangles where pictures had hung, staircases, windows, sometimes a rag of a curtain still stirring in the breeze.

I looked forward to school more anxiously than expectantly, despite Alma's assurances. What I remembered of school in Mexico City (I could hardly hope for a return to the earlier, happier days in Cuernavaca, where I attended a small private school with a single, very friendly teacher) was a grim and boring perpetuity, day after dreary day, of meaningless tasks ungraciously rewarded, and, worse than that, of being a stranger, by dint of my race and by dint of the sheer inhuman enormity of the school, without any prospect of relief other than my family's constantly postponed embarkment for Europe. But, as it turned out, Alma was right. There were several wonderfully friendly boys in my class who took me under their wing from the first day. They seemed to be proud of me, showing me off to kids in the other grades. When I mispronounced a word, they would call their friends' attention to it, not mockingly, but as if I were a first-rate humorist; I was included in their amusement, and they always took care to clue me in on the joke. Thanks to them, I began to feel at home where I was, and within a year my German had become fluent, with hardly a trace of an accent.

I do remember one instance in which I became the laughingstock of ten or fifteen kids who had the good fortune of being present when I launched into a pedantic lecture on sexual intercourse. My mother had solemnly informed me of the unsuspected uses to which genitals could be put, and of the wonderful biological function their coupling served. That this procedure was accompanied by pleasure I also knew. I felt terribly enlightened and considered it a good deed to pass on this rare knowledge. It took me quite a while to realize that I was the ignorant one, not they. As I started explaining, supplementing with gestures what I couldn't supply in words, an extraordinary hilarity began to develop around me. I took this for a sign of ignorant disbelief, and earnestly continued my disquisition: yes, it was admittedly very funny, this manner of making children, but that was the true state of affairs. My audience increased rapidly, and for the benefit of latecomers I was urged to tell it all from the beginning.

⟨The facts of life according to the students of the Zentralgrundschule Gross-Glienicke were less lyrical than my mother's version of them, but no less interesting. A case in point was a certain graffito, a rhomboidal shape with a vertical slash in the center, scrawled on countless walls, sidewalks, and dusty windows by dozens, maybe hundreds of little boys who swarmed about with pieces of chalk in their pockets, perpetuating the mystic emblem all over the village, secretly, assiduously, like those pre-Christian zealots who announced the coming of the Messiah with the sign of the fish. Some adults seemed to have something against this image, they kept wiping and scrubbing it off, especially in school. I suspected some sexual significance, but couldn't imagine what it might be, and preferred not to ask, and pretended to know what I was doing when I, too, drew the picture: one-two-three-four and *five*, tee-hee-hee. Then, one day, someone scribbled the sign on a mural that graced the back wall of our classroom, placing it with unmistakable intention on the exact midriff of the woman who stood gazing upward and hugging a sheaf of corn in either arm, and someone else drew a lengthy garden-hose-like extrusion that emerged from the loins of the (similarly upward-gazing) man next to the woman and curved very peculiarly around her hip to connect with the suddenly not so mysterious vertical slash in the center —*her* center. The scales fell from my eyes: so that's what a vagina looked like! It was so much clearer, in this dia-grammatic form, than Alma's attempt once, in Mexico, to show me the real thing at the back of a cow ("There, beneath the tail—don't you see?" Bent forward, I peered: I saw nothing. Then some people came along, and Alma pulled me away by the hand). Jürgen Manusch gave a finishing touch to the mural by changing the legend be-neath it: the word *"Ernährung"* in *"Die Bauern sichern uns die Ernährung"* (The peasants secure our nourish-ment) became *"Vermehrung"* (reproduction).

Fräulein Friedemann, our biology teacher, was the first to discover the defacement, and called in Herr Dreifach, the school's principal. This was something *unerhört*—outrageous, unheard-of—a regular *Schwein-erei*: who did it? Of course, no one raised his hand. In that case, said Herr Dreifach, the whole class would suffer—we'd have to stay after school. No one really minded.

Those kids weren't just savvy about sex, they were casually acquainted with death and gore as well. A little girl, for example, brought in a globulous cow's eye with pale wet noodle-like muscles or veins hanging from it; and once a bull's testicles were thrown around the schoolyard, amid a great deal of shrieking, until they were confiscated. And there were frequent stories told about the exciting things that happened when some-thing went wrong during slaughter time, including some tales that bordered on the fantastic and were de-bated as to their veracity: the pig that divined its impending murder and became a rampaging and dan-gerous beast; the beheaded chicken that ran right across the frozen lake to the West, never to be seen again; the unkillable bull; the heartbroken cow that sought to avenge her slaughtered calf and had to be shot. I certainly was in no position to doubt any of these stories. I believed and admired my friends wholeheartedly, and sought in all ways to be like them: dress like them, talk like them, act like them. How pleased I was (and how mortified Alma was) by the remodeling of my skull at the hands of the village barber, who made it look angular, almost square, with a clean strip of hairless scalp around the back of the head reaching up to about the top of my ears, and above that a mop of hair sliced off precisely at the edge of the no-hair zone. Now all I needed in order to be like the others was a slingshot, or *Katschi*, as it was called. This Alma and Bodo resisted: it's too dangerous, they said, and what's more, you can't *buy* a slingshot, and we don't know how to make one. That was a mistake, for Jochen, who had overheard the conversation without picking up my parents' unexpressed opposition to my owning any sort of weapon, offered to make me a Katschi. Now there remained only the question of its danger, and here again, Jochen, the undisputed authority on Katschis among the four of us, unwittingly overrode my parents' objections by laying down some simple precautionary rules: make sure no one is in your line of sight when you shoot, make sure no one is about to step between you and your target, keep your thumb out of the way, and make sure you don't shoot at useful birds. When Alma heard Bodo's translation of that last rule, she turned passionately against Jochen: "He must not shoot *any* birds, or any living thing. That's the most important rule." She turned to me now, speaking English. "You aren't going to shoot birds, are you?" "Of course not." But I was lying. The main purpose of a Katschi was to wreak destruction of some sort, and the usual targets, in order of their prestige value, were birds, squirrels, street lamps, windows, and, very rarely, other boys wielding Katschis. No, it was unavoidable that I would shoot at birds. I couldn't afford to be squeamish; my future depended on it.

Jochen made me an excellent Katschi out of an old inner tube, a piece of leather, and a forked branch, and showed me how to use it. What a thrill to feel the rubber stretched taut, the fork quivering in my left fist, the stone in its leather thong pinched between thumb and forefinger of the right hand and held at eye level, lining up the target—a fence post, say—with the upper ends of the fork and with the stone, as Jochen had shown me—a deadly straight line—then to let go, and hear the stone whiz and strike against the wood. My friends inspected and tested the Katschi. It was good, I could tell before they said so; anything that made them thrust out their lower lips and sagely nod their heads had to be good. Then we went hunting.

I had received a package of books from Jim, my father in America, among them Howard Pyle's *Robin Hood and His Merry Men*, with its lusty protagonists, hospitable inns, bouts with broadsword and staff, stout ales and goat cheese with fresh-baked warm bread, all in the greeny fastness of Sherwood Forest. On that first forage into the woods, eight or ten boys strong, with our slingshots in our belts, ducking gratuitously into the brush whenever an adult came into view, I was choking with the desire to tell about Robin Hood, and to transform my friends into the Merry Men, with myself in the title role. But they had their own mythology, derived, as I later learned, from Karl May's Winnetou books about the American Wild West. An older boy who had been kept back a grade, and who could fight, skate, play soccer, and shoot a Katschi as well as anyone, elected himself Winnetou, the noble and fearless Apache with the finely tuned senses; and a friend played his loyal and adoring German companion, Old Shatterhand, the intrepid trapper. The rest of us were anonymous Indians, and it was our duty to avoid snapping twigs and, eventually, to help shoot down an eagle.

It's difficult to shoot a bird with a slingshot. The slight curve of the trajectory varies with distance and with the angle of the shot, so it's difficult to gauge; branches get in the way, and of course the bird doesn't hold still. When I saw how the others consistently missed, I aimed a little below the bird—I didn't really want to hurt it. But at the same time I wanted badly to prove my mettle as a marksman. The ensuing tension gave me a stomachache. Eventually one of us did bring down a bird—a starling, a bona fide harmful bird, undeserving of pity. But it was pitiable nonetheless. I think we all felt this, because no one moved to do anything to it after it fluttered down to our feet and lay on its side, waving one wing and hissing at us, nor did anyone laugh or say anything, nor did we move on until after a quivering spasm went through the bird's wing and head, and it sank back limply. Later I walked home with one of my fellow Indians, a new boy named Uwe, whose father was a general and who had just moved into our neighborhood. Uwe said: "I felt sorry for that bird." I liked him very much for saying that. "I felt sorry for it, too," I said. "I'm never going to shoot at birds again," he said. "Neither will I," I said. I told him about Rolf, our lamb-like German shepherd, and how his former owner, a political commentator whose voice Uwe had heard on the radio many times, had tried to make Rolf vicious by feeding him fresh blood and frightening him. Uwe, too, had a dog, a Scotch terrier named Lady. He also kept pigeons —beautiful pigeons. How could he have shot at that bird? With swimming eyes, he recited a poem his mother had taught him:

> *Quäle nie ein Tier zum Scherz*
> *Denn es fühlt wie du den Schmerz!*

> *Never torment an animal in jest,*
> *For it feels pain as you do.*

How virtuous we felt, walking through the woods and professing our faith in the kinship between man and beast. What joy in meeting another soul responsive to noble and elevated feeling.

I'm sorry to say, though, that it wasn't long before we converted to the very unmerciful pleasures of fishing. Valentin Birkelbach, a poet and painter who often came to visit from Berlin, showed me how to cut a springy willow branch for a rod, how to fashion a float out of a cork and a feather, what size hooks and lines to use, where to dig for worms, how to impale them on the hook, how to tell a nibble from a bite, when to yank the line, how to mercy-kill our catch by jamming a finger in its mouth and bending its head back sharply, cracking the neck. I was repelled at first; but I was at war with my childhood and hated all vestiges of innocence I could recognize in myself. I knew how not to cry when I was injured in a soccer game, I'd passed tests of endurance swimming and running . . . I'd have to pass this test, too. All boys went fishing, it had to be done. Also, Valentin expected it of me. He looked so disappointed by my misgivings. And then he explained that fish and worms have inferior nervous systems and don't feel pain as we do, that their writhing and thrashing are mere reflexes, and that, furthermore, one mustn't be sentimental about animals, it's human suffering one should reserve one's compassion for.

It was the earnestly friendly tone of his argument that persuaded me, rather than its logic. The honor of being apprenticed to an adult, no matter in what sort of skill, was an irresistible lure. Having learned all that Valentin could teach about fishing, I taught it to Uwe, assuring him, as Valentin had assured me, that the repulsion he felt would go away with some practice. But Uwe was nowhere near as squeamish as I had been.

I learned to enjoy fishing: the long wait filled with daydreams, if I was alone, and with quiet talk when I was with Uwe, and often with fantasies of fat carp or knife-toothed pike approaching beneath the dark-olive licheny surface of the lake and staring at our freshly hooked worms; the thrill of seeing the cork-and-feather contraption dip and bob up again, or tilt and float sideways and gradually sink out of view, and of lifting one's wriggling catch out of the water; and the pride of looking at the day's bounty laid out in a row according to size. For a while, the nasty business of hooking the worm and dispatching the fish still felt nasty, but I could go through with it. Eventually it was as simple as walking, as easy as handling a fork and knife. The main trick was not to think of the pain I was causing.

As for Katschis, I found a relatively harmless substitute in the common rubber band. Let me explain right away that our use of this weapon in Gross-Glienicke had nothing in common with the limp, short-orbited flights rubber bands are sent on by American schoolchildren. They fail to understand that the rubber band's elasticity makes it a good gun and a lousy projectile. By folding a strip of paper about an inch wide and eleven inches long into a tight little roll and then bending it in the middle— so that it's V-shaped—you can create a bullet with which a good marksman can kill a fly at ten paces. That is precisely what I practiced at home—shooting flies. When the rubber band eventually became enormously popular during the ten-minute breaks between classes—bullets whirring from everywhere and everyone crouching behind their desks or behind barricades of books—I became a feared sharpshooter indeed and could adopt any name in our pantheon of martial heroes without danger of being challenged.

❨[In several conversations, Alma impressed on me her wish that I take to heart the fact that we were Jewish; and not only that, but that we were Jews in Germany. It meant something. It meant, on the most basic level, that we were different and, perhaps purely by virtue of this difference, in some way nobler, more lovably human, than Germans. Of course, Alma never put it in such bald terms; but the idea crept in whenever she was talking about someone like Einstein or Yehudi Menuhin, for she spoke of them with prideful affection, as if they were family members. They weren't just great men, they were Jews, and this Jewishness seemed to form an integral part of their excellence.

At first I took pleasure in the self-conceit of belonging to such illustrious company. But when I talked about these things with my friends, I felt embarrassed. I didn't like thinking of myself as different. I was relieved when they shrugged at my announcement. That I was American or that I had lived in the wilds of Mexico—these were, for them, interesting truths about me: but that my mother was Jewish—what difference did it make?

Until today, I always took that response for granted as something normal and natural (which, in fact, it was, under the circumstances); just as I took for granted that, during the twelve years I lived in East Germany— right after the Second World War—no one ever used the word "Jew" as an epithet against me, not even by implication. Now, upon reflection, I see what a truly astonishing fact it is, and what a feat of statecraft it represents.

For it was the government's doing. Making racist remarks, let alone disseminating them through the media, was a punishable offense. A chalk-drawn swastika on a sidewalk would attract an inquest by plainclothesmen and detectives. The virtue or villainy of fictional characters in children's books, while it was often rather crudely linked to social class (workers good, bourgeois bad), was never established by reference to race or nationality. Our schoolbooks and the movies we saw were designed to instill a respectful and friendly attitude toward foreign cultures. In 1951, an International Youth Festival took place in East Berlin—tens of thousands of young people from all over the world dancing in the streets beneath their countries' flags and sending up clouds of balloons and pigeons, all the world's color come to gray Berlin; and nine months later, the many babies born with African hair and Oriental eyes and tan skin. In the spring of 1952, the first in an annual series of gigantic bicycle races took place, a sort of Eastern-bloc "Tour de France." Droves and droves of stoop-shouldered, frantically kicking men flew along highways and country roads through Poland, East Germany, and Czechoslovakia. For several weeks you could hear the sportscasters discussing carbuncles and trophies and cheering the weary stragglers (turbaned and bearded Indians, usually) along with the leading team (always distinguished by Picasso's peace dove emblazoned on sky-blue jerseys) and celebrating the lasting friendships that had developed between Germans and Frenchmen, Egyptians and Czechs, Russians and Italians. "Peace and Friendship among the Peoples!"—this slogan was everywhere, for many years.

And all East Germans were informed of what the Nazis had done. Whether they liked it or not, they were informed. Especially schoolchildren. (On some children, though—Stefan was one of them—this reformatory zeal had unfortunate psychological effects. But of this later.) Once—to give an example of many lessons of this kind—a former concentration-camp inmate, an astronomer and mathematician, came to tell us about Dachau. He spoke with an eerie sort of humorous self-depreciation, almost like a veteran shyly boasting of his participation in some great campaign. Everything had its good side, it seemed, even floggings and torture—you could look back and say with a grin: Here I am, still intact, isn't that funny? He had even derived some profit from spending several months in nearly perpetual darkness and solitary confinement by mentally reconstructing the proportional tables of logarithms for finding the planets' positions. It wasn't worth much as a skill, he said, but he could always impress people with it, and back then it had helped him keep his bearings.

Alma was aware of these big political changes, and applauded them, just as I took them for granted. But I felt at home in Germany and she didn't. Partly that had to do with the way she looked. Her straight, long, black hair arranged in a wreath around her crown and pinned tightly above the temples, which gave her eyes a faintly Asiatic slant; her bold use of mascara and lipstick to *paint* her face, not just retouch it as German women did (if they used makeup at all); her thick American accent —these outward signs alone set her apart, made her appear foreign, even exotic. And she had no intention of adapting her appearance to the norm of East German womanhood. Sometimes she wove thick strands of brightly colored wool into her hair, or stuck flowers in it. Dancing even to the most four-square East German polkas, she tended to move her head, shoulders, arms, and hips—not just her feet. She chain-smoked indecorously, letting the cigarette dangle from a corner of her mouth. Once, at a public dance, a drunken man with dueling scars on his cheeks slapped a cigarette out of her mouth and exclaimed: *"Deutsche Frauen rauchen nicht!"*—"German women don't smoke!" It helped that he was immediately made to leave, and that everyone present, strangers and friends alike, expressed sympathy for Alma. But there was a second, much more frightening incident at a pub in Schierke, a winter resort in the Harz mountains. Alma was sitting at a table with Bodo and several friends, talking and drinking. A man leaned over from an adjoining table and shouted something at Alma. At that time she spoke very little German, so she didn't understand his words: *"Verdammte Judenhure!"* —"Damned Jew whore!"—but there was no mistaking the look of menace and lechery on his face. A man at Alma's table leaped up and threw a glass at him, and then the other man's friends jumped up to defend him, and there was a good deal of shoving and shouting, until someone called the police and the anti-Semite and his friends hurried away. Bodo never pressed charges— I imagine he didn't consider the matter important enough to warrant his attending a trial way up in the Harz. But for Alma, that encounter wasn't so trivial. She was shaken. It was as if the specter of Nazism had risen up and stared at her through the beer-slackened mask of one man—one among many who, for all she knew, may have been sober enough to hide their true feelings.

Even though these were the only incidents of the kind, they probably reinforced whatever anti-Teutonic sentiments Alma had brought with her to Germany. I remember sitting with her in some grim cafeteria watching hundreds of stolid, tight-lipped men and women walking by stiff-backed, unhappy. "Just look at them," she said, snorting with derision. "The master race." The violence, the meanness of it were so unlike her. Race—what did race have to do with anything? *She* was being racist, not those people out there. And if they were German, so were my friends, and so was I, for all practical purposes. Later I realized that, on the very rare occasions when she came out with this sort of icy judgment, it was invariably because Bodo had hurt her. She told me so herself. If it hadn't been for him, she would never have come to Germany. She didn't really belong here.

I was ten or eleven—I'm not sure—when I went down to Bodo's Laube in search of something to read and found a book full of facsimiles of Nazi documents and photographs taken in concentration camps. I already knew about the cattle cars and the gas chambers and the mountains of shoes and hair and the lamp-shades made of human skin. I also knew that children just like me had been hanged, burned, asphyxiated. Nevertheless, I was not prepared for that book. No, not the book, just one picture, one among dozens. All the others I've forgotten, but this one photograph I remember clearly. It shows a skeletally thin man standing inside a swimming pool, his hands gripping the stone edge. The water looks dark and opaque. It reaches up to the man's chest. On his face is a look of mortal anguish and exhaustion, and also of supplication. There are two other men in the picture. Both are comfortably seated in chairs by the side of the pool. One of them has a uniform on, the other is wearing a suit. The uniformed man has one booted leg crossed over the other, and he is holding a stopwatch in his palm. The man in the suit is taking notes on a pad in his lap. There seems to be a smile on the face of the man with the stopwatch. He is looking down at the man in the pool, and the man in the pool is looking up at him. The caption beneath the photo identifies the two seated men and explains that they are measuring the human body's tolerance to extreme temperatures.

Coming upon this picture was like discovering a door through which I could step directly into hell. No one reckons with such a door until it appears, and once opened, it can never be closed again. I could turn away, of course, I could close the book. But I don't know how many times over the years, at troubled and unguarded moments—sitting by the lake fishing, or just before falling asleep—I have returned to that glance exchanged between those two men—the suffering man begging for mercy and the smiling man in the uniform of cruelty. The enormousness of it. The wrongness, unfathomable. And that this moment, which should never have been, was given a bland unalterable duration by a finger pressed on a shutter. And by myself.

❡Trying to remember the village from which I've been absent for so long, I find myself floating over it, like a ghost. But it's difficult to haunt a past that is itself becoming ghost-like, losing its features. I see people walk-

ing, hanging up laundry, shopping, sawing logs with a
shrieking band saw, riding bicycles, bundling hay, milk-
ing cows, driving trucks, gossiping, fishing, quarreling,
calling their chickens ("Puuut, putt-putt-putt-putt"),
drinking beer at Niemann's café, cheering at the Sunday-
afternoon soccer game, cursing the kids who broke all
the street lamps again. These people have no faces. (Of
course, I'm not counting Jochen, or his wife, Irma—
they were practically part of our family.) I see postures,
gestures, baggy trousers and dresses, gray cloth caps on
the men, blond or gray bristles growing back where the
barber's electric shears denuded the scalp, deep cross-
hatched creases in the backs of thick and thin reddish
necks, women grown dumpy with middle age, and
sometimes bloated and bowlegged, kerchiefs tied over
curlers, brown stockings held with elastic above the
knee, wooden clogs. These are no longer real men and
women, they've all started sinking back into a blurred
composite picture of stereotypical North German peas-
antry. Even our immediate neighbors have started to
vanish. Some voices linger, laughing or talking—their
sound and pitch rather than actual words. Of a middle-
aged couple next door, only the woman's large blue coat
continues to walk past our front gate in a stout, rectitudi-
nous manner, accompanied by the clop-clop of invisible
heels. Further down the road is a villa that, I believe,
housed a family; but I can no longer summon so much as
a squeaking hinge or a flutter of cloth by which to recall
them. Next, there's a house someone disappeared from
overnight, sometime in 1953. Several policemen escorted
him out of his home and into their car. He was an engineer and he had black hair; that's probably all I ever noticed about him. The whole town murmured about his
arrest for a while. He was surely innocent, people said; it
was surely political; such a nice man wouldn't commit a
real crime. But no one could find out for sure. The man's
wife left with their two children a day or two after her
husband was taken away.

Now I see a recognizable figure: the Count, der Herr
Graf. Here he comes, all wounded arrogance, dispossessed
of his landed estate, of his sharecroppers, of everything
except a lifetime's habit of self-esteem, enhanced now
by a well-tended white chin-beard and white close-cut
hair on top of his head. He wears a tweed suit and spats.
Some of the villagers lift their caps and bow as he
passes by on his constitutional—treading carefully, for
he's old and beginning to stoop and a little unstable, but
still jerking his cane forward with an air of jaunty authority, and rapping the pavement with it.

"*Morjen, Herr Graf!*"

"*Guten Morgen.*" (They speak in dialect, not he.)

"*Wie jehts der Frau Gräfin?*"

"*Gut, danke.*"

He doesn't reciprocate the polite inquiry, nor does he
stop walking as he answers the interlocutor graciously,
though always careful to keep the distance befitting his
rank and the dignity of his years.

And there's the Countess. Her face is very pale,
deeply lined, but her blue eyes are bright and curious,
like a child's. She, too, is dignified, but it's a dignity that
needn't fear simplicity. She sits on a bench in the back
row of a class of ten-year-olds in the Zentralgrundschule Gross-Glienicke, wearing a black peasant dress
and a black bandanna that contrasts with her hair,
dyed nearly white-blond, and her pale broad forehead.
She's learning Russian. Some of the children's parents,
just a few years ago, were tenant farmers on her estate;
now they own parcels of what used to be her property.
Why was she learning Russian? Why in that place?
Why wasn't she proud? An explanation occurs to me,
probably it's a fiction, but maybe it's true. Maybe she
was glad the Russians had won the war. Maybe she felt,
as I've heard many others felt, often secretly and halfheartedly, a stirring of hope and renewal breathing
from the pages of even the most arid propaganda of that
time. Maybe she liked hearing the children singing the

old, gentle folk songs and the new ones, like the one
Brecht wrote: *"Und nicht über und nicht unter/allen
Völkern wolln wir sein"*—"and not over and not under/
every nation let us be." Maybe she was glad not to be
the Frau Gräfin anymore—though people still called
her that. But all this may be sentimental conjecture.

Deep in the woods, in a wooden house I have to
imagine because I never saw it, there's another set of
faces, much cruder than those of the Count and the
Countess, and somehow less distinct; partly because I've
begun to forget them, but also because their features
were blunted by congenital idiocy. A hulking, thick-
boned, shaggy-haired family of eight or ten, they had an
uncannily appropriate surname: Baer. Two of the Baer
sons, Helmut and Hubert, sat in the back row of my
class: the law required their presence in school, and no
special program was available. An older sister, raven-
haired, with deep-set suspicious black eyes, was pregnant—some murmured, by a member of her family. The
older Baers were rarely seen in the village.

Sometimes we taunted Helmut and Hubert—especially Hubert, whose name lent itself to being pronounced in an imitation of his thick-tongued, low-moan-
ing way of talking: "Oobet Baeh." He pretended to be
amused, and that made it easier to dismiss what scruples we had. Otherwise, I don't remember anyone mis-
treating the Baers. The administrators of the school
very sensibly seated Hubert and Helmut together, even
though they were two years apart in age, and promoted
them to a higher grade as a reward for a year of uncom-
prehending docility.

The last house on the dead-end street where we lived
was a wooden shack that had been painted yellow a long
time ago. It was hedged in by lilac bushes on one side and
by cornstalks on the other. Several tall sunflowers shaded
the wicket gate. From certain angles all you could see was

smoke rising up from among the greenery. This was the
Gontscharoffs' place. Their western fence formed part of
East Gross-Glienicke's border; that is, the garden adjoining theirs was in the British sector. Strange to think that
in those days the East-West border, or at least that part of
it, was made of chicken wire, and that it was patrolled by
an old couple against incursions by rabbits and little boys
who might damage their vegetable garden.

Herr Gontscharoff was a Bulgarian. He had pale, watery blue eyes, white hair, and a mustache which he
twirled upward at the ends. He was frail and rather timid.
From our house, we could hear his German wife shouting
at him. Sometimes she was shouting at her goats; it was
hard to tell the difference.

The big dirt field in front of our house belonged to
the Gontscharoffs. They were nice enough not to object
to Alma's jumping hurdles on it with her horse, Roland,
or to my playing soccer there with my friends. Not that
they could have made much use of the field. They were
too old to cultivate it. Their pensions and the yield of
their large garden were sufficient to keep them going.
They sold their corn to the local farmers for pig feed, and
Frau Gontscharoff thought us very peculiar when we
asked for permission to pick a few ears for ourselves.
But she had to admit that the boiled product wasn't unworthy of human consumption. Once she and Alma met
in a food store. Alma bought a pound of peanuts, a new
import from the Soviet Union. Frau Gontscharoff had
never tasted a peanut, but took Alma's word that they
were good, and healthy too, and bought some herself. She
came by the next day to complain that these peanuts refused to get soft, even though she'd boiled them for many
hours.

We bought eggs from the Gontscharoffs for a while,
before we got chickens of our own. These eggs had a
strange fishy taste, not bad really, once you got used to
it, but hard to explain. Eventually we learned that their
chickens were fed with fish heads.

Herr Gontscharoff never said or did very much that I can remember. Mostly he sat on the porch surveying his luxuriant and untidy fenced-in part of the world through those watery eyes of his, and when something alien intruded—that Uhse boy, for instance, come to search for a soccer ball that had flown over the fence—Herr Gontscharoff seemed to give it no more importance than he would have a bird or the shadow of a cloud passing over his garden. He responded feebly to greetings, to apologies not at all. After a while he became so weak that he could no longer call his chickens for feeding, a chore which until then seemed to have been his exclusive responsibility. Herr Gontscharoff was dying, and his wife was furious at him for it. She scolded him throughout the day: a good-for-nothing she'd married, a useless lazybones— she'd have him put away if he didn't get moving.

One day Alma accidentally ran over the Gontscharoffs' little dog with her car. It was killed instantly. She carried it to where Herr Gontscharoff was sitting, in his usual place on the porch, and said what had to be said: that she was terribly sorry, and that the dog had just come shooting under the wheels, and again that she was sorry. Herr Gontscharoff didn't say anything, he just held the dead dog on his lap and looked at Alma and cried. After that Alma couldn't stand hearing Frau Gontscharoff yell at her husband. Once, when she knew the old woman was out of the house, she went over to visit, and asked Herr Gontscharoff whether there was anything she could do to help, since he was so weak. You could rub my feet, he said, they get numb and hurt. She visited him frequently after that, to rub his feet and talk. I don't know what they talked about; they couldn't have had much in common, except maybe the fellow feeling of strangers in a strange land, and a liking of each other beyond the words they used to communicate. In his living room was a photograph of a group of workers assembled under a banner with a revolutionary slogan in Bulgarian. One of these men was Herr

Gontscharoff in his youth. The photograph was a me-
mento of something extraordinary he had accomplished,
though I don't remember what it was. Maybe he had
organized a strike. It was Bodo's idea to honor him
with a celebration of the Bulgarian national holiday.
Friends from the village and from Berlin were invited.
Never had there been so many cars parked in front of
the Gontscharoffs' shack. Never before, I'm sure, were
speeches given there and champagne bottles decanted.

Eventually Herr Gontscharoff was hospitalized in
Potsdam. I visited him there with Alma. I remember the
impact of his almost repulsive frailty as we stepped in,
and the shock of pity I felt. So this was what dying
was like: white flaccid limbs on a white bed in a white
room, a blood-red rose in a vase, a faint sickly-sweet
smell, as if he were already rotting; his face denuded of
all adult knowing and strength, the awful nakedness in
his eyes as he forced the words out, almost voiceless:
"*Frau Uhse . . . ich hab' Angst . . .*"; his waxen, blue-
veined hands clutching at Alma's sleeve and relaxing
gradually as she sat down on the bed and very gently
stroked his forehead and cheeks, smiling and looking
into his eyes and saying, "It's good. Really, it's good. It's
like peace. Life is much harder than death."

Across the lake from our house lived Herbert Gessner, the radio commentator who had tried to make a
bloodthirsty monster out of Rolf. I liked Herbert. Instead of plying me with questions about school, as most
adults did, he gave me enthusiastic accounts of his own
hobbies. I don't think I'll ever forget his inspired recreation of a great automobile race. By holding the rim
of an ordinary water glass to one corner of his mouth
and deftly modulating the cupped palm of his free hand
over the mouth of the glass (like a harmonica player)
and roaring at the same time, he could produce an
astonishing *EEEEEEEEAAAAAOOOUUUUUUgggr-
grhhmmrmrm*, followed by a frenzied announcement

that the highly favored So-and-so had taken the lead once again in his Mercedes-Benz but that the indomitable Carraciola, handicapped by his inferior Porsche, was in hot pursuit and actually *EEEEEE*UNBELIEV-ABL*YEEEEEEEEAAAAAOOOOUUUUUU* PASSING HIM IN THE STRETCH! *gggggrrhhrgh* ... Another time he gave a blow-by-blow description of a boxing match he'd seen in West Berlin between the American Sugar Ray Robinson and the West German middle-weight champion, Gerhard Hecht. Hecht was floored and incapacitated by a blow to the kidneys, a blow which Herbert said was permitted by American but not by German rules. Thus Robinson was innocent of any intentional foul play. But no one knew that at the time. The audience went berserk and threw bottles and tin cans into the ring. A man sitting behind Herbert called Robinson a black swine: "*Schwarze Sau! Schwarze Sau!*" Herbert grabbed him by the shirt collar, held his fist under his nose, and said, "Shut up, you *weisse Sau*, or I'll knock every tooth out of your mouth." Herbert was tough. It showed in his radio commentaries. You didn't have to understand much of what he said, you just had to hear the glee with which he exposed the crimes of Nazis holding office in the West. It wasn't just a job for him, attacking Nazis and racists—it was a passion.

Herbert also told me about his exploits as a schoolboy: dropping rotten eggs on a hated teacher, disfiguring portraits of Hindenburg and, later, Hitler, covering the school's skeleton with phosphorescent paint and darkening the room before the teacher came in. I couldn't hear enough about Herbert's pranks, and on the second or third telling he tried to temper their timeless appeal with remarks that emphasized their historical specificity and political justification. That portrait of Hitler was a portrait of *Hitler*, not just any old big shot, *you* understand that. And you don't drop rotten eggs on

somebody just for the fun of it—not unless it's a
Schweinehund like that teacher, who liked to beat little
boys on their calves with a cane. These precautions
couldn't quite forestall an influence he might have deplored, had he lived long enough to hear about it. The
trick with the skeleton, in particular, came in handy
several years later.

⟨[Four-year-old Stefan invented a persona for himself:
Herr Ganzmacher (Mr. Fixit), modeled on all the
plumbers and electricians he'd seen, and also, and especially, on Jochen, who was always the chief *Ganzmacher* in our household of technological cretins. Herr
Ganzmacher would, as a rule, knock three officious raps
on the living-room door, whereupon the adult-in-resi-
dence would exclaim in a tone of glad expectation:
"Who is it?" "Herr Ganzmacher!" "Oh, I'm so glad it's
you, we were just wondering . . ." etc. But Herr Ganzmacher had no time for small talk: "Is something *kaputt?*" Why yes, the record player seemed irreparably
kaputt, and the vent in the fireplace was clogged, and a
window was stuck. Herr Ganzmacher marched in
briskly, lugging a large briefcase filled with tools, inspected the damaged object (which, of course, had to
be in perfect condition if he was to fix it), and got to
work. Usually he'd have everything tiptop after some
diligent tinkering, but sometimes he'd sit back scratching his head, looking stumped. "I will have to come
back with some special tools," he'd say then, walking off
in a hurry and turning briefly at the door with a reassuring "It won't be long" sort of gesture. He'd be back with
something invisible and bulky to which he gave a buzzing sound. That, then, would do the trick. Quite often
he was so gratified by the admiration and relief he'd
caused (though he tried not to let his pleasure break
through the Ganzmacher's mask, which at most allowed

for some businesslike satisfaction) that he'd leave without charging a pfennig. And sometimes, when he did charge, he'd make out a hastily scrawled bill in imitation script with the words running from right to left, enumerating the costs he'd incurred, and the time he had labored. Herr Ganzmacher was a harried fellow, but dependable.

A very different sort was Herr Balitz, an invisible personage with whom Stefan conversed at great length (he must have been five then), always in a leisurely unhurried tone: "Good morning, Herr Balitz, how are you today? . . . (a pause while Herr Balitz responded and Stefan nodded his head in acknowledgment) . . . I'm glad to hear that . . . my wife is fine, thank you, except she was kicked by the horse last week and had to be hospitalized . . . and how is *your* wife? . . . And your husband, how is he? . . . (for some reason Herr Balitz had both) . . . I see, I'm glad . . . and how are things at work? . . . *Ach!* . . . (heaving a sigh, and beginning to pace with his hands behind his back, no doubt accompanied by Herr Balitz in the same position) . . . The situation at work is very difficult, very very difficult. The other workers don't work enough, so I have to work more. That makes me too tired. The doctor says I need a lot of rest. What does *your* doctor say? . . . Yes . . . yes . . . aha . . . yes . . . yes, my wife smokes too much also . . ." and so on. When they weren't pacing side by side, Stefan and Herr Balitz stood facing one another, and then it became apparent that they were exactly the same height.

Maybe there really was a little Herr Balitz who visited Stefan. Would an imaginary creature go on a business trip to Leipzig and leave his creator in a state of listless suspension? For a whole week?

Most probably, though, Herr Balitz was a compensation for loneliness. There were no children Stefan's age in the immediate neighborhood, and only one within walking distance—and Willi was a "fair-weather friend," as Alma aptly and bitterly called him: here today, so long as Stefan was pliable to his every whim or had a new toy for Willi to play with, and gone tomorrow, sometimes along with the toy. Disagreements between Stefan and Willi were invariably and quickly settled by force, always to Willi's advantage: sitting on Stefan's chest, he'd pin his wrists to the ground and grind both knees into his biceps (a practice known as *Muskelreiten*, "muscle-riding"). In this way he exacted penance, confession, surrender . . . any or all of these, as he saw fit. But sometimes Stefan refused to give in. Then Willi punished him by staying away for several weeks. When he came back, he was always welcome; after all, he was Stefan's only friend.

It is painful for me to write about Stefan's very sad childhood in any detail because I contributed to it, both actively and by default, out of jealousy and out of a need to dominate. I excluded him from my games with my friends, insisting that he was too young for us, and at other times, when I did condescend to play with him, it was with a kind of pushy superiority—natural, perhaps, in brothers six years apart in age, but still a source of shame and self-reproach when I think back on it. There were times when my jealousy materialized as physical disgust—the pale freckles covering his face, his habit of saving his desserts and sweets revolted me. Nor could I forgive him the only weapon he had against me, which was to tell on me. It infuriated me that his complaints were always believed and always dignified with the most serious attention (in large part owing to the fact that he told the truth), while on several occasions mine were dismissed as lies or exaggerations (which they often were). The immediate facts had little bearing on my feelings. I felt victimized by his existence.

Stefan, who worshipped me and wanted to be like me in all ways, even to the color of my hair, unwittingly sharpened my envy by drawing, painting, writing, and studying much more energetically than I ever had; and after a while it would no longer be a clear case of his emulating me. By the time he was nine and I was fifteen, he would be attracting attention with solid accomplishments in the form of illustrated manuscripts, regular little works, whereas I would be busy hiding my unfinishable poems and my unpresentable pornography. He would be the creative one, I the dreamer. Stefan would be Bodo Uhse's remarkably talented son, Joel his problematic and rather woozy stepson.

When Stefan was six and I was twelve, we both contracted scarlet fever. The law required that we be quarantined in a hospital, together with other children afflicted with contagious diseases—all sorts of diseases. A boy with diphtheria shared our hospital room in Potsdam. Stefan was infected, and very nearly died. Shortly after recovering, he developed pneumonia—a common complication of diphtheria, the doctors explained. The pneumonia in turn led to an inflammation of the tonsils. A tonsillectomy was performed. Two months later the inflammation returned; apparently the tonsils hadn't been completely removed. The chief doctor at the hospital felt responsible for Stefan's condition, although he kept repeating that it wasn't really anyone's fault. Not even the law could be faulted. Given the nationwide shortage of hospital beds, the state had to choose between two unfortunate alternatives: protecting the healthy while endangering the sick, or the other way around. As for the failed tonsillectomy—such things happened once in a while, that was no one's fault either. Still, the doctor felt sorry and responsible. He offered to treat Stefan gratis in his private clinic in Berlin. He would personally supervise the operation, not because anything was likely to go wrong, but just to make sure. Stefan would have to be quarantined again—just for a week. Hospital regulations, standard procedure. No, certainly not together with a diphtheria case again. He would be alone, in a private room.

Alma objected that keeping a six-year-old alone for a week might not be advisable. To this the doctor replied that most mothers rebelled against the idea at first. The children disliked it too, for understandable reasons. But once Alma and Bodo were gone, he said, Stefan would adjust. He would not, as a matter of fact, be *alone*, strictly speaking, since doctors and nurses would be looking in on him frequently; and he could always read or listen to the radio. And he could receive visitors, certainly. But not in his room; they would have to communicate with him from outside, through a closed window.

Alma never forgave herself for consenting to this arrangement.

After the operation—a successful one, this time—Stefan was put in an open-topped glass box that was ordinarily used as an incubator. (This, too, was due to the shortage of beds.) There he lay for a week, alone except for a daily checkup and the times when he was fed or bathed or his sheets were changed, and visiting time. He begged Alma and Bodo to take him home; he said he was frightened. But, having once accepted the rules—signed their names to an agreement, in fact—they were unable to help him.

Not long before this nightmare, Stefan and I had seen a movie about the men who planned the extermination camps. It was compulsory viewing for all children in Gross-Glienicke, perhaps for all in the DDR. *Der Rat der Götter* it was called, *The Council of the Gods*. There was a scene in which several animals—a lamb, a hen, a mouse, and a puppy, I seem to remember—were asphyxiated in a glass gas chamber while several statesmen and scientists looked on with interest. That experiment was repeated in Stefan's dreams night after night for several weeks. What could anyone tell him? That it was just a movie? Just a dream?

It seems more than likely that, lying in his glass incubator several months later, Stefan's night fears were restimulated in ways that it would be useless to imagine. It was at this time he developed asthma, which kept him periodically bedridden and gasping for breath until he was fourteen years old.

〔I was, for a while, a good student—"brilliant," in fact; "exceptionally gifted." Everyone agreed on that. When I was twelve, I was promoted a year ahead of my age group—a decision that may have contributed to my eventual academic collapse. It seemed a mistake even then. Being the youngest in the class exacerbated my shyness. Nor did I take well to the high expectations placed upon me. Flattering though it was to be deemed exceptional, it involved a frightening isolation. I would much rather have had dashing good looks, or superlative skill in soccer or ice skating. I began to avoid all those cultural temptations—literature, piano teachers, a prospective study course with a famous boys' choir—that threatened to elevate me still further above my friends. Instead, I devoured and helped circulate forbidden books, such as Karl May's Winnetou saga and, especially, the murky adventures, smuggled across the border, of a pathologically fearless New York detective named Tom Brack.

Detective Brack had a swarthy unassuming poolshooting Mexican cohort named Manuel or Pablo or José Martínez or Gutiérrez or González, who was constantly being compared to a cat—with good reason, since he was lithe, agile, sleek, swift, sinewy, silent, and intuitive. Tom Brack—a Caucasian, of course—had brains, an unchallenged preeminence as problem-solver and leader of men, and a glorious musculature. However, he had no sinew to speak of, nor a sensory apparatus worth mentioning. And since his sleek sidekick had neither brains nor muscles, the two crime fighters needed each other, sometimes desperately. Divided, they invariably fell; united, they knew how to adapt to every challenge.

They also provided excellent personas for me and my friend Uwe to slip into each day after school. I remember well my cat burglar's stunts on top of the chicken coop, and Uwe's King Kong-like way of heaving boulders into the lake. (Since Uwe was rather bulky and I was thin, there could be no question as to who played who.) My parents never objected to their son's willful plunge into the lowest kind of pulp. They were confident that some innate sense of values would buoy me up to the surface again. To the heights, actually— quatrains by Heine: that's what I interrupted for the sinewy-muscular prose of *Tom Brack*. A protest delivered to Bodo by our new maid, Anneliese (Jochen's sister), impressed this fact on my memory. She had seen me lying on the floor, day after day, poring over a volume of verse. Finally she asked me what I was studying so hard. "Heine," I said. Later that evening, after Anneliese had gone home, Bodo told me and Alma what a dear girl she was, how she cared for us children so much that she dared to confront Bodo angrily for what she considered to be an abuse: "Why does a twelve-year-old boy have to read Heine?" "But he *doesn't* have to read it. He's reading it because he likes it." Ironically, just a day or two later, a teacher found the latest Tom Brack in my desk and informed Bodo of my misdemeanor—so unbefitting the son of a Communist and a writer. "What *are* you reading," Bodo asked, "Tom Brack or Heine?" "Both," I said. But soon after, it was Tom Brack all the way.

(Bodo was consistent in his toleration of pulp literature. Once he discovered a Zane Grey thriller, in German translation, under the car seat where Jochen had hidden it. Jochen, shamefaced, admitted to preferring Zane Grey—Tsahn Greh, he pronounced it—to the Socialist Realist books available in the East, and to the classics. Bodo asked to read the Zane Grey when Jochen

was finished. "Not bad," he said when he returned it.
Apparently he meant that sincerely, for he defended
both Jochen and Zane Grey at one of the weekly political classes all employees of the Aufbau publishing
house were obliged to attend; Jochen, though still
Bodo's private chauffeur, was now on Aufbau's payroll.
The chairman of the meeting had asked everyone to say
what they were reading, and Jochen boldly confessed:
Tsahn Greh. The predictable lecture on reactionary
bourgeois literature followed—how it distorts reality
and stands in the way of progress. Then Bodo raised his
hand and said he had looked into the writings of this
Zane Grey and they weren't at all objectionable, and
in fact were quite well written, and very entertaining.)

At the opposite end of the village from where we
lived, about half a mile along the road to Potsdam, was
a pine forest containing patches of heather and a marsh.
That was the play- and battleground of a group of boys
who had formed a kind of Karl May cult. They read
all his books, got dressed up as cowboys and Indians,
built campfires, tied one another to trees, shot arrows,
emitted war cries, and all the rest of it. They were, for
the most part, older than Uwe and I, and a lot tougher,
so we stayed away from them. Only once did we participate in a horrendous battle between the Comanches and
the Apaches. Having painted our faces and stuck feathers
in our headbands and table knives in our belts, we
tramped along the Seepromenade toward the appointed
meeting place, dodging the amused glances of people we
passed. Two of the oldest boys were, by general consent,
the chiefs (one of these being Winnetou). They took
turns selecting braves in the order of their reputation for
fierceness, which put Uwe and me humiliatingly near the
end of the list, just ahead of some small-fry from the
fourth and fifth grades. The chiefs exchanged a gallant
"How!" and went trotting off in opposite directions, followed by their respective tribes. A half hour later the

forest was humming with menace. From time to time twigs cracked and birds nervously fluttered and squawked in the trees. Suddenly, several hundred yards from where Uwe and I were squatting behind a clump of tall dry reeds (we'd been sent to scout behind enemy lines), a ferocious whooping and howling broke out, followed by a cry of "Halt," a scream, the sound of crying, and merciless commands: "Get up! Keep moving! Faster! Shut your mouth! Crybaby—some Indian you are!" One of our men, a ten-year-old, had been captured. No chance of rescuing him: we were outnumbered, our troops nowhere in sight. "Surrender, wherever you are! Or else you'll be tortured!" A stone whirred through the air. Three boys approached with loaded slingshots in their hands. Their faces were streaked with red and green paint. They stopped just ten steps away and shot another volley of stones, fortunately not in our direction. Apparently they knew we were somewhere near, but couldn't see us. "If you come out right away, we won't hurt you. If you don't, you'll be sorry." No Indian scout worth his salt surrenders to threats of torture. Besides, our chief had told us the Apaches might torture us just for being afraid. We lay low, quivering. After a while the boys walked away. We didn't dare move for at least a half hour. Then we had a whispered argument—not a powwow, we were through with being Indians—as to which was the safest way to get home. There was no sure way of telling, we didn't have Winnetou's instincts to guide us, just our five senses quickened by terror. Never again!—that much we agreed on. Never, never again! These kids are crazy, they're playing war for *real*. Stop cracking sticks or they'll hear us! We should never have read Karl May or Tom Brack. Oh, God, don't let them catch us. I promise, if you help us get away I'll never tease Stefan again, I won't cut classes, I'll even go to church on Sundays, I'll pray every night, I'll brush my teeth, I'll be a model Young Pioneer—just don't let them catch us!

Well, the Great Spirit led us directly into the enemy's hands. Fortunately, they'd used all their rope to tie up several other Comanches, including our chief. We were simply told to sit down. The war was almost over. To our surprise and relief, the Apaches weren't torturing anyone. They were busy roasting some stolen potatoes over a fire. Our fettered chief clenched his teeth and gazed yearningly over the treetops. Then something amazing happened. One of the Apaches betrayed his own tribe! He had been lingering behind the tree where our chief was bound, and in an unguarded moment cut through the rope. They ran away together—fled leaping into the woods, like deer, and were out of sight by the time the Apaches dropped their potatoes and scrambled into pursuit. Now was our opportunity. Could we dare to run? We probed one another's eyes for assurance. Yes. We ran all the way back to the Seepromenade, then dragged our feet home, ashamed of ourselves. Why didn't we untie the other Comanches? Someone else probably did. But we should have. Some Indians we were.

Just a few years earlier, in the winter of 1946, eight boys were playing war in the woods. They were between thirteen and fifteen years old. Since the landscape was littered with weapons at that time, they had plenty to play with: hand grenades, submachine guns, undetonated bombs, steel helmets, and uniforms. Russian soldiers discovered their cache and arrested the boys. Their teacher, too, was arrested. The boys were accused of belonging to a neo-Nazi Werwolf detachment, the teacher of leading it. The boys were beaten and terrorized into signing a "confession," written in Russian; and when the teacher was shown their signatures, he, too, acquiesced and signed, since a denial would have been useless. All were interned in the former concentration camp at Sachsenhausen, which was now a Soviet prison. Later they were transferred to a prison in Bautzen, under German auspices—a much

harsher place than Sachsenhausen. Five of the boys returned to the village in October 1950, bloated and
flabby and sick with tuberculosis of the lungs; one of
them had bone TB as well. Of the other three boys, two
had died in prison and the third had vanished—none
could say whether he was dead or alive. The teacher
was released from Bautzen in 1952. He came home
shockingly aged and by all accounts "kaputt," a sick and
brokenhearted man.

⦗Gross-Glienicke, as I remember it, was clustered alongside the lake (Glienicker See) in the shape of a fish-
hook. My school, the mayor's office, and the church
were near the upper end of the hook, and our house was
at the lower end. Probably, before the country's political bisection had lopped off what was now perforce
called West Gross-Glienicke, or West Glienicke for
short, the village had been more or less circular or oval
in shape, with the lake at its center. The western part of
it had a public beach of sorts, a grassy meadow that
bordered on the lake. We East Gross-Glienickers had no
beach on our side of the lake, but, as if to make up for
that, the politicians had accorded us another, larger
lake, Sacrower See, just a half hour's walk through the
woods. This lake had several coves that were so secluded you could swim in the nude, and also a more
public beach, sandy and framed by banks of tall reeds,
that was used by West and East Gross-Glienickers alike.

The border was open during those years, except for a
red-and-white-striped toll bar that was raised and lowered to let cars and bicycles through after some (often
perfunctory) baggage and passport control. Once in a
while you'd hear of someone, a peasant woman or an
older boy, who had been caught smuggling meat or
eggs to the West. By selling the goods there and then
buying East marks from a bank, one could quadruple

one's profits. This sort of economic crime was punished severely, sometimes with a long prison sentence. But I think anyone my age could have safely made a small fortune smuggling, for my friends and I were never stopped on our way past the toll bar.

We didn't go to the West very often—just occasionally on Sundays, to watch a soccer game; and this only when our home team, Rot-Weiss Gross-Glienicke, was playing out of town. I don't remember there ever having been a game pitting East against West Gross-Glienicke, but if there had been, all of us would have rooted for the East—not for political reasons, but because they were "ours." (The West and everything connected with it—sports, politics, citrus fruits, espionage, money, modernity, glamour—was *"drüben,"* "over there." And regardless of how you felt about it, *"drüben"* was a foreign country.)

For a while, I had the impression that soccer was played at a higher level or was at least more exciting in the West than in the East. That probably had to do with the surrounding fanfare—frankfurter stands, newsboys, little trumpets being blasted by the onlookers. Also, interesting people came to these games, interesting because one never saw their likes in the East: British and occasionally American soldiers, for instance, including blacks, always a great sensation. There were usually a few fancy cars parked near the soccer field, and it was easy to spot the slick people who had come in them, people of some significance, you could tell by the curious-polite reactions of the ordinary folk; aristocrats who stood apart from the crowd, even if rubbing shoulders with it, and who never really joined in the cheering and booing. Applause—yes, that much they would grant. They were appraisers, connoisseurs of the game, and their presence lent it an aura of importance.

Tucked away in the pine forest near Sacrower See was a Soviet encampment. As far as two or three miles away you'd run into crude wooden signs forbidding unauthorized entry and warning trespassers of various dangers and punishments—very explicitly, but in Russian. These signs were, at any rate, not meant for me and my friends; we walked past them often to spend an afternoon with the "Russkies." The soldiers greeted us from afar with waving hands, sometimes in the middle of a drill. We were always welcome in their volleyball games, small and incompetent as we were. More than once a group of Russkies took us for a ride in an army truck (which was against the rules) and would tell us to duck low when we passed an officer. The smaller the child, the greater the friendliness almost invariably elicited in any passing Russian. I remember a bus ride from Potsdam to Gross-Glienicke during which a Russian soldier, ignoring the stiff embarrassment of many of the German passengers, spent twenty minutes entertaining a fascinated and delighted two-year-old across the aisle with grimaces and fluttering hands. German adults, in general, were bent on maintaining a definite hierarchical distinction between themselves and children; they were rather stern, and bestowed friendliness in a clear exchange for good behavior. The Russians, on the other hand, seemed to enjoy the anarchic element we brought to their often severe barracks life. Even the officers must have liked having us around, otherwise they wouldn't have tolerated it; but they seemed, on the whole, more bound by their regulations, or perhaps by their rank, and hence less free to play with us. And we—we felt flattered more than anything: it was a privilege to have strong soldiers for companions. At the same time, though, that we marched through the woods to visit them, my friends often told stories about the almost unbelievable primitiveness the Russkies had exhibited in the course of occupying Germany in 1945; how, ignorant of modern plumbing, one man would shit in a kitchen sink, while another hacked a hole in a wall, jammed a faucet in it, and cursed because no water came out; how the Russkies had marched from house to house demanding *"Uhri, Uhri!"*

—watches and clocks; how they would cut off a finger if
a ring refused to come off it; how Anneliese K. of our
class, who had been only five years old at the time, had
been raped; how one day a decree came down from
Stalin ordering the death penalty for rape, looting, and
pillage, and how a soldier caught with several wrist-
watches too many in front of Niemann's café was put up
against the wall and shot then and there without any
legal ado. Many of these things, if I was to believe my
friends, they had witnessed themselves; but some of
their terminology, for example the satirical use of the
Russian word *"kultura,"* usually to denote some slovenly or inept workmanship or behavior, must have come
from their parents. So, I assume, did jokes that portrayed Russians as outlandish yokels with a misplaced
superiority complex, for example the one about the Russian soldier who, seeing a squirrel, exclaimed: *"Armes
Deutschland! Kleine Füchse!"*—Poor Germany! Such
small foxes!

That many Germans held the Russians in contempt
became palpably evident wherever Russians strayed
into the daily life of the village—when shopping, for
instance. My toes still curl in my shoes at the memory of
a young soldier requesting some groceries with an air of
meek self-effacement, in clumsy but perfectly understandable German, and of the other shoppers' and the
salesgirl's sarcastically feigned incomprehension, and
the sneers and winks exchanged behind the man's back,
and my cowardly complicity in their mean joke. But
everyone, even the most contemptuous, would grant
that the Russkies produced some superb musicians,
singers, and dancers (that they made superior soldiers
as well was something only Communists were happy to
admit). It didn't take much discernment. A truckful of
Russian soldiers would roll by, all singing some vast and
sorrowful song in three-part harmony—it couldn't fail
to astonish and move you. (Their German counterparts,
the border police—stationed in a training camp across

the lake from us—also sang in chorus, while marching or while being transported on trucks, but their music was choppily martial, more shouted than sung.)

I remember the evening when Gross-Glienickers were treated to an exhilarating "friendship performance" by a Red Army cultural ensemble at Niemann's café. It made you wonder which was the disguise, the costume: the familiar, drably uniformed, vodka-soused muzhiks staggering into a bar to demand yet another *sto gramm*, or these dashing, mustachioed men in wide-sleeved silk shirts riding the air with effortless leaps and cartwheels. Hard to believe that these shining girls in embroidered dresses, singing songs of such sweet melancholy it brought tears to your eyes, were the very same officers' wives you'd see walking around with their heads wrapped in polka-dotted kerchiefs, smelling of cheap perfume, interrupting one another with high-pitched, throaty, quarrelsome-sounding voices. A homage to German culture was also presented: a Bach toccata played on a harmonica, and a tender rendition, sung by a blue-eyed man with a pink spotlight on him, of an old-time favorite called "Domino," which melted the German women's hearts (you could hear the collective female "Aaaah!" filling the applause at the end). The show concluded, and was intended to climax, with a lovingly produced *tableau vivant*. The performers rushed about on the darkened stage—slipping into costumes, moving props, shifting the spotlights, getting into position. Then the lights went on, and lo! there before us in the flesh was an immortal masterpiece of nineteenth-century Russian realistic painting no one had ever seen. At the center, seated before a table of rough-hewn wood, holding a white quill poised over a sheet of paper, was a man with a wryly humorous expression on his face. His black hair had been moistened and brushed down over his forehead so that it resembled a large skullcap. Next to him, on his left, stood one of the men who had danced before—I could tell by his beet-

ling eyebrows, the scowling expression of which he had
intensified for the purposes of this performance. A
heavy handlebar mustache was pasted under his nose,
there was a fur hat on his head and a pipe in his mouth
—a pipe that was actually lit and through which he was
blowing a thin cloud of smoke. He was clutching the
head of the pipe with his left fist in a very dramatic
manner, as if he had just finished dictating whatever
was making the scribe smile so wryly and was taking a
pensive puff in preparation for the next flash of wit. His
black eyes, burning beneath those aquiline eyebrows,
were fixed on some point above and beyond the heads
of the audience. His right hand was placed on his hip, a
gesture that caused his elbow to stick out at a jaunty
angle, and at the same time drew attention to the
gleaming hilt of a saber. Next to him stood a fat man
with a tall white fur hat, holding his belly with both
hands as if afraid it would burst, his head thrown back
and his mouth open in a frozen guffaw. A man with a
glistening bald pate was leaning back in our direction,
balanced precariously on a barrel, apparently laughing
so hard he was about to fall off. Another bald man, with
a strange wisp of hair growing out of the top of his head
and hanging over his brow, was sitting at the table, leaning on it with both elbows, his massive torso naked, a
round-bellied lute on his lap. He, too, was equipped
with enormous mustachios. His mouth was open, as if in
speech, and he was looking at the scribe, so perhaps he
was adding something to the scowler's dictation. A man
standing behind him was belting a mute laugh up to the
sky, and had simultaneously laid or more likely
pounded a fist upon the bare back of the man with the
lute. A smaller character, also bald (shaven heads
weren't hard to come by in the Soviet Army), and wearing a gray forelock, had crow's feet and wrinkles
painted on his face. Evidently he represented a wizened
old man. He, too, was holding a pipe, which he had just
pulled out of his mouth, it seemed, to permit himself to

laugh (motion- and soundlessly, like the others) in a puckish, toothless sort of way. Immediately next to him was a saturnine character whose grave expression and solemn mustache suggested something deeply serious afoot, which the laughing men were choosing to ignore. Way over on the right stood an august figure, his back turned to the audience, a yellow hooded coat slung over his shoulders, the sleeves hanging loose. He appeared to be neither watching nor listening to the scene before him, but to be attending to something far away or deep within himself. In the background, a laughing man was holding up a hat, while another pointed excitedly into the distance behind him. The actors held their positions bravely for several minutes, while the smoke continued to curl from the scowling man's pipe, refusing to hold still. The lights went out. The audience responded with bewildered but polite applause. Then all the performers stepped out and bowed, hand in hand, and the scowling man, still wearing his fake Cossack's mustache, said: "Long live friendship between the German and the Soviet people!" The audience responded ecstatically—not, I'm afraid, to the offer of friendship, which was a too familiar and hollow rhetorical phrase, but to the best show Gross-Glienicke had seen in years.

Occasionally the Russkies would ask with a sly leer whether we had any big sisters, and then we were expected to put on the same sly leer while making a ring of the thumb and forefinger of one hand and sticking the forefinger of the other hand in and out of it: that always produced loud laughter. I knew very well what that sign meant, but why it should be deemed *that* funny made me wonder.

Probably sexual frustration had something to do with it, for Russian soldiers were forbidden to socialize with German girls (though some officers did have their wives with them). Everyone had heard about the drunken Russian who was seen fucking a chicken-wire fence.

There was one truly weird notion I developed about Russians. Maybe it was just an elaborate fantasy, but who knows? There could be a simple explanation: a unisex cologne, or the chemical makeup of the diet of Soviet citizens in the fifties, or something like that. I detected among Russians the presence of a certain smell, a finely pungent, not unpleasant odor that was distinct from all other peculiarly Russian smells, such as the smell of cabbage soup or makhorka tobacco or boot polish, or of the sweat-soaked rags the soldiers wrapped around their feet instead of socks. This smell, I discovered one day, was identical to the smell of a live anthill. Having once made this correlation, I became hooked on it, and found myself sniffing whenever I came across either a Russian or an anthill, refining my knowledge of their respective odors and becoming increasingly convinced that they were indistinguishable. One day I saw two soldiers spreading handkerchiefs on an anthill—to perfume them, it turned out, for I was bold enough to ask, and they answered with deep inhalations and facial expressions indicative of relish. The riddle appeared to be solved. But when, some time later, I sat next to the wife of a Russian officer in a bus, and smelled the anthill smell strong and clear beneath, or beside, or in addition to, a cloud of lilac perfume, a doubt appeared; and that doubt grew every time I noticed a Russian smelling like an anthill. Could it be that all these people had ants perfume their handkerchiefs? There weren't that many anthills around. The doubt deepened into mystery when, years later, Ivan Ivanovich Anisimov, literary scholar and president of the Gorky Institute for World Literature, came on a semi-official visit from Moscow. Bodo was chosen, or volunteered, to be his escort, and so it happened that I came to sit next to Mr. Anisimov at a David Oistrakh recital. A dour, self-important, obviously influential man, he was absolutely not the type to scour the woods for an anthill—yet he, too, had that

smell, and he was Russian. Probably David Oistrakh
smelled that way, too.

For a couple of years our next-door neighbors were Alfred Kantorowicz and his very friendly and kind wife,
Friedel, who, I believe, played the piano. (I do know
there was a grand piano in their house, for I remember
the timidity and unworthiness I felt when I first sat
down before this musical shrine, so obviously not a toy.
Friedel opened the lid and removed a silk cloth from
the keys. Then I carefully pecked out the notes of a
nursery tune under the somewhat oppressively encouraging observance of Friedel and Alma, until they moved
into another room, after which I gradually sank into a
trance in which my command of the instrument appeared consummate, and the cacophony I was no doubt
producing, sublime.) I've learned recently that Kantor,
as he was called, was a university professor and the
editor-in-chief of an academic magazine. He impressed
me then as a quick-witted, intensely impatient, tall and
thin man with worried eyebrows and a habit of frequently bringing his fingertips to his nostrils and sniffing them.

In 1951, Kantor left Friedel, moved to Berlin, and
soon after could be heard ranting on the West Berlin
radio, attacking everyone from the Minister of Culture
on down to people who had done him no harm and
considered him a friend—Bodo among them. Three
years later, Friedel vacated the house next door, taking
with her the piano, her library, her delicate coffee cups,
and her elderly Persian cat couple, and in moved a
Soviet platoon. The change was drastic and immediate:
balalaikas, harmonicas, an accordion, and a loudspeaker
trilled and lilted and boomed out one folk dance after
another, and often the men's voices, inside and outside
the house, joined in. Much of the day was spent in drill:
"*Raz! Dva! Tri! Chetyre!*" Presenting arms, falling,
standing, creeping, running for miles laden with full

gear. Most interesting for us who watched over the
fence was bayonet practice—everyone taking turns
feinting and stabbing a sack filled with straw. The
commanding officer was a humorless, splendidly built
man who liked to exercise on parallel bars, wearing nothing but the briefest of gym shorts and covered with glistening oil, which set off his muscles to advantage. I don't
remember him playing volleyball with his men; maybe he
was disdainful. He didn't swim with them either, but that
was because he didn't know how. One day the soldiers
threw him into the lake (in his gym shorts), just like
that; swung him by the arms and legs and threw him in
with a great big splash. Uwe and I saw it because we happened to be swimming at the time. He was shouting in
anger and fright as he flew, and the soldiers were laughing. He went down with much bubbling and gurgling,
came up briefly, splashing and trying to hold his face
above water, let out a cry, and sank again. Several soldiers dove in after him and hauled him onto the shore,
where he stood bent over, choking and cursing. The soldiers laughed and clapped him on the back to help him
cough up the water he'd swallowed.

A volleyball court was set up on the field before the
Russians' house and ours, the net strung between the
two posts of a soccer goal Jochen had built for me and
my friends. At first we feared the goal had been expro-
priated, but the net was put up for the duration of a
game only, and we were always welcome to join in, as
the soldiers were welcome to take part in our soccer
games. As soon as they saw Roland, Alma's horse, some
men volunteered to groom him, and Alma let them take
turns riding him around the field.

Anneliese, our maid, had left us to enter a nurse's
training school, and my parents had just hired a young
girl named Christel. When one of our new neighbors
offered to help her beat a rug, she came running into
the house, terrified: "Frau Uhse! . . . The Russians! . . . I
can't work here!" Outside, the soldier had started beat-

ing the rug. Alma went out and somehow, across what would seem to be an insuperable language barrier, she apologized for Christel, explaining that the girl had heard bad things about Russians, and he said that he well understood and felt sorry about Christel's fear, but that she should know Russian women were also raped, and by Germans; and that his name was Yuri; that he had only wanted to help Christel, and perhaps talk to her; and that he was homesick. All this Alma told Christel later. He did do a good job with the rug, Christel admitted, and that was nice of him; but the thought of herself standing face to face with a Russian and conversing with him still filled her with fear and revulsion. "Never," she said. "They're ugly."

These neighborly contacts ceased very soon after they began. All Soviet troops in Germany were under strict orders not to fraternize with the population, and the officer in charge next door had obviously felt it necessary to enforce this rule. Children, however, were exempt from it, as I already knew from my visits to the encampment near Sacrower See. Our joint volleyball games continued unimpeded. Jochen, too, for some reason, remained always welcome to join in (but he preferred soccer, despite the preeminence his tall, lanky build gave him on the volleyball court), and I often saw him hobnobbing with the chauffeur of the Russian army truck that brought provisions (lots of cabbage, I remember, and potatoes, and black bread). Jochen evidently had a way with Russians, and the most peculiar thing about this way was that frequently it consisted of loudmouthing them: the ruder he was, the more they seemed to appreciate him. Bodo once gently questioned the appropriateness of Jochen's blustering, bullish manner when speaking across the fence to our new neighbors. Jochen explained that he was in fact being friendly, and that they knew that. He had learned Russian ways from an officer and his orderly who had taken up quarters in his home right after the war. Russians, he

said, don't respect a man unless he shows a big mouth.
I don't believe this holds true as a generality; but
when Alma got arrested by the Russians, it was Jochen's
method that brought quick and favorable results, while
Bodo's soft-spoken politeness proved ineffectual and
very nearly calamitous. Here is the story as I remember
it from Alma's, Jochen's, and Bodo's accounts (though
Bodo had the least to say). Alma went horseback riding
in the woods. It was a balmy spring afternoon, already
drawing toward evening, and enticing all creatures, including Alma and Roland, to venture away from paths
beaten by the weary tread of habit. She cantered past
the Russian warning signs and past three Russian soldiers who stood smoking and quietly conversing. *"Stoi!"*
one of them shouted. Alma was at that moment becoming aware that it was getting late and that she ought to
turn back, so the soldier's cry registered less as a command than as a suggestion in the direction her own
thoughts were taking. She wheeled Roland around and
came trotting back, smiling apologetically as she passed
the men, who were staring at her with eyes widened by alarm, it seemed. *"Stoi!"* From the shrill and
frightened tone of the voice, she could tell that she had
best stop immediately—which she did. An excited and
of course fruitless interrogation in Russian followed.
Then one of the men walked off, while the other two
stayed behind with Alma—one of them holding Roland's bridle, the other Alma's wrist. After a while the
third man returned, said something to his friends, and
then they all walked together through the darkening
forest to the Soviet encampment near Sacrower See.
There Alma was briefly, and again fruitlessly, questioned—no one could be found who spoke English, or
sufficient German to overcome her rudimentary grasp of
that language. Several soldiers and officers parleyed,
disputed, attempted a telephone call: there was no answer. It was finally decided that she should be driven,
and Roland ridden, to Krampnitz, near Potsdam, where

there was another encampment. However, Alma didn't know this. All she knew was that she was told to climb into the back of a truck, the kind that was painted olive, with two long benches made for two rows of soldiers to sit facing each other. She sat on one bench and a soldier whose job it was to guard her sat opposite her on the other bench. The truck rumbled along the Potsdamer Chaussee, with Roland galloping behind, ridden by a soldier who didn't know how to ride but who managed to hang on precariously while the stirrups, which were set much too long for the man's short legs, dangled and bounced in the air. At Krampnitz, Roland was tied to a fence and Alma was led into a barracks building, then into a room dominated by a large photograph of Stalin. There she was subjected to a long stream of questions, again in Russian, this time by about seven men, all officers. One of them looked her up and down in a calmly appraising manner. Another, very handsome and arrogant, was evidently convinced that Alma really spoke Russian and was pulling the wool over their eyes—she could tell by the gestures and faces he made while he talked about her to the others. The only relevant Russian words she could muster were *"amerikansky"* and *"kommunistka,"* a combination that made little sense to her interrogators. Intermittently, they all went into a huddle, planning a new line of questioning, but not a change to another language. Once Alma asked if she could use an ancient-looking telephone on a wall near her (it had to be cranked before dialing). Permission was granted, but the phone didn't work.

At long last a man was found who claimed to speak German, and who did, at least, manage to present Alma with an intelligible question: *"What agency do you work for?"* (He had led her into a small room containing a table, two chairs, and a smaller version of the same portrait of Stalin.) A much greater impediment than the language barrier was this man's unwillingness to doubt his own presuppositions. His goal was to break down her resistance by constantly repeating the above-quoted and a few other leading questions in rhythmic counterpoint to smacks delivered against the top of the table with a riding crop, *smack, smack, smack,* asking questions and refusing to listen. All Alma could do was repeat her unbelievable story: that she was the American wife of a Communist German living in the Soviet zone of Gross-Glienicke. "Just call him up," she said, "I'll give you the number." "I'm not so stupid," he said. "Now tell me: what agency do you work for?" Eventually he gave up. He led her back to where the other officers were waiting. She felt exhausted and near to tears. One of the men offered her a piece of candy. Then he brought her a glass of water. She drank a little of it. Very soon after that she had an idea. She asked for a piece of paper, a pencil. They were brought to her. She drew a picture:

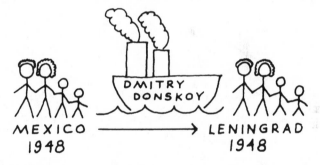

She pointed at the woman on the left side, and then at herself; at the woman on the right ride, and again at herself.

That did the trick. "Dmitry Donskoy! Dmitry Donskoy!" These words kept appearing in the lively discussion that followed. An atmosphere of relaxation, almost of relief, began to develop. The glances cast at Alma became friendlier, though the handsome skeptic still seemed wary of her. Just then the door opened and Bodo was led in.

He had begun to worry about four hours after Alma

had left, and asked Jochen to drive him and Stefan into the woods to look for her. (I think I was at Uwe's, target-shooting with his BB gun.) They followed Roland's tracks up to the place where they veered from the path and led past the Russian warning signs into the forest. Jochen stopped the car and, leaving Bodo and Stefan behind, began following the tracks. It was growing dark, and the tracks were difficult to discern in the thick pine-needle carpet, so he had to walk bent over and slowly ("Just like Winnetou," he said later). Three Russian soldiers leaped out of the brush: "*Stoi!*" This is where Jochen's theory of the big mouth was put to the test. "*Was du machen!*" he shouted (that's how I, too, learned to converse with Russian soldiers—in a lingo consisting of about thirty German words and predominantly Russian syntax and pronunciation, a precise mimicry of the way they talked to us). "What you do? Stop! Put down guns! Me: driver! He: big man, big Communist!" Then he saw that Bodo, the big Communist, was standing near the car with his hands up. Two soldiers were pointing submachine guns at him. One of the three men with Jochen was an officer. Jochen berated him, shouting and waving his arms: "That big, big man! Bad heart! He die: you . . ." and he made a throat-slashing gesture. The officer laughed and started trudging down-hill toward Bodo, followed by Jochen and the soldiers. "Big man?" the officer said to Jochen, still chuckling. Then he ordered the soldiers to put down their guns. He looked very proud of his power of command. According to Jochen, Bodo was "*volkommen kaputt*"—completely wiped out. White as a sheet, he grabbed for a cigarette and lit it with fumbling, quivering fingers. Stefan, then, was nowhere to be found—not in the car, not in the surrounding bushes. After several minutes of searching, Jochen discovered him, very frightened, wedged underneath the back seat. He helped him out and comforted him and assured him that they were all safe. The officer had in the meantime examined Bodo's papers, which included a pass identifying him as a member of the People's Chamber—a big man indeed. He lifted his hand to his cap and saluted. Bodo asked if he knew the whereabouts of his wife, who had gotten lost riding a horse somewhere in that area. Jochen translated: "Woman! Here: on horse! Where?" Aaah, the officer knew all about it: "Krampnitz," he said. That explained everything. Jochen drove Bodo and Stefan to Krampnitz.

The sentries welcomed Bodo like a guest—they had already been advised of his imminent arrival and statesmanly importance. A soldier escorted him to the room where Alma's picture was working its magic. A brief inspection of Bodo's papers, and she was free. Jochen, Bodo, and Stefan drove back home on the darkened Potsdamer Chaussee, slowly, followed by Alma on Roland, who was in an irritable, unresponsive mood—understandable after that afternoon's many discomforts, not the least of which was that he'd been haltered too short in a spot where there was nothing to nibble.

The Russians next door moved out after about a year, and I had less and less occasion to visit the troops in the woods near Sacrower See. The soccer field in front of our house had become an attraction for boys from all over the village; there was no need to go in search of amusement. And there was always the lake, a source of adventure at all times of the year—especially since part of it was off limits by law and closely watched by the People's Police. Fortunately, they never chose to feel provoked when we dared one another to swim or paddle westward in great haste and in full view of their binoculars.

On the way home from school one day—it was my first year in high school, I remember, so I was fourteen —I approached a group of Soviet soldiers who were busy sawing off all the branches of the linden trees that lined the Seepromenade. They were turning them into supports for an electric cable which one man was just beginning to drag off the back of a truck. *"Warum?"* I asked him (giving the word, as usual, a Russian pronunciation)—"Why?"—and held out my hands to emphasize the question. It was not the right question to ask, certainly not in a tone of reproach. The man looked at me with his mouth open. I repeated the question in Russian—*"Pochemú?"*—thinking he hadn't understood. I felt angry and hurt on account of the trees, but also afraid because some of the other men had stopped their work and turned to look at me, without humor, with cold dislike. I sensed obscurely that I had strayed into a labyrinth of political considerations in which trees, human beings, and simple questions have no meaning; that in the eyes of these men I was not a child but a German, a half-grown German who had the effrontery to complain about a few paltry trees after what the Germans had done to the Soviet Union. I turned around and took a detour home, with a knot in my throat.

¶[Herr Bender, our extremely erudite history teacher, gave dazzling and confusing demonstrations of dialectical reasoning. Class Struggle, Contradiction, Thesis-Antithesis-Synthesis, Capitalism-Socialism-Communism, Necessity, Just Wars, Unjust Wars, Private-ownership-of-the-means-of-production (Capitalism), From-each-according-to-his-abilities-to-each-according-to-his-work (Socialism), From-each-according-to-his-abilities-to-each-according-to-his-need (Communism), Periods of Transition (we were in one), Formal Logic (old, abstract, useless), and Dialectical Logic (new, concrete, useful): these were the phrases he used, and it was important to know their meaning if we were to decipher his questions on a test and answer them to his satisfaction. The *Concreteness* of dialectical logic was exemplified in the facts of history itself: capitalism superseded feudalism, and socialism superseded capitalism. If in some countries a revolution leaped directly from feudalism to socialism, bypassing capitalism completely, as had been the case in Russia and China, that was allowed for in dialectical logic also, for, according to Engels, Nature was fond of leaps and disliked smooth transitions. *Contradiction*, we learned, was the hallmark of dialectical reason, and this stamped Herr Bender as a competent dialectician indeed. He gloried in contradiction. Not only did he use the word a great deal, he missed no occasion to demonstrate that something could be the case and at the same time not the case; false, but in a sense true; a victory, nevertheless a defeat; retrogressive, but, in a larger, dialectical perspective, a great stride forward. Nevertheless—and this was the very appropriately paradoxical cornerstone of his philosophy—there was an inexorable force that had no opposite and admitted no exception. Its name was *Necessity*, and there were no two ways about it. Necessity came like an avenging angel to fight by the side of the oppressed; soldiers who believed in the cause they were fighting for were *necessarily* victorious over soldiers who didn't. That was why the United States would of *Necessity* lose the war in Korea, and why Communism would of *Necessity* triumph all over the world—as surely as the sun rose each day in the East. The seesaw of contradiction was of *Necessity* tipping in our favor (thank God!) and to the detriment of the West. We were strong, they were weak; we were good, they were bad; we were progressive, they were reactionary; we had the benefit of dialectics, they were hamstrung by formal logic.

In a way, Contradiction and Necessity complemented one another. When speaking of Contradiction, Herr Bender seemed to be climbing about in a maze, it made one dizzy to watch him; and if he went on for too long, we'd lose interest. Then along came Necessity, like a drum roll, like a dust cloud announcing a herd of buffalo in one of Karl May's novels; Herr Bender stopped wavering, and so did History. His gestures became broad and sure, his chest full, his eyes bright. No one else in Gross-Glienicke, not even Herbert Gessner, the radio commentator, or, for that matter, the clear-eyed, silver-haired pastor with his air of quiet, humbly knowing assurance, could summon up such mountainous strength of conviction. *Necessity!* What a mighty force, and how fortunate that it was our ally and not the West's! After a while, though, Necessity lost its power to fascinate. Someone would start reading a greasy Tom Brack beneath his desk, others would gaze out the window or doodle. Then Herr Bender would toss out some question like: "Was Napoleon progressive or reactionary?" and you just knew this was of the Contradiction variety and called for a complex answer—and not simply "Both," but why both and how both. Thus he'd capture our attention again.

But there were times when a deep sullen lethargy took possession of our brains, like an opiate, and no amount of dialectical shuttling could lift the weight off our eyelids. Then Herr Bender would be reduced to two options: waking us up with a written test, or entertaining us with what he professed to regard as the anecdotal trivia of history—actually the human and narrative meat of it, much more engaging than the dry bones of theory. I think Herr Bender himself enjoyed these excursions, otherwise he would have given us more written tests.

I remember the day he told us about the Greek myths, a subject very far removed from the official curriculum. Aphrodite rose from the sea, Zeus hurled thunderbolts and made love to young girls in the form of a swan or of rain, Poseidon churned up the oceans, Apollo plucked his lyre, Dionysus danced, and for about ten minutes, until the bell rang for recess, the wild fresh wind of poetry wafted around the classroom. There were sacred fountains, explained Herr Bender, where poets and artists prayed to the nine muses for inspiration. History, too, had a muse, he said proudly. "And music?" I asked. "Music, too—but," he said, with a downward twist of his mouth, "it doesn't have a muse of its own. Music shares the same muse with lyric poetry." "Why is it called music, then? Doesn't it have the word 'muse' in it?" "That is true," he said, with a surprised expression, blinking pensively. "I don't know," he said then. "I really don't know *why* it's called music. It's an interesting question."

What a triumph! The all-knowing Herr Bender foiled by my interesting question! Maybe I'd stumbled on something important. Maybe there was a mysterious affinity of names for their proper objects, and maybe by studying the meanings of the roots of words one could find something out about the things they signified. (I knew nothing of etymology, hence the excitement.) *Music*, for instance . . . Obviously the name signified that, among all the arts, music was the most favored by the muses, the most *musical, muse*-like par excellence (in German, I had the word *"musisch"* for extra support)—just the opposite of what Herr Bender had intimated by pulling down the corners of his mouth when speaking of music and lyric poetry, ranking both beneath his own boring subject in a single breath. Ha! Surely the muse ruling music and lyric poetry was the most bountiful of all, since she patronized two arts at once. What was her name? I looked it up: Euterpe. I resolved to pray to her. Why not?

When, I wonder now, did I first become conscious of her (as yet nameless) existence? It would be impossible to resurrect a precise beginning, and a sacrilege to invent one. But without a doubt, the priestess presiding over my initiation in music was Alma. On and off, she'd get together with other musicians to play string quartets, and then she would practice for hours each day on her viola. Stefan and I liked to watch and listen, or just be there, reading or playing with blocks. I liked the way she stood with the viola tucked under her chin, the gently watchful look in her eyes as she read the notes, the clever way her fingers walked on the strings, the slow elegant sweep of her right arm drawing the bow. She would patiently repeat the same series of sounds until all the flaws were worked out of them, over and over, until it was all beauty. She too became beautiful, her brow smooth, her lips relaxed and faintly smiling, her body swaying in unison with the clear, warm, swelling and subsiding sounds. Often she'd lie on a deck chair in the garden singing Mexican ballads and accompanying herself on a guitar. Sometimes we sang together: Mexican songs like *"La Llorona"* and *"Malagueña,"* and American songs like "Careless Love," "St. James Infirmary," "As I walked out in the streets of Laredo," "Oh Katy dear." She wasn't afraid of expressing the feelings in these songs with simple and direct commitment, and never ironized them, as some friends did who may have found them too sentimental. Sometimes, in a silly mood, she'd sing a song that was popular when she was a girl. "A man gave me a Cadillac . . . Oh, tell me, is there anything wrong in that? Boop-boop-a-doop?" And there were her records—classical records, and those wonderful old New Orleans jazz records (to which she liked to dance, with loose arms and slightly bent knees). Unintentionally, without effort and therefore without provoking resistance, the joy Alma found in making and listening to music communicated itself—first to me, and, a few years later, to Stefan.

¶[Some boy robbed a magpie's nest and gave me one of the young ones. I called it Jakob (on the assumption that it was male). Jochen built a large cage out of several slats of wood and some chicken wire, and we put it on the balcony, right outside the door to my room. I fed the bird earthworms and mealworms and pieces of meat, carefully pushing each morsel down its gullet.

After a while I could leave the cage open, allowing Jakob to hop about freely on his springy legs, and, eventually, to flutter from the balcony to the trees in the garden and back. He never learned to fly like a real magpie. But he did have the proverbial magpie habit of bringing home bright little things like glass shards, bottle caps, pieces of paper, as well as food, and of hiding his treasure, not just in his own chicken-wire coop, but in all the rooms of the house he was permitted to enter. I remember opening a book and being startled by an outpouring of dried-up wood lice that Jakob must have pecked out from underneath a stone or rotting log, killed, and deposited there for a day of need. He liked to perch on top of Bodo's head, and of course the day came—Alma and Stefan and I all waited for it, knowing Bodo's extreme squeamishness—when Jakob shat down his collar. He would frequently leave his nearly perfectly circular and almost flat droppings on the polished edge of a dresser or neatly placed on a windowsill, where, if the light fell at a certain angle, they looked just like coins. Inevitably someone would in passing swoop one of these little discs into his palm. Once Alma, an inveterate sun-worshipper, lay dozing naked and supine on the balcony. Bodo and I sat at a table nearby, discussing my homework, while Jakob went about his usual impish business. Attracted by the unaccustomed sight of pubic hair, he skipped onto her belly, cocked his head, and delivered a peck that sent her yelping out of sleep. Bodo and I laughed, and Alma didn't seem sure whether to be annoyed, embarrassed, or amused.

One day some wild magpies discovered Jakob. They didn't like him. They called other magpies from across the lake, and when those came they joined in the calling, until magpies came flocking in from everywhere, circling and screaming at poor Jakob, part bird, part human, squatting on the railing of our balcony. I took him in. After a while the birds gave up their clamoring and flew away. The next day, after I let Jakob out, they came back—an even greater and angrier mob. Again I took Jakob into my room. He pecked at the window and squawked; it seemed he was asking to be let out. Maybe, I thought, they were actually calling him, and their cries seemed like threats only to my human ears. Also, I couldn't keep Jakob inside forever. Still, I felt afraid for him. I waited another day or two, and let him out at a time when no other magpies were around. Everything seemed all right. But when I came back from school, he was gone. I hoped he had been adopted by the flock; but that evening, when I discovered some black and white feathers in the neighbor's yard, and some more floating on the lake, I knew Jakob had been killed.

❲On March 5, 1953, Joseph Stalin died and the Zentral-grundschule Gross-Glienicke closed for a week. All the children ran out of school screaming with glee. But even a second-grader like Stefan, even the dimwitted Baer brothers couldn't help noticing, that day or at the latest the next, that if there was cause for satisfaction in the great man's death, it was in bad taste to flaunt one's pleasure. Wherever you went, gloom and depression pre-vailed, even when the radio with its stream of tragic music and mournful communiqués was turned off. You felt guilty cruising the lake in a canoe with too obvious relish, or taking a spin on your bike, just for the fun of it, heading nowhere in particular. We played soccer after a while—no one was telling us not to—but kept our voices below their usual frenzied pitch, out of respect for our mourning elders. Both my parents seemed genuinely sad. Alma, looking at Stalin's portrait hanging over the piano in the living room, remarked, as she had at previous times but with more feeling, what a remarkably *human*, *kind*, and *wise* face the man had; and I, looking at his enigmatically twinkling eyes, dimpled chin, and pic-

turesque mustache, and hearing how lovingly she spoke
of him, and how grandly Mozart's *Requiem* commended
his soul to the highest heaven, I was deeply moved, and
felt privileged to be able to join, if only for a moment
and to a feeble, juvenile degree, in "the world's deep
sorrow and gratitude." That's how one radio commentator kept putting it, with curious persistency. "The light
of the world," another man said, a poet: "a light that
can never be extinguished." I remembered *The Fall of
Berlin*, a Soviet movie in which Stalin was portrayed in
distinctly solar terms—as a beneficent but at close distance almost unbearably radiant being. Inspired, I went
to my room and tried to write an ode to Stalin. I found-
ered, as usual, against the difficulties of the strict rhyme
scheme and meter I had chosen, in misplaced allegiance
to my favorite poet, John Keats—misplaced because
free verse was quite acceptable in odes to Stalin and
would have been easier to imitate. All the other requirements I was able to meet: the bombastic, expansively
trumpeting sort of voice, the similes derived from the
most grand and elemental manifestations of nature, and,
easiest of all, lots of exclamation marks, like visual hur-
rahs!

Meanwhile, day after day, the newspapers displayed
the same portrait of Stalin we had in our house, and also
another photograph of him smoking a pipe; these pictures were framed with black borders. Even the humor
and entertainment magazines abandoned their frivolous
functions almost completely to pay homage to "the
greatest son of the working class." The men and women
of the radio never tired of repeating (as if they still
couldn't believe it) that "*Josef Wissarionowitsch Stalin
ist tot*"—a statement that gained in purely incantatory
sonority what it was losing in news value. It went on for
weeks. RIAS, the West Berlin radio station, on the other
hand, and Radio Free Europe and other Western radio
stations exhibited the most vulgar contempt for the
world's sorrow and gratitude. They were actually cele-

brating! A group of comedians, famous for the rather grim volleys of barbed and poisoned jokes they sent eastward over the air, suddenly put paper hats on their wit and became truly funny. A certain news commentator, too, was lacing his ordinarily boring and transparently malicious invective with a champagne-like froth of heartfelt exhilaration—or did it just seem that way by contrast to the official gloom in the East? The Western musical programs, both classical and popular, seemed to be outbidding one another with happy-go-lucky tunes. One station even offered a medley of Eastern European folk music, under normal circumstances a staple of *our* programs! No, I wasn't mistaken. I could recognize a slap in the face when I saw one. I felt offended—on behalf of Stalin, of Socialism, and of all good and noble things.

⟨[One morning, around the beginning of the eighth grade, a bald, rosy-faced man with steel-rimmed spectacles entered our classroom. He introduced himself as Herr Fischer, and told us that he would be replacing Frau Kluepke, our kindly, incomprehensible math teacher; no explanation was given, but he made it clear that he intended the change to be drastic. While he spoke—in a resonant, level baritone—he whittled the bark of several sticks he had brought with him, letting the shavings fall to the floor. He had memorized our names and the order in which we were seated, and one by one he fixed a cold blue gaze on each of us, and not so much called us by our names as let us know that he knew well who hid behind each name, and was not to be deceived. Still whittling, he said that he had been informed of the practice, on the part of "certain elements," of doing homework in school during recess, despite explicit prohibition by the principal. He warned us not to try this on him, since he could tell by the ink how long ago something had been written, and he would not accept work done in pencil or ballpoint pen or any medium other than telltale ink. By now the sticks were ready—four rods of varying length and flexibility. He eyed them with satisfaction. Then he informed us of their purpose, which all along we had dreaded without quite believing he really could have this in mind: offenders would be punished with a whipping.

During the days that followed, however, his behavior was reasonable, even pleasant, and after a week the rods disappeared. So by the time Advent came around, Herr Fischer looked innocuous enough for a little fun at his expense. We decided to celebrate the season by pulling the shades to darken the room and planting lighted candles in our inkwells. No gentler mutiny could be imagined, but it kindled a monumental display of wrath in Herr Fischer. As soon as he walked in, he switched on the light, and we saw that his face and bald head had turned almost purple. With a terrifying roar, he had us spring to our feet; with another roar, we were ordered to blow out the candles; next, all those with candles on their desks were commanded to step out in the hallway. From the hallway he led us in a brisk march to an empty classroom. I shivered at the thought of those rods. But his punishment was unforeseen, as befitted the crime. He had us walk single file past him and out the door, and each boy and girl was given a crisp hard slap on the cheek. When my turn came, I winced, and the blow glanced off my head. He pulled me back and slapped me solidly across the cheek— harder, it seemed to me, than he had hit the others— and twice, to boot. I was outraged.

I told my parents what had happened, and Bodo came to my defense, quietly and mildly, I'm sure, but with all the weight of his Old Communist, Member of the People's Chamber importance weighing against Herr Fischer's known background as an officer in a Nazi submarine. There was no more slapping after that, or even threats of corporal punishment, which in any case was forbidden by law. But Herr Fischer avenged himself subtly. He did it mainly with his eyes. He would be joking with the rest of the class, and as soon as I joined in the general relaxation, I'd get one of those implacable blue stares. That frightened me; and then the fear would subside and settle into a darkly turning pool of guilt and self-doubt. I had always had difficulty with mathematics: now I didn't understand it at all. This offered him more opportunities for terrorizing and humiliating me. Nor did he overdo it to the extent where I might have had occasion to denounce him to my parents again. He did it so well that I didn't realize he had it in for me until, as a matter of fact, now that I think back on it. I always felt that I was at fault in some deep way that only Herr Fischer's eyes could fathom, and that the judgment issuing from them was just, if terrible. It was true, after all, that I didn't comb my hair properly, that I wasn't good at math, that I had a tendency to drift off during class, that I always had ink smeared on my hands or face; and it was also true that Herr Fischer had become the most popular teacher in school, that his jokes stirred us out of our boredom, that he was popular in town as well, that he had the most powerful right leg on Gross-Glienicke's soccer team ever, and, finally, that this universally liked and respected man despised me. When one day he said, "*Uhse*" —he could pronounce my name in a way that spelled doom—"*dein Schicksal ist besiegelt*," it seemed that my fate was indeed sealed and that judgment was at hand. I had failed a crucial test, and Fischer was informing me of the likelihood of my failing the grade altogether; but I felt overtones of a wider and more far-reaching threat, and I believe he meant me to feel that.

I began to play hooky.

In this connection, I have to mention my friend Uwe, without whose encouragement and assistance I would never have played hooky as intensively as I did. Acknowledgments are also due to Mark Twain, especially for *Huckleberry Finn*; also to Thoreau and to several Chinese loafers who wrote poems and painted, because, though I didn't know them yet, I'm sure I was anticipating their companionship; and to an Austrian writer whose name I never learned, who read on the radio an exhilarating essay in praise of laziness—something about lying on a hill in an ocean of clover and blissfully "wasting his life."

Uwe's interest was mainly in building an elaborate hiding place in the woods, and adding each day to the interior decoration—now a rug, next day a stool, or a board set up as a shelf for our books. His was a builder's enthusiasm, mine a dreamer's, but we got along fine; I helped him build, and he tolerated my dreaming. I can't for the life of me remember what those dreams were, but I know for a fact that I spent a lot of time staring vacantly, because my mother once took me to a doctor to remedy this condition, along with another supposed disease she inferred from my habit of drawing phlegm up my nose by means of loud snorts. The doctor agreed that the bridge of my nose was rather narrow, but he was opposed to the idea of cauterizing the nasal passages, since the discomfort was located mainly in Alma's ears; he also said that getting rid of phlegm via the throat was more natural than using a handkerchief. Turning to the subject of daydreaming, he reproved her, gently but firmly, and in my presence, for suggesting to him—and to me, since I was present when she brought it up—that there was something wrong with me on account of my daydreaming. "He's not lethargic," he said. "He's just a typical thirteen-year-old." Sometimes I'm still a typical thirteen-year-old.

(My mother ought not to have been so surprised by this penchant for dreaming I showed—it is one of her own most marked qualities, and probably a source of her considerable artistic gifts. I think she was ashamed of what she considered her "vagueness" and didn't want to see such an unpractical quality perpetuated in me.)

Uwe returned to going to school regularly, but I continued to set out, on many a morning, always with the
excitement of a first venture, for the woods. I had several hiding places besides the one I had built with Uwe.
One was on an embankment next to the Seepromenade,
a dugout from which some German soldier may have
murdered American troops when they marched by in
the spring of 1945. It was exciting to see and not be
seen. Some of my friends walked by on their way to
school. About nine-thirty, every few days, Jochen and
Bodo would drive past on their way to Berlin. Sometimes
Alma would pass by on horseback. When policemen or
soldiers passed, I ducked especially low, because I assumed they had a special instinct for hidden people. Occasionally a dog would discover me and bark, and I'd
seriously worry about being found out.

When this place got boring, I ventured deeper into
the woods, past another large lake, past the Russian
soldiers' encampment, and off all beaten tracks, so as to
run the risk of getting lost and maybe having a real adventure. Nothing dramatic like that ever happened, but
I did catch glimpses now and then of foxes and wild
geese and hares and deer; and lying in a grove of young
pine trees, I would let my body become so immobile
that it seemed to melt into the cool damp earth and
moss, and I would open my sense of hearing as wide as
possible, to take in every creak and cry, rustle or song
around me. If I got up and walked, crows and magpies
fluttered before me, screaming as if to alarm the whole
forest, and in the brush I could hear the commotion of
the general flight.

¶ One of the books I took with me to the woods was *The
Morning Watch*, my American father's novella. I lay
down to read it in a clearing by the edge of the lake, not
far from the invisible boundary separating East from

West. I remember the location because, instead of making me forget my surroundings, as books usually did, this one made me more acutely aware of them. A certain phrase, a few words describing the corrugated bark of a tree, lifted off the page and settled on the trunk of a pine right near me, not only describing but revealing it. There was another, not quite as startling moment a while later. I had closed the book and was distractedly looking at the picture of a bell on the dust jacket, when, from a chapel hidden on the opposite side of the lake, there came a single, faint chime. I had heard that bell ring many times all morning without ever hearing its thrilling sweetness. And it was my father's writing that had opened my ears. What other writer could charge words with this kind of magic? None! I felt hugely proud. Was it farfetched to imagine that he had written this for me, or at least with me in mind? Why else would he write about a thirteen-year-old boy? But Alma had told me that Richard, the boy, was really a portrait of my father when he was my age. And, obviously, Jim couldn't possibly have known I would steal away on a forbidden walk through the woods just as he had a long time ago. So Richard had nothing to do with me, at least not directly. But if I disregarded the incomprehensible churchy emotions—the constant guilt, the wish to suffer for Jesus, or with him—then I could imagine that I was like Richard, and therefore like my father. I even tried writing a story about a boy who avoids school, displays a great deal of morbid sensibility, experiences a kind of animal pleasure while roaming in the woods, and is discovered and finally punished for truancy. I never got past the first two or three pages, which were a virtual translation into German of passages near the beginning of *The Morning Watch*.

I had never known my father—unless one counted the first year of my life, when he and Alma still lived together. Alma had left him—she told me this herself—because he was in love with another woman and was staying away days and nights on end while she took care of me. She felt betrayed, she said, and was very angry, even though at the same time she never stopped loving him. He, too, loved her and didn't want her to leave; but he kept visiting the other woman. So one day Alma packed her bags and went to Mexico with me. There she met Bodo, and married him soon after. Three years later, when I was four, she returned to New York for a few weeks, taking me with her; and there I met Jim. But Alma and Jim had agreed not to tell me that he was my father, since I already had a father in Bodo and it would be Bodo with whom I would grow up. They felt it would confuse me to have two fathers. When Alma told me this a few years later, she said she wasn't sure whether it had been the right thing to do—depriving me of my one chance to get to know my father.

But I remembered him. He was that big kind friend of Alma's who used to pick me up at the house where we lived on Gay Street in Greenwich Village (for years I remembered it as Gray Street, maybe because it was winter and the street was in fact gray); from there we would walk to Washington Square Park to feed the squirrels peanuts. One day a squirrel bit my finger. I was hurt, more by the feeling that the squirrel had been mean to me than by the sudden little pinch. Jim squatted down next to me and kissed the hurt finger and explained that the squirrel hadn't *meant* to hurt me, that it had thought my finger was a peanut. That didn't make sense to me at first, but then Jim held up the tip of my finger and said, "Doesn't it look like a peanut?" and it did. We laughed, and he dried my tears with his hand, and then we walked on. Some time later I was sick for a day—I had a fever and my throat hurt. Actually it was pleasant being sick, because Alma kept giving me hot milk with honey and reading to me from Kipling's *Just So Stories*. In the evening Jim came into my room and softly closed the door. He sat down on the edge of my bed and took my hand in his. Then he touched my forehead with his cool palm. That felt good, and we both smiled. Then he held my hand between his two hands and gazed into my eyes, smiling gently, for a long time. I didn't feel at all uneasy, as I might have with someone else. The room became very, very still. A strange thing happened. It was as if he were talking, as if he were telling me everything with his eyes. If the words "love" or "father" had been spoken, I might not have been able to understand. But this way, no misunderstanding was possible, and there was no confusion. I felt wonderfully content. I don't remember Jim leaving the room or saying anything. Maybe he sat with me till I fell asleep.

([In Germany and probably elsewhere in Europe, and maybe all over the world, the rich American relative is a commonplace of novels, movies, and jokes. No ordinary person is really presumed to *have* such a relative, any more than one is likely to be seen walking a gryphon on a leash or conversing with angels. But I grew up with the knowledge and the glamour of being the grandson of just such a mythical creature.

Not that my mother's father showered riches on us, but from time to time the postman would deliver yet another package from . . . (and before uttering that golden and fabulous word he paused and raised his eyebrows) . . . "*Amerika*."

My friends usually came by on the day after the package arrived, tipped off by the mailman. They left their footballs and slingshots behind to see what Grandpa had sent this time. There were always comics, a book or two, sometimes a toy. The most amazing thing he ever sent was a "G.I. Joe" in a jeep. The jeep was endowed with foresight. When you wound it up and set it loose on a table, it didn't fall off, but veered as soon as it reached the edge. G.I. Joe, on the other hand, was bereft of all intelligence and dignity. His hands whipped the steering wheel from side to side, he bounced in his seat, his steel helmet teetered on top of his head and kept falling into his face.

Actually, everything Grandpa sent was intriguing simply because it came from the West. Gum, Jell-O, jeans, powdered milk, canned foods, cocoa, Camel cigarettes, Nescafé—they all had the glitter and sheen of the unfamiliar. Those objects that had the least utility for me—coffee and cigarettes—appealed to my imagination the most. There was poetry in the picture of nesting birds on the label, in the heady aroma rising from the jar, in the yellow desert landscape encased in a box of glass-clear paper. Bodo knew how to fill this box with smoke, burn a circular hole in the bottom end, and send blue smoke rings quavering into space.

The Nestlé birds reminded me of something Alma had told me about Grandpa. He was a hard man in some ways, she said, caring only about money and his immediate family—a typical capitalist. The rest of the world could go to hell. Except for flowers and birds: for these he reserved an extraordinary affection. He had arrived almost penniless in America, a refugee from the poverty-stricken Austrian village where he'd grown up. His first source of income was selling whips (those were the days when people still drove in horse-drawn carriages). He stood next to a basket full of whips, shouted something, and cracked a whip. One day as he snapped the whip he accidentally killed a sparrow in mid-flight. That was the end of the job. He couldn't bring himself to crack the whip any more.

Occasionally Grandpa sent photographs accompanied by a letter. One picture was of his office—no one in it, a big leather armchair, black, a heavy desk with a leather-bound blotter, a marble inkwell with two pens sticking up from it, a picture of the American President on the wall, and a rug on the floor. There were several pictures of his matronly second wife gardening with a fancy dress on, but in sandals and with a big straw hat on her head, and pictures of Grandpa putting seeds in a bird feeder in front of a gorgeous house with an enormous window that reached from one side of the house to the other. He had built this house himself—not with his own hands, of course, but he had helped an architect design it. Inside were many impressive gadgets, appliances, and conveniences; but the most important thing was the garden. It was not only large but landscaped. A great many beautiful, sweet-smelling flowers bloomed there most of the year, and there were trees and shrubs that stayed green through the winter. All over the garden were small and large fountains and birdbaths and feeders and birdhouses, and Grandpa filled the feeders with seeds every day and sat down in an armchair in the living room to watch the birds through the enormous window. That was what it was for.

There was only one thing wrong with the house— Grandpa wrote Alma a letter about it—one really serious fault, for which he hadn't yet found a solution. The house killed birds. The trees and shrubs in the garden were reflected in the picture window as in a mirror, and birds, especially the swift-flying swallows and cardinals, kept smashing against it. So Grandpa was always digging graves for birds in his garden.

Fortunately, some years later, someone suggested the simple remedy of attaching to the window a big red ribbon tied in a bow. That was enough to warn the birds away.

❨[A black-haired, blue-eyed girl sat in front of me in class. Her name was Ursula—Ursel or Uschi for short. She'd been there all along, but suddenly everything about her was different. The outline of her neck, the gentle oval of her face, the confident slow grace of her limbs in movement, the curve of her small breasts, her bright laughter, her low voice in quiet speech, the pleated skirts and white blouses she wore, her little hand winding a lock of hair behind her ear, as if beckoning me—what painful bliss it was to be near her!

I don't know how my attachment began, but I do remember a critical moment in its development. Uschi and her freckled friend, Erika, Uwe, two other boys, and I were running around in a pine-tree-studded valley right across from the People's Police Station; or, rather, the boys were chasing the girls; or actually, to be really precise, Ursula was inviting us to catch her, and Erika was tagging along, giggling, with her hand over her mouth. Uschi was caught and rather roughly tumbled. I personally held her in much too precious esteem to lay hands on her so rudely, but my friends, including Uwe, were less inhibited. They dragged her by her feet, uphill, in the direction of some bushes. Her skirt slid up, revealing thighs—a sight that meant nothing to me until her hand shot out to hold the hem of her dress, and her eyes, meeting mine in a deep, lowering glance, put the seal of erotic supposing and meaning on the moment; a moment later, Erika had begun to shriek and make loud mentions of the People's Police. Ursula's abductors, still holding her captive, hastened to put her in a position less compromising to themselves, in case anyone was watching—seated, that is, held by the arms, with her feet pointing downhill and her skirt pushed down to her knees. It was then agreed that she be set free, provided she would state her preferences among the four of us, in descending order. She named me third and Uwe fourth. I knew why she named him fourth—because he was fat and had a squeaky voice. But why was I third, I who loved her so much—yes, that was it, I *loved* her!

Uwe's feelings were hurt. On the way home, in a bitter rage, he declared he found Ursel repulsive. "Her skin is ugly! Take a good look at her—she's got acne all over her forehead!" I knew, of course, that Ursula was without blemish. Clearly, Uwe was deranged with the pain of thwarted love.

As soon as I got home, I informed Alma that I was in love, and that my love was unrequited. She didn't seem at all sorry; she looked serious and very alert, but surprisingly unsympathetic. She said this was a matter I'd have to work out on my own; I was a young man now.

How could I be a "young man" already? Alma was overestimating me. My voice had just started to change, and still cracked undecidedly between high and low; pubic and chest hair was just beginning to sprout—a promise, yes, but certainly not a badge of manhood; and wasn't I still waiting for Sperm, that mysterious substance, to emerge from one of those throbbing erections that overtook me at odd and often embarrassing moments? And what did she mean by "working it out"? She couldn't actually be implying sex? Was it that I should "court" Ursula, or "flirt" with her? I'd heard Alma use these expressions, and had seen the process depicted in books and movies—a kind of diplomacy, a maneuvering with looks, talk, and gestures, that required a lot of charm and savoir-faire. It also presupposed an established friendship or at least an acquaintance between the prospective lovers, not to mention a faculty, on the part of the male, to express in well-chosen words his heart's passion, and to awaken, by the ardor and painstaking thoroughness of his attention, a reciprocal tenderness from the woman's heart (which, as a rule, seemed reluctant to be touched). How could I talk to Ursula, about anything, about homework, let alone about how I felt? I couldn't even find adequate words for it in my journal: "I'm sick, I'm actually sick with love." It was true, but I couldn't *say* that. I did manage to write letters to her. Yes, it was possible to write: "Dearest beloved most beautiful Ursula, I love you, I dream about you, I think of you all the time"—but to give or send her those words, that was impossible. It wasn't simply that I lacked the courage. What I lacked was all sense of worth in relation to this radiant angel whose very name spelled perfection, this enchantress who had reduced me, in complete innocence of her great power, to a condition of chronic astonishment. How could I expect a requital of such adoration? Wasn't it enough to just be intoxicated by the sight and thought of her, to catch a smile from her now and then and carry it home with me, nurture its memory for a few hours? Wasn't it enough just to love? The rhetorical question called forth an existential answer: No, just loving her wasn't enough. I desired her. It had to do with that moment in the valley in front of the People's Police Station: her white thighs, raised and separated slightly by the boys' hands holding and pulling her feet, her fist clutching the hem of her dress, and that look she shot at me—such a strange mixture of fear and mischievous provocation. Yet when I sought her eye in school, she was cold, she ignored me. What to do, what to do? I offered to carry her books for her in an attempt at chivalry, but she laughed and shrugged. I turned to Bodo's library. There were two books whose titles at least sounded promising. The first, Ovid's *The Art of Love*, announced a generous program in the very first line: *This is a book for the man who needs instruction in loving./Let him read it and love, taught by the lines he has read.* "Loving," in Ovid's usage, evidently meant seduction. I hadn't thought of it that way, but was willing to learn.

But Ovid was addressing elegant grown-up Romans, not a thirteen-year-old barbarian with a crush on the village beauty. I couldn't very well conspire with Ursula's handmaiden, as Ovid advised me to do, unless I translated that to mean Erika—in which case I still couldn't. Nor was I about to send Ursula wax tablets inscribed with an announcement of an imminent visit and all kinds of coaxing promises. *What if she reads, and won't answer? Do not attempt any pressure./Only supply her with more flattering missives to read.* Absurd! I sat behind her in class! *Meanwhile, if she is borne through the streets on a litter with cushions,/Go to her side, but take care—don't give your mission away./Hide what you really mean in cunning, equivocal language,/Don't let anyone hear words that might cause him offense./Or if she loiters afoot, by the colonnades and the porches,/Dawdle along nearby, either ahead or behind,/Or, now and then, cut across, if the columns are rising between you;/With no apparent design, take a few steps at her side./Also, be sure to be near when she sits in the theater watching;/You will have something to watch, her shoulders, the curve of her dress./Watch her as much as you please*—Well, I'd been doing just that for weeks now. What was the next step? There was no next step. Without any transition, I was presumed to be sharing my bed with a woman. How did we get there? No explanation, except that Bacchus was supposed to be of some kind of help. Oh, now it turned out we weren't alone with one another: this was a banquet, held on my bed for some reason, and among the guests I should make sure to befriend *her husband*, give him my garland to wear, say how becoming it seems . . .

I shut the book in despair and turned to the other: Stendhal's *On Love*. There are four kinds of love, Stendhal said: passionate love, gallant love, physical love, and vainglorious love. No question but that my love was passionate, the true and only love; and that Ovid had no conception of it: "gallant," "physical," and "vain," these words well described the love he taught. Didn't he recommend deception and even force in the pursuit of one's goal? That was all well and good if one's love was gallant, physical, and vain. But true love forbade manipulation. The fragrance of passionate love was awe and tenderness, it bloomed without design or method. That was a beautiful way of feeling, but it left the recurrent image of Ursula's thighs unaccounted for. Maybe my love was really physical love . . . What to do? Where to turn? Ovid's book had a chapter called "Remedies for Love." Maybe I should study that.

One day I was called into the principal's office—I no longer know for what reason—and when I stepped in, Ursula and Erika were there, too. The principal was out of his office, the girls said he'd be back in ten minutes or so. I sat down and tried to avoid looking into Ursula's eyes, which were looking at me with what seemed like mocking directness. Nor did I want to seem to be avoiding her. I felt called on to talk, but had nothing to say. When I did finally come out with some remark, my voice sounded hoarse, and the girls looked at one another and laughed. Then they looked at the ceiling with lingering smiles on their faces, until Erika burst into giggles and Ursula poked her with an elbow. I felt ashamed. Then Ursula began scratching her leg, slowly and with exaggerated attention, just around the knee and then a little further up. It was as if she'd been reading my secret thoughts and was teasing me with this proof of her knowledge. She looked at Erika, still scratching, and Erika covered her mouth with her hand and laughed. I looked away. "It itches," Ursula said. Why was she doing this? If only the principal would come. "What's so funny?" Ursula said. "If it itches, shouldn't I scratch?" I suddenly felt abysmally sad. But at the same time I wanted to look again. I wished I were dead. But I also wanted to see what was making Erika giggle so. I looked. Ursula's hand had pushed the hem of her dress way up, and she was scratching the inside of her thigh. I looked away again. I could hear her fingernails scrawling the skin. "Mmmm," she said, "that feels *good.*" Erika sputtered. The principal's feet could be heard approaching. Erika sat up straight, and Ursula pulled down her skirt and folded her hands, looking her usual queenly self. When the principal came in, we all stood up, and I noticed my whole body was quivering. Fortunately, he spoke to the girls first, giving me time to recover. Ovid was right—love was a sickness, a festering wound. I could feel it aching in my heart.

Between Herr Fischer's attention and Ursula's indifference, going to school became depressing indeed. I took to the woods, sometimes for days in a row, with an almost mystical sense of unburdening.

Surprisingly, the teachers had full confidence in the excuses I proffered—colds, viruses, an occasional voyage. Not even Herr Fischer questioned me, at least not verbally. He just probed my innermost soul with his eyes, focused on my guilty secrets, subjected them to a brief ironic appraisal, then dropped them as not worth any further regard. Sometimes, if the weather was bad, I stayed at home, pretending to be sick. It wasn't difficult. I was a passable actor, and my parents were trusting. Only once did I run into difficulty—when Alma and Bodo were away on a trip, leaving Stefan and me in the care of Anneliese, Jochen's sister. Was it that I overacted, or did I fail to emphasize my suffering enough? She forced a thermometer on me, even though I insisted I didn't feel feverish—just dizzy and very very weak. "If you have no fever you go to school." I heated the thermometer on the radiator and showed her the resulting temperature—not so high as to give cause for alarm, but enough, one would think, to arouse some concern, some solicitude. After all, Anneliese was responsible for my welfare. She took one glance at the thermometer, shook it down, and told me to put it back under my tongue. This time she sat on the edge of the bed while I stared through heavy-lidded eyes and made my breathing sound effortful and rasping, as if even the involuntary movement of my lungs was afflicted by my mysterious fatigue. No use: when the three minutes were up, Anneliese squinted briefly at the thermometer and said, with merciless matter-of-factness, "You're all right. Get up. Go to school." "But I'm weak." "Then you must creep." I spent the day in the woods, hoping I'd get really sick from the wet and the cold—maybe die! How sorry everyone would be then. Ursula would repent her indifference, and mourn having frivolously toyed with the feelings of one who truly loved her (but before dying I'd first have to leave written testimony of my love). Herr Fischer's heart would be pierced by a stab of remorse, unameliorable for many years, and this remorse would run like an electric tremor from heart to heart through the entire village. My parents, above all, would be sorry for not having loved me enough and, worse, for having loved Stefan more, and for what reason? Merely because he was small and sickly and freckled and cute, and not old enough to be held responsible for his mistakes and hence to disappoint.

It was during this time that I discovered Eduard Fuchs's *Illustrierte Sittengeschichte vom Mittelalter bis zur Gegenwart*, a six-volume history of sexual mores, concealed behind several dictionaries on a high shelf in Bodo's studio. I remember my first glimpse into one of those tomes—it must have been the volume dealing with the eighteenth century, to judge from the style of the allegorical copper engraving I opened the book to. The title was *"Die Wollust"*—"Lust." A woman with beautiful naked breasts, lots of jewelry, and curly, disheveled hair was holding a goblet of wine in one hand and playfully handling a snake with the other. The snake was nibbling one of her nipples, and on the woman's face was an expression I had never seen before: a slackness and at the same time a peculiar fullness around the lips, which were smiling and slightly parted, while her eyes were narrowed almost to slits. This face became my sphinx, the keeper of the distilled essence of a secret knowledge that, in the hundreds of more pornographic pictures presented by Fuchs, was—I could feel it—diluted, even hidden in the act of being revealed. Those images did serve, of course, as costumes and stage sets in which to try on and, to a degree, experience my own carnality; but of its object, woman, and the love of woman, only that smile and those low-lidded eyes provided any more than gallant, physical, and vain intimations. Not that this "Lust" had anything to do with passionate love either; it was a completely other category, not of the heart or of the sensual surface of the body (though these factors came into it, surely), but of a mystical interiority where two beings united in a secrecy and pleasure that were immense and un-utterable—otherwise, among all the thousands of pages in those six volumes, some description should have cropped up approximating the delicious promise given and withheld by that bewitching smile. My own mother had dropped a hint of this knowledge when she discov-ered me sleeping with a hand on my genitals and, warn-ing me of the dangers of masturbation (I believe she mentioned insanity), said: "I know it must feel wonder-ful." "What must feel wonderful?" "Playing with your penis." She had it all wrong: far from playing with it, I liked to hold it, scepter-like, in a condition of firm im-mobility; and though that felt good, I knew greater plea-sures. The enigma remained, and nothing would lift the veil, no amount of research in Fuchs's *Sittengeschichte*, not prolonged contemplation of the lady representing *Die Wollust*, nor efforts to imagine myself the cause of her pleasure by presenting to her the blind questioning eye of an erection.

Of course I showed Uwe these books. It was gratify-ing to find him as ignorant of the essential knowledge as I was, and just as eager to find it out. We felt certain that we were on the threshold of an extremely exciting discovery as we gloated over the pictures and texts and discussed our differing tastes in women and very similar responses to erotic stimulation. It was reassuring that he, too, was plagued by erections at odd times of the day, and useful to learn that he dealt with them by pressing his member (that's what Fuchs called it) against his stomach with the elastic waistband of the athlete's training suit he frequently wore, and that he, too, had not yet experienced Sperm, though he seemed to have had a nocturnal emission, proof positive that he had the stuff, even if in truth it wasn't much that came out. In a full-grown man, he said, it comes out in amazing quantities, he'd seen gobs of foamy sperm in a urinal; and he knew for a fact that a woman becomes several pounds heavier after coitus: some of the weight being urine—for the man loses control of his bladder in the spasmodic relaxation called "orgasm"—and some of it Sperm. Through Uwe, the fame of the *Sittengeschichte* spread and attracted a number of boys who were all suffering the same preinitiatory agitation. Having savored and drooled over the books for a few days, we rehearsed the task that lay ahead of us with a series of little skits that always ended in a simulation of coitus, variations on the theme of seduction and conquest of the female libido, deceptively hidden, we knew, under skirts and prim attitudes, just waiting for a skillful male hand to manipulate one of several so-called erogenous zones and set in motion an elemental tide of deep breathing, wiggling hips, sighs, moans, and cries of delight.

One question that concerned us all was whether normal adults really did these kinds of things with any sort of regularity. Uwe was firmly convinced that his parents had renounced sex completely ever since he was born. The way he said this, he seemed to fear losing respect for them. When I considered his father with his silvery temples and pink double chin, and his mother with her timid wrinkled forehead, her pursed smile, and her permanent, I had to agree it seemed, on the face of it, pretty unlikely that they would indulge in anything so primitive and messy as sexual intercourse. It wasn't likely of my parents either. They liked to sleep back to back, a position that would seem to preclude conjugation. Also, they were never erotically affectionate with one another during the day, nothing more than friendly kisses for greeting and parting, a pat on the back of a hand, things like that. Quite possible, though, that they were hiding their true feelings, just as Uwe hid his erections, just as everyone hid away what the German language bluntly labels the *"Schamteile"*—"shameful parts" of the body. Just as Bodo had hidden Fuchs's *Sittengeschichte*. Why had he hidden it? To keep me ignorant of the fact that he, too, perhaps, would like his penis to be an object of female adoration, as in that picture of nymphs attending the god Priapus with his rather smug smile and long, almost vertically upward-pointing phallus?

Setting aside the riddle proposed by *Die Wollust*, there was something manifestly uncivilized about sex, undignified in the extreme. The grandeur and beauty of the human body and spirit, exalted in music, glorified in poetry and art—what could they have in common with this lewd murky groping and fumbling and peeking, or with some of the more grotesque postures of copulation? Fuchs's books gave the impression that for centuries there had been a silent war between sex and civilization, and that it was waged just about everywhere in the arena of daily life, in the sanctuaries of art and religion no less than on streets and in bedrooms, with bosoms and calves the contested treasure, and hems and décolletés the constantly shifting battlelines. There seemed to be always two images of mankind, as in those erotic parodies of famous paintings: on the one hand, the human body in the clear daylight of public morality, chastely aspiring and often suffering for some lofty purpose; and on the other hand, steeped in a kind of lurid twilight, the same human body, mirroring the first in almost every respect but deprived of decency as of a mask, and possessed by sex. I could see it in my own life, the ridiculous contradiction of being a Young Pioneer with a blue neckerchief, the statutes of a high code of honor printed on imitation parchment and framed in my room, proudly greeting other Young Pioneers with our salutation: *"Seid bereit!"*—to be crisply answered with *"Immer bereit!"*: "Be prepared!" "Always prepared!"—always ready to help the old carry their bundles, to help our misguided peers mend their ways, ready to grow up to be a patriot and a Communist, perhaps to provide a fifth superhuman semi-profile for a grateful posterity to add to the faces of Marx, Engels, Lenin, and Stalin on the giant billboards of the future . . . and to be at the same time perpetually preoccupied with erections and lecherous daydreams. It was with some justice the Niemann brothers parodied our slogan with *"Seid bereit!"* *"Beine breit!"*—"Be prepared!" "Spread your legs!" If only some girl of our acquaintance would evince this kind of pioneering readiness—oh, we would be ready, too, Uwe and I! Ursula? She was too frighteningly beautiful. Her oval, enigmatic face and lithe, small-bosomed figure belonged to the order of noble values, in a league with great music and art.

❦There came the day of the midterm reports. I was failing the eighth grade—a real disgrace for an offspring of the Intelligenz. The one-paragraph commentary on the bottom of the report card deplored my dreamy disposition and frequent absence from class. A few probing questions from Bodo brought out the truth: that I had been lying, to my teachers as well as to him and Alma. Why? Why are you staying away from school? It's boring. What about it is boring—specifically? I don't like math. Any other reason? I don't like some of the kids in school. Who? (Uschi Tunger, I thought.) Dieter Kunz, I said. What's wrong with him? He keeps putting my head in a nelson.

It was decided that I needed tutoring, particularly in math and the sciences, and to this end I was sent once or twice a week to a man who lived near us in the woods, in a small, overheated wooden house crammed full of plush furniture and porcelain knickknacks. Behind the house was an equally crowded garden overflowing with tomato vines, cabbages, chickens, and earthenware dwarfs. Inside, the air was dense with fine grains of dust floating and dancing in the shafts of sunlight that fell through the windows. My teacher paced the floor in wooden clogs while I worked. He wore short pants that revealed a deep shrapnel wound on the inside of one of his thighs. When he wasn't pacing, he brewed Muckefuck, a brand of ersatz coffee my mother couldn't hear mentioned without laughing; or else he read magazines or rolled cigarettes. For some reason, he saw fit to have me copy newspaper cartoons and picture postcards. He seemed fascinated with the results.

When my math tests showed no improvement, Bodo, unaware of Herr Fischer's hatred of me, turned to him for help, and abruptly Herr Fischer, disarmed and flattered by Bodo's humble appeal, became friendly.

On the wall of his living room, where we worked, hung a color photograph of a thinner, younger Herr Fischer, with an officer's cap smartly tilted on his straw-blond head, gazing into space through unpleasantly hard, cold blue eyes, like colored glass buttons on a doll. But the real Herr Fischer no longer pierced me with his malignant stare. He actually took a liking to me. Together we pored over graphs and equations, like alchemists over their bubbling alembic, both of us glowing with excitement; for the task of transmuting the leaden dross of my mathematical idiocy to a pure golden A in the finals was as much of a challenge to him as it was to me. "You can do it," he said. "With your intelligence . . ." And with that incomplete sentence, and with the expansive gesture that indicated the unlimited possibilities of its completion, he returned to me a hundredfold what he had taken from me during the time of our enmity.

I stopped playing hooky completely. And I studied, crammed, practiced for hours on end: not only math, but biology, physics, chemistry, history, the hundred-meter dash—all my weaknesses. I did it for Herr Fischer, who believed in my intelligence.

One day, just three weeks before the finals, without any announcement in class and without saying goodbye to me, he moved to another town (much later I learned he'd been offered a job as school principal there). But the momentum of my studies was too great to allow me to withdraw to the woods again. I felt no need for it. I passed the examinations with honors.

A year later, Herr Fischer came to Gross-Gliencke to watch a soccer game of decisive importance in the regional championship. He waved to me from across the field, and I went to talk to him. The first thing he wanted to know was how I did in the exams.

As it turned out, that eighth-grade graduation was to be the pinnacle of my scholastic career. It was downhill from then on, and the descent and eventual withdrawal took more than a decade to accomplish.

It was an hour's ride to my new school, in Potsdam. After several months, I still had the feeling of exile I'd had on my first trip there. On the way home, looking out the bus window, I would imagine I was a German prisoner of war returning from Siberia and recognizing with profound gratitude and mounting exhilaration the half-forgotten landmarks of his village, until, walking down the last stretch of dirt road, where the house and its wire fence become visible and the tall poplars sway in unison, as if to greet him, his weary feet break into an eager trot, transported by wings of joy. Once through the front door, of course, home was just home and I was I—and that was good enough. It was a pleasure to dive into the lake and wash off the gray despair of a wasted day. Inconceivable to sacrifice what was left of it to homework.

My midterm grades were poor. Naturally, my parents were troubled, and questioned and counseled me as best they could, and of course the school warned me of my

impending failure. But my mind was set. Only a Herculean, or rather Sisyphean, effort would launch me into
the tenth grade; it hardly seemed an attainment worth
the sacrifice of all my free time. Ninth grade, tenth
grade, what difference did it make? I'd still be imprisoned behind a school bench.

Most adults who knew me spoke about my problem
with puzzled but sympathetic interest. Always, in the
midst of tongue-clicking, head-shaking consternation
over my 4's and 5's (the equivalent of D's and F's in
American schools), there was praise, reassuring, confident mention of my *intelligence, talents, gifts*, which, if
I only saw fit to use them, would scatter dazzling 1's all
over my report cards, as had happened just the previous
year. It certainly helped soothe the dull pain of ig-
nominy that was making itself more noticeable each day
as the term drew to its close. I tried to regard those 4's
and 5's as badges indicative of a noble disdain of mere
credit. Let others strive for high grades in school; I
would withhold myself for a more deserving contest.
Only one person, a stern Russian teacher, turned the
usual flattering formula inside out when she passionately denounced me in front of the class: "The only 5 in
this test comes from Uhse. And I want you to take a
good look at him, if you haven't done so already, because he is *talented* and *intelligent* as perhaps no one
else in this class, maybe this school. But he is lazy—
damnably, unconscionably lazy!" "*Faul wie die Sünde*"
was her sonorous German phrase, underscored by a
stabbing forefinger. I let it thrust me right back into the
woods, and to simplify matters, I composed a letter, in
what Bodo considered to be his inimitable Gothic handwriting, explaining that I had been stricken with a bad
case of pulmonary bronchitis and would be conva-
lescing in a sanatorium for an indeterminate length of
time.

Imagine spending every weekday morning in the
woods by yourself, keeping clear of all human contact

and taking care all the time to maintain complete secrecy about what you're doing. Subtle and surprising
changes take place. Solitude becomes a pleasant companion, and relative immobility, without books or
flights of the imagination, is full of romance and adventure. To come upon a fox's lair, for instance, and recognize the tiny tracks before the entrance, and hide behind a rock on a patch of emerald moss and wait for
hours, and gradually feel the immense luxury of existence in your nostrils and traveling up your spine in
happy shudders, until you start laughing out loud, infected by your own deliciously absurd lightheartedness;
and then the magpies go screeching in all directions to
warn the forest of the madman in its midst, and, of course,
the fox never shows its face, and you come home flushed
with radiant satisfaction. Then, not to tell anyone, and
go again the next day.

"How are things going in school, Joel?"

"Oh fine, I'm starting to like it."

In the afternoon I'd play soccer till my knees got weak.

In April, shortly before the end of the school year, a
letter from Jim arrived, offering the intriguing possibility of a change. Actually the letter was addressed to
Alma, but it was all about me. Jim wanted me to come
to America. He seemed to be very anxious not to be
misunderstood: it was not for political reasons, he said,
or for nationalistic reasons; it had something to do with
one's place of origin, in a cultural and perhaps in a
mystical sense—Jim himself didn't seem able to explain
it very clearly. But it was important, he said, that I get
to know my country now or very soon, or else a vital
connection would be lost. It was a long letter, full of
repetitions, and half of it didn't seem to make sense, to
Alma any more than to me. But what was clear was that
Jim wanted me to come to New York, and that—Alma
pointed this out to me—he wanted very much to get to
know me, more perhaps than he wanted me to get to

know my American heritage; but that he felt it would be wrong or indelicate or divisive to say so.

Alma discussed Jim's idea with Bodo. They didn't seem opposed to it; but they weren't sure either. The whole thing would have to be discussed in detail. That could be done when Jim came to visit sometime soon (he had written earlier that work on a movie version of *Moby Dick* might bring him to Europe). I looked forward to being with my father again. And I thought it would be wonderful to go to school in America, at least for a while. Just to get away!

Then came the final exams. In a last-ditch attempt to save my skin I prepared some tiny cards densely covered with information that would help me pass a crucial physics test. Everyone in class was impressed, and I was more than willing to share my treasure. Unfortunately, I was caught passing one of the cards: there was a sickening sensation of cold inevitability as the teacher's gaze rose from something she was reading and her eyes came to rest on my hand frozen halfway behind my back. Had she found only that one card, I might have been pardoned; but beneath my desk were seven or eight others—massive evidence of malice aforethought. She told me to hand in my exam paper and go home.

Three days later we were given our report cards. Up to that moment I had tried to stave off the inevitable, at least in my imagination—I would be given another physics test, my many 4's and 5's would be forgiven by a fiat from the Board of Education, I would be promoted because of my recognized capacity to make up for time wasted and lessons not learned. That afternoon, I stood waiting for the bus in Potsdam, my disastrous report card folded up in my shirt pocket. The square was empty, an enormous asphalt floor with white lines marking where the buses were to park. The sun was beating down—the first day of a long vacation. I felt dizzy, began to black out, almost lost consciousness. For a moment I felt a peculiar, melancholy elation, as if I were actually falling, finally, after teetering on the edge of an abyss without ever being sufficiently fascinated or frightened to either leap into oblivion or else climb to safety.

¶[That summer we went to Vienna to spend a week with my American grandfather and his wife. Because they were Jewish and the Nazis had murdered most of their relatives, they wouldn't set foot in Germany. Perhaps they didn't know that Hitler had been welcomed enthusiastically in Vienna.

I wasn't at all interested in what the city had to offer in the way of museums and architectural splendor. Instead, the giant ferris wheel and the ghoulish chamber of horrors and the miniature racing cars lured me to the Prater each day. It was Stefan's favorite place, too. Once Walter H., an amateur jazz pianist and a writer of popular books on physics, went along with us. I asked him why the noise of those racing cars seemed to increase in pitch whenever the cars turned a corner, even though it was impossible to accelerate the motors. He didn't know. Several hours later he said: "You really put a flea in my ear with that question about the cars." On the day we left Vienna he was still trying to figure it out. That made me very proud: I, who had flunked the ninth grade, putting a flea in a physicist's ear!

Grandpa's wife was one of those people whom memory has rendered almost incorporeal, a powdery essence of pink kind cranky freckled softness. She was afraid of nearly everything: afraid of traffic, the weather, the German language, and "foreign food." She spent her vacation eating only oatmeal and salads and drinking American—not Viennese—*American* coffee. She kissed Stefan and me a lot—moist, sweetly perfumed kisses on our cheeks and foreheads—and bought us lots and lots of chocolate.

My grandfather resembled a cartoon capitalist: a wall-eyed old man with a big belly, wearing a three-piece pin-striped suit and a watch chain. He seemed to love me and Stefan, even though we had hardly ever written to him, despite Alma's frequent prompting. Stefan, he found, resembled a son who had drowned many years ago. ("A good boy he was . . . smart too . . .") As for me, he wanted nothing more than for me to cherish the fact that I was an American: "American-born, of American parents." Whenever these subjects came up—America and the drowned son—Grandpa would pull out an enormous handkerchief with a graph-paper design on it, wipe his eyes, and snort. I had never seen a man cry before. Grandpa also approved of Bodo, even though he found his Communism deplorable. "Does he take care of you right?" he asked Alma in his gruff, raspy voice. "He don't go after other women? He brings home good money? That's good."

Grandpa in his munificence had arranged for me to have a large room of my own—cork-paneled, thickly carpeted, furnished with a chandelier and several mirrors and a vast bed above which hung a reproduction of a Watteau: a bucolic scene where elegant shepherds and lasses made music and danced and played blind-man's buff. More precious than all these signs of luxury was a key which permitted me to lock myself in with my fantasy women, secure against sudden intrusion by my parents or Grandpa or hotel staff—though I did welcome the *image* of one of the maids, idealized in the manner of Watteau's girls, high-bosomed and with dark thick-lashed eyes. There she was, blissfully writhing beneath me, breathless, pierced by pleasure . . . But what would that pleasure feel like in my own body? Trying to imagine it was like trying to slake thirst with a picture of water. Of course I knew that orgasms (what a soundy word: "*der Orgasmus*") could be procured by a generally condemned practice called *Selbstbefriedigung*, self-gratification; I even knew something, from

books and from hearsay and from my own instinctual
groping, of its mechanics. But I had no idea of the need
for persistence in applying this knowledge. I could only
conclude that I wasn't ready, and hope that, some day
soon, the Great Pleasure would fall into my lap like a
fruit that ripens in its own time.

In the meantime, though, I was impatient, and willing to settle for any profane substitution. I bunched
blankets and pillows and sheets into a rudimentary but
at least tangible effigy of a recumbent woman, indented
and puffed her out at the appropriate places, insinuated
myself in the sheath I had prepared between her spread
thighs, and abandoned myself to passion. In no time at
all, her form, tenuous to begin with, had reverted to
chaos. Need made me inventive: I borrowed from my
mother's wardrobe a brassiere, a pair of tights, silk under-
pants, a slip. These garments helped buttress the much
too soft material with which I was sculpting, allowing
me to stuff and wedge it tightly enough to achieve a
simulacrum of fleshy resiliency. The result was pleasing
to the eye as well, especially when I dimmed the chandelier. Again I embraced my creation. She neither resisted
nor welcomed my ardor, as could be expected; she was
altogether stupidly unresponsive, and once the erotic
qualities of silk, nylon, and cotton had been explored,
the sight of those flaccid provocative limbs splayed on
my bed became loathsome and I kicked her onto the floor.
Why wasn't there a bell one could ring, in addition to
the one for room service, that would summon a young
girl, warm and passionate, into my bed. I groaned with
frustration.

The telephone rang. It was Alma. "Are you ready?
We should leave in five minutes, we're waiting in the
lobby." I had completely forgotten—we were going to
the opera. I quickly dismembered the rejected bed-
puppet, hid Alma's lingerie under the mattress, hur-
riedly showered, got into a suit and tie, plastered my
hair to the right and left, insisting haphazardly on a

zigzag part, and rushed off with Alma and Bodo to a performance of Mozart's *Abduction from the Seraglio*. We arrived just in time to take our seats as the lights dimmed and the curtain rose—*before* the overture, a departure from custom that gave rise to alarmed murmurs among the audience, relieved by a delighted "Aaah . . ." as the stage set came into view: a gold-and-white palace with minarets and filigree lattice work on the windows, by the edge of a blue sea shimmering with the tender rose of a sunset. Reflections of water played on the walls. Against a crooked tree stood a white ladder. The conductor's baton rose from the pit, and the overture, like a band of nimble genies, sprang up to carry away palace, ocean, ladder, tree, orchestra, and loges with their cargo of shining faces, lifted us all, swiftly, gaily, away to some splendid, festive place of high enchantment. A chime leapt alongside the general jubilation: *bing-bing-bing-bing*, like a child, or a young goat, and was joined every few beats by a threefold clash of cymbals. The gay invisible swarm danced rings around itself; held back, and quieted, walked in a noble, stately round; leapt back into turmoil; paused. A sadder, plaintive tune set in, as of something lost and sorrowed after, and half-despairingly longed for; repeated itself; returned to the gay prancing march with its clashing and steadily tinkling chimes. A short man with boots and a sword at his side stepped onto the stage and began to sing the sad tune we had just heard, with a voice of searing purity:

> *Hier soll ich dich denn sehen,*
> *Constanze, dich mein Glück!*
> *Lass, Himmel, es geschehen,*
> *Gib mir die Ruh zurück.*

> *Here then is where I'll see you,*
> *Constance, my happiness!*
> *Ah, heaven let it happen,*
> *Please set my heart at rest.*

He stood raised on tiptoe, leaning toward one of the latticed windows in a yearning sort of way, one hand on his heart, the other as if holding aloft an invisible apple:

> *Ich duldete der Leiden,*
> *O Liebe, allzuviel!*
> *Schenk' mir dafür nun Freuden,*
> *Und bringe mich ans Ziel.*
>
> *Too long I've suffered sorrow,*
> *O love, within my soul!*
> *Make me a gift of pleasure,*
> *And bring me to my goal.*

The words were moving enough, but the music was uncannily beautiful; I pressed my lids shut to prevent the tears from flowing. The song, unrelenting, repeated itself, and the singer's voice swelled with the tender, supplicating urgency of his, of my heart's prayer:

> *Make me a gift of pleasure . . . of pleasure!*
> *And bring me to my goal!*
> *And bring*
> *And bring me to my goal!*
> *And bring me,*
> *Bring me to my goal!*
> *And briiiiiiiing . . .*
> *Bring me to my goal!*

The floodgates opened. I watched the rest of the show through a blur of periodically replenished tears— tears of happiness, and of gratitude for this happiness. Bodo passed a handkerchief on to me via Alma, and I made use of the fortissimo passages to clear my nose. Such happiness! From what? Beauty? Love?

Early next morning I woke up to the sound of a woman humming in the courtyard just outside my door.

I got dressed and took a brief walk around the block. Most of the city was still asleep. The sun had just risen, and was pouring streaks and puddles of burning red-gold on the blue cobblestones, and igniting the same blaze on the gilded wings and wind-curled garment of a statue on top of a building. All the sounds and motions of people and cars were tentative, muted, as if everyone felt touched by the same tenderness and peace and didn't want to disturb it. A bell struck twice, very gently, in a distant church, like a benediction.

The spell evaporated at the breakfast table with the usual Let's-go-to-the-Prater and Eat-your-eggs-dear sort of conversation. And not long after that—it was raining and I was locked alone in my room—*Die Wollust* was to have her due, and I mine; we had waited long enough for each other, and when would we ever again find such a propitious combination of solitude and mirrors? From the ideal world of the *Sittengeschichte* (forever redolent of the hayshed where I so often hid to read it) her slender arm reached into a tall mirror to fondle my reflected penis (in substitution for her pet adder) with delicate knowing fingers, while my own bodily arm, hand, and penis supplied the necessary models for the illusion. Never had my imagination been given a more challenging assignment: to project into the empty space to the right of this mirror (from where her arm came) as lifelike a reproduction of *Die Wollust* as possible, and at the same time to weld sensation and image indivisibly together. *Die Wollust*, in turn, tightened her grip and gave to her playful manipulations an ever more earnest, rhythmic intensity. She seemed to know what she was doing. A darkly imploding force began to agitate and gather itself in my loins, so utterly unforeseen and so astonishing in its momentum that I had no thought of fearing or welcoming it, and noticed only that it was eclipsing the pale lunar gleam of my fantasy, then the mirror-image, the room, and finally everything. A moment later I was staggering on stiff legs, gradually recovering my sense of

sight (perhaps I had just closed my eyes), and recognized
with tremendous relief and excitement the evidence of
my manhood copiously distributed on the rug.

([In September I was transferred to another school in
Potsdam, not far from the old one. In addition, my parents arranged for me to move into an *Internat*, a kind of
rooming house for male high-school students. Living
away from home would be good for me, they said; and
there was a pedagogical look in their eyes, a look of
inflexible kindness, with which, I knew, there could be
no arguing. I tried, of course, briefly—but their minds
were made up. (*Something* had to be done.)

At the Internat there were a great many boys between the ages of fourteen and eighteen, and we were
watched over by a tall, dignified, fat young blond
woman with corkscrew locks, who floated about in
ample, lavender, somehow Grecian robes. After about
half a year, I realized I had gained, both at the board-
inghouse and at the school, a reputation for dullness, if
not downright stupidity. I'd suspected as much but had
trusted in my prowess at German composition, thanks to
which several illiterate seniors finagled a surprise A at
the bottom of their homework assignments.

In the eyes of the majority, however, I was definitely
one of the less brightly shining lights around. No doubt,
failing the ninth grade had something to do with that.
And I was shy, and a clumsy conversationalist. Not much
of an athlete either, can't spike in a volleyball game.
Nothing. How I envied the bright ones, the grace and
lightheartedness with which they wore their success.
Grau, for example. He was known by his last name as I
was, as many were, but in his case it tended to sound
like Mozart, Shakespeare, Lomonosov. Considered a
genius by some, he had written several plays, one of
which was soon to be produced in Mecklenburg. On top

of that, he was a crack athlete, and was making a name for himself at track meets in the Potsdam district; there was talk of preparing him for greater things. Everyone wanted to be his friend; he attracted girls, applause, respectful recognition from high and low. A medal, too, I don't remember for what. Even his hair was superior: if it ever came into disarray, perhaps during a soccer game, one toss of the head and each ash-blond strand fell neatly into place, impeccable part and all. And for a finishing touch, in shameless favoritism, Fortune had tinted his eyes a smoky blue-gray, in stunning coincidence with his name. From these eyes, as if from some blessed mist-shrouded region, he would occasionally notice me vegetating in darkness, and pass on to more interesting objects.

One day, though, during a volleyball game, Grau and I became forecourt rivals on opposite sides of the net. He teased me good-naturedly: "Have you learned to spike yet, Uhse?" I didn't know what to say. His teammates set the ball up for him perfectly. He slammed it right at me, saying, "_Na, Uhse?_" I parried the shot, deflecting it overhead toward the back of our court—pretty heroically, it seemed to me, even if my backward fall in the dust wasn't the most graceful. My teammates returned the ball to me. I slammed it directly at Grau, saying "_Na, Grau?_" The ball bounced off him and hit the ground, and a round of laughter raised me up in a brief effusion of glory. But Grau, smiling and tossing his hair back, drew the laughter around himself with a simple offhand remark: "He's not _completely_ witless, is he?" It was almost admirable, how deftly, with how little effort, he'd managed to yank out from under me the little strip of status I'd gained.

There was a second hierarchy, in addition to the social (though partly congruent with it)—the political; the first and topmost, actually, as hierarchies go. I had joined the FDJ (_Freie Deutsche Jugend_—Free German Youth) of my own free will and without question (how could I _not_ join, coming as I did from a "progressive" family?). It was as undemanding an outfit as the Young Pioneers had been. You got a brilliant blue shirt with the emblem of a rising yellow sun sewn on the left sleeve, and in exchange for a nebulous sense of belonging, all you had to do was attend three or four fantastically boring meetings in the course of the year, and wear your blue shirt neatly pressed on festive and official occasions, or whenever you wanted, provided it was neatly pressed. I wore it often unpressed, and no one made anything of it. At the same time, though, that the FDJ offered communion in a nationwide blue-shirted family of equals, it also provided a ladder, let down from above to recruit the most promising among the younger generation, the most responsible, the most ambitious, the most mature—climbers, in short—into the bureaucracy. They were called *Funktionäre*, as distinct from the rank-and-file. Most of them developed unattractive symptoms of adulthood: humorless, in some cases fanatical purposiveness; philistine smugness masked (especially to themselves) as pious devotion to the principles of Marxism-Leninism; in general, a passion for principle and a distrust of play and imagination. Most pathetic and, to me, disgusting was their constant effort (it didn't come naturally) to exemplify an idea of "forward-looking" youthfulness—pretending to be excited by the newest phony agitprop youth song, smacking their hands above their heads in rhythmic unison to celebrate the tedium inflicted by some politician at a mass rally (and there were always hundreds of oafs who joined in), referring to one another as "*Jugendfreunde*," youth-friends (it sounds as silly in German as it does in English— Jugendfreund Schulze, Jugendfreund Schmidt). How anyone my age could contrive to forget that "youth," in particular adolescent youth, does not look forward to the constrictions of adulthood with unquestioning glee—is not, in fact, "forward-looking"—was beyond me; and besides, I was too indolent to set foot on even the lowest rung of that ladder. The great majority didn't want these "functionary" positions, because of the work involved and because of the attendant deformation of character; so there was no stigma attached to being an anonymous, functionless blue shirt among millions. It was as a social being that I wished I could climb just a little higher in the estimation of my peers; at least high enough to be noticed.

Toward this end I signed up for dancing instruction under the tutelage of a Fräulein von N. (she insisted on both the "von" and the "Fräulein"), a time-encrusted remnant of the turn of the century, haughty, bone-thin, sour, pale, and fantastically wrinkled, with strings of pearls and sometimes a furry carcass or two slung around her neck. Once a week we assembled beneath darkening portraits of Fräulein von N.'s ancestors in a long, chandeliered hall in her mansion. A sickening odor of cologne and shoe polish emanated from the boys lined up along one wall. At the opposite end of the room, four chandeliers and seven portraits away, stood a parallel row of girls, giggling and making their dresses sway. My immediate neighbors would argue over priorities: "The fifth one from the left, that's mine." "What, that crow? You can have her." "Not that one, you idiot, the fifth, the one with the breasts." "Let *me* have her, you danced with her last time." "Shut up, everybody, first come, first served." The terror of imagining similar conversations at the other end of the room. Now Fräulein von N. calls for silence. "As always, the gentlemen are to *walk*, not *run*, toward the ladies, and ask them to dance, with a bow, please. Is that understood?" We nod. Then she bends over the phonograph, and by the time she sets down the needle, the stampede of swiftly walking gentlemen is already underway, and I'm setting my course in the direction of a slim black-haired creature who faintly resembles Uschi Tunger. But the closer I get, the less she resembles her, and the more unappealing she looks. Swerving off to the left, I collide with several crisscrossing male bodies, sidestep them, and come up short against a tall blond pudgy-cheeked girl with a blue ribbon in her hair. I bow. She steps forward and puts one palm on my palm and the other on my shoulder, while her eyes, which have the color and approximate hardness of Meissen china, look past me with indifference. "*Eins*, zwei, drei, *eins*, zwei, drei," says Fräulein von N. "This is *not* one of those new American dances, so please do *not* stand too far apart." My partner and I step closer together—too close, it seems, but how exciting! I can feel the double mound of her bosom pressing against me, her blond perfumed curls tickling my nose, and my thigh gently wedged between her thighs as we whirl, *Eins* zwei drei, *eins* zwei drei, breast to breast, thigh to thigh, in near-coital embrace. Does she like it? What a small ear she has. My heart's in my throat. "That is *too* close," says Fräulein von N., tapping me on the shoulder. At the same time, the record stops. We step apart. My partner is blushing and looks angry, or disturbed. I feel ashamed and sorry.

I had no intention of ever dancing with her again, but thanks to the caprice of random selection, or else to some weird powerful chemistry that works at long distance, I found myself eye to eye with her the following week. For a moment her pupils widened. Then she put on her mask of indifference, and placed one palm on my palm, and the other on my shoulder. Once again, our bodies met and, instead of instantly retreating, drew closer together. But her face looked enormously bored, her lips wore a pout of dissatisfaction. I tried to make conversation. "Do you like dancing the waltz?" I inquired. She shrugged. Then she looked at me with straightforward dislike, which I reciprocated. That was my first experience of that horrible dissociation of the emotions from the body I read about in Robert Musil several years later: "Two heads can turn upon each other the most terrifying coldness, while the bodies below stream into one another, resistless and burning. There is something malignantly mythical about it, like a two-headed god or the devil's goat-foot . . ."

❲One day I had a long talk with Alma and Bodo. This Internat, I said, was doing me no good at all. I felt lonelier there than I would at home. And I wasn't able to study, I said—there was too much noise (that was not true). And I was just plain homesick, weekend visits just weren't enough. Maybe next year I'd be ready. Couldn't I please stay home?

They gave in. Unfortunately, my argument that coming home would improve my grades was given the lie very soon after. I started failing again. Intensive conferences took place—between Bodo and my teachers, between me and my teachers, between me and my parents. Bodo took hours off from his writing to coach me in mathematics and physics (which he wasn't too skilled at himself), and I resented him for it. Through my window I could see the lake, some boys paddling by in a boat they had made out of a bomb casing. At least let me enjoy my weekends!

My fourteen-year-old world was bleak indeed. I had no friends. Uwe and his family had moved to another town. I learned that Ursula was engaged to a local soccer hero with short powerful bowed legs. He was so unlike me that it hurt. The soccer field in front of our house no longer drew crowds of boys from all over the village. Many of them were working seven days a week on their parents' farms now. Others were apprenticed to some craftsman or other, or working in factories in Potsdam; what free time they had they probably knew better ways of spending. Sometimes I'd run into them, and I found we had little to say to one another. I noticed they were wearing creased slacks and pointy-toed shoes from the West, and their hair was slicked back in the brand-new *Entenschwanz* (ducktail) fashion—as if by choosing work they'd become instantaneous young adults, while I, by settling for more school, had condemned myself to remaining an oversized child, wearing the same old sneakers and shorts and crowned with the same old mess of unmanageable hair.

One afternoon in May, just a year after Jim's invitation to come to the States (his trip to Europe had been canceled, since another writer had been given the job of writing the script for *Moby Dick*), the telephone rang and the operator announced an overseas call for Alma Agee. I said she wasn't home, and neither was my father. The voice at the other end—a male voice—asked if this was Joel Agee. I said yes, it was. "Hello," said the voice, "I am calling to tell you . . . I have to tell you some sad news. Your father died yesterday. He had a heart attack. Please tell your mom. Tell her Jim died yesterday. Okay?" "Okay." "I'm sorry . . ." "It's all right." "Goodbye." "Goodbye."

When Alma and Bodo came home soon after, I told them the news. Alma said: "No!" and shook her head. "Jim? It can't be! He can't be dead." Then she sat down and put her hand to her forehead and shook her head.

Later, when we were eating dinner, I said: "I guess there's no reason for me to go to the States now, is there?" and Alma burst into tears.

❴[I no longer enjoyed reading. For all I knew, I was a rather trivial mistake of creation, just a tiny nucleus of private gloom, rather shoddy in appearance, pulsating uselessly and without much vigor, sometimes on a school bench, sometimes in my dugout in the woods, sometimes at home in my room—it hardly made a difference where—while around me was a universe marked by purpose, efficiency, order, usefulness, and productivity, if not exactly happiness. There were political troubles, of course—border disputes, spies and saboteurs put on trial, quiet worried talk among my parents and their friends about some trials in Czechoslovakia that somehow hadn't seemed quite right; and there were memories, still fresh, of the airlift that sent American planes roaring over our heads toward the Tempelhof airport in West Berlin, of the rumble of Russian tanks suppressing the revolt of June 1953, of the war in Korea, which, though far away, provoked mutterings among adults that a third world war might erupt. But these seemed very minor disturbances to me, faintly alarming and even faintly entertaining, then quickly submerged in the forward march of Five Year Plan here, Marshall Plan there. The world would continue, and so would the purposeful, industrious people who drove the tanks and flew the planes and were attempting to educate me in school. The real disorder was in me: I had no purpose in life.

The idea of suicide began to appeal to me, not just for the soothing balm of self-pity, but for the apparent logic of it. It seemed right—almost beautifully right, like the one simple solution to a complex equation, the door leading out of the maze. It beckoned.

Suddenly my parents were fighting. It was very surprising. They never fought—disagreements, yes, a petty quarrel occasionally, but never a violently angry scene. They loved one another. But I came home from school one day and found Alma in a tearful rage, Bodo alternately depressed and angry. The horse, the dog, the maid, my brother, and I slunk off to a safe distance. That Sunday Bodo drove off to Berlin, ostensibly to work, and Alma, seeing in me her only ally in this cold country, told me, half in tears, half vengefully, all about Gertrud, his secretary: how Bodo had brought her to visit; how Alma had liked and trusted her, even asked her to model (Alma had begun painting in oils); how Bodo had had an affair with Gertrud; how they had betrayed Alma, exploited her naïve generosity; how deceptively affectionate and thoughtful Bodo had been throughout this time, bringing Alma flowers, taking her to the opera. This episode had an enlivening effect on me. Here I was, abruptly promoted from the level of problem child to a rank above Bodo's (now a scoundrel): Alma's confidant, mature, compassionate, neutral but understanding. Even after the fabric of domestic harmony had been mended, with Gertrud's dismissal (insisted on by Bodo's superior at Aufbau Verlag) and the passage of some time, it was obvious that my parents, too, had their problems; they weren't so wise, nor was I altogether useless. School also changed for the better. Somehow I managed to pass the ninth grade the second time around.

I wrote in my journal (in English, for some reason): "I feel like a character in a play. He's just emerged from obscurity into unexpected brilliance. No, not brilliance, visibility. Curtain. I can hear the stage mechanics rumbling, preparing the new set. We'll be moving in two weeks." The move was to an enclave of artists, writers, and bureaucrats in the district of Niederschönhausen in Berlin, an area that had either suffered little damage from the Anglo-American carpet bombing of the city or else was completely rebuilt, for there wasn't a single façade chipped by so much as a bullet, while a little farther off there were still blocks of buildings reduced to rubble and shattered glass. Our new maid, Margot, came with us. But Jochen, whose home and family were in Gross-Glienicke, would have to find a new job. We were all sorry to part from him.

Our new house had two stories, like the one in Gross-Glienicke, and a garden—not as large a garden as the old one, and it lacked the tall fir tree and the lilacs and the magnolias, but still, a garden. The big loss was the lake. You had to take a subway to get to the Spree, and a train or bus to the Müggelsee and its beaches. No more running out of the house on a midsummer day and flying down the hot flagstone path in seventeen steps and leaping high and far off the wooden platform into the delicious coolness . . . But there was a forest not very far off—especially if you went by bicycle. These were thick-stemmed old leafy trees, not pines, as in Gross-Glienicke. A little way into this wood and you'd come to the palace where the President, Wilhelm Pieck, was said to reside. Many black limousines stood in front of it, and armored cars and jeeps. A ring of barbed wire surrounded the place, patrolled by guards. You could sense it was best not to go too near it. There was another, taller, barbed-wire fence further on. That was the border. I was told there were guards keeping a lookout for saboteurs and for *Republikflüchtige*, people fleeing to the West. Who in his right mind would flee to the West here? You could just walk across at Friedrichstrasse—not with all your belongings, of course, but safely.

I asked Bodo about *Republikflucht*. Why do they want to stop people from going to the West in the first place? Why do the newspapers talk about it as if it were a major crime? Because people are needed here, he explained. They're needed to work, to teach, to write books . . . all the things that people do. It's because people are valuable that we want them to stay.

"But what if somebody wants to leave anyway? Let's say they have part of their family in the West. Why can't they leave?"

"I personally think in such a case people should be allowed to leave," Bodo said. "But it's difficult to make exceptions to a rule and not weaken the rule itself. The reason for the rule against moving to the West is that in our country, which is a socialist country, everybody gets a free education. The state pays the cost of training a doctor, for example—which is a lot of money. And that money is produced by the working people themselves, by their labor. So, when a doctor goes to the West, because he can make much more money there than here, it's as if he were robbing all the people in the DDR of the fruit of their labor. They paid for his train-

ing because doctors are so badly needed. And then he
leaves. That's why it's considered a crime. But I agree
with you that in some cases exceptions ought to be
made. It's a very difficult problem—the problem of the
individual and society . . . of the common rule and the
private exception. When this problem is solved, we will
have Communism. Then there will be no more state, just
people living and working together and helping each
other. And enjoying it, too. Ultimately, joy is what it's
all about."

I loved him when he spoke to me openly like that,
instead of evading my questions with half-finished
phrases and cryptic wags of his head. Even if I didn't
understand everything he said.

There was a *Republikflüchtiger* in our circle of ac-
quaintances, I learned soon after that conversation—
Bodo told me himself. It was Herr Kohlmeyer, one of
the masons who had built a garage next to our new
house. He had actually told Bodo about his thoughts of
leaving—told him because he trusted him, despite his
Party button—and Bodo had not objected, and certainly didn't denounce him to the authorities, as he might
have a real criminal. Herr Kohlmeyer's motive was
pecuniary, just like that of the hypothetical doctor Bodo
had talked about. Maybe, I thought, the state had in-
vested very little in Herr Kohlmeyer's education and
training, so that he was in effect worth less, in terms of
money, than the doctor; and maybe that was why Bodo
felt his leaving was okay.

I asked Bodo about that. He seemed upset by the
question, even annoyed at me: "People are valuable regardless of how much money they make or how much
money went into their training. Money has nothing to
do with the value of human beings."

"But the other day you said—"

He interrupted me, intensely irritated. "You are confusing things. I thought I explained!" Then he broke
into a violent coughing fit, as he often did when he got

upset. He went into the kitchen to get himself a beer. I felt guilty for having agitated him like that; he had a bad heart, I should have been more careful.

When he came back with his beer, he put his arm around me. "You're right to keep asking like that. You must always ask questions. You know what Brecht said about questions, don't you?"

I shook my head.

"He said that instead of putting all the answers we're proud of on billboards and banners, we should publicize the questions we haven't found answers for." Bodo didn't elaborate any further on the answer he had given me.

My parents attributed my improved psychic condition and academic performance during the first half of the previous school year to the bracing effects of life in an Internat. Accordingly, they were dead set on putting me in one again. I objected with more determination this time, though again I could feel there'd be no prevailing against their fixed opinion (whether they were right or not was a question that didn't concern me). "I don't need discipline, I need a home!"—that one almost worked with Alma. Then I made the acquaintance of a boy who was to be sent off to a boarding school in Thuringia, and who didn't seem quite as unwilling as I. Peter Vogel was his name. "It's supposed to be a good school," he said. "You live right where the school is." "That's terrible," I said, "that means there's no getting away." "That's true . . . but there isn't anyway." (Well, I knew better than that.) "It's high up in the mountains," he continued, "really beautiful. There'll be lots of skiing. I wish you'd come, too. We could live together in the same room." That sounded appealing.

The more time we spent together, the more we found we had in common. We both liked to talk about girls, for one; though Peter seemed a good deal cannier and bolder in sexual matters than I was, at least judging by the way he talked. Also, he liked to paint, just like me. He was quite ambitious about it. When we painted together, there was a certain element of friendly competition, right from the start—nothing really contentious—that I found stimulating and that seemed to improve my ability. Peter knew how to pass pitiless judgment on an artist after a single glance at his work. Extreme verisimilitude in a painting, for example, was a sure index of a complete absence of talent in its creator; such mere technicians did not deserve to be called artists. Even among genuine artists, there were scores of lesser lights, called "epigones," condemned to flicker ineffectually in the glaring radiance of geniuses with resounding surnames. It was a shameful thing to be an epigone. But the most unforgivable fault of all was pretentiousness, transparent immodesty of ambition. (Alma, too, for some reason, had it in for pretentious people, not necessarily in the arts. She'd spot them unfailingly; at least that's the impression she gave. She'd endure their presence, and then nail them, after they'd left, with that cruel epithet, scornfully muttered: "Pretentious.") Peter and I did our best to steer clear of these aesthetic hells in our painting. But from what I remember of our work, we were promising to become epigones of Impressionism.

I think our friendship was in large measure founded on a capacity to infect each other with uncontrollable laughter. This nerve-shaking cachinnation came and went like a grace, it couldn't be brought on at will. But when it came, it announced itself as a sort of spiritual ticklishness; everything that was meant to be serious became at first vaguely, subversively amusing, and eventually ludicrous. How purposefully everyone strutted about! How *earnestly* these people rode the streetcars, stood in line before shops, stepped in and out of urinals, exchanged money and merchandise over counters, picked their noses, criticized jaywalkers, pushed baby carriages, led their dogs out to pee, directed traffic, chewed on their bockwursts!

We walked the streets like twin tuning forks vibrating exquisitely to this citywide concert of duty-bound commotion, until the slightest sour note (the finger in the mustard, the salesgirl's hiccup, the jerking streetcar shaking its unresponsive sullen-faced freight back and forth, back and forth, like sacks of potatoes) sounded loud and clear and irrepressibly funny, like a fart in a cathedral. Later on, we were to meet and team up with other boys prodded by the same demon of silliness. It must be the province and privilege of adolescence to laugh good and hard at the spirit of gravity before it begins to lay claim to one's soul.

When Bodo asked me one day, point-blank, whether I'd like to go to school in Thuringia with Peter, I smiled and said yes.

Bodo, late 1950s

Alma, mid-1950s

Stefan, ca. 1953

Alma with Roland
(the horse), ca. 1953

1955-1958

The Thuringian Forest contains lovely winter resorts and one big dreary boarding school commemorating the name of Friedrich Ludwig Jahn, patriot and gymnast. We slept five to a room—five beds, five wardrobes, one table, and five chairs were the furnishings. All two hundred boarding students had their breakfast and dinner (and on Sundays lunch as well) in a great hall with vaults and arches in Gothic style. Before eating, we had to stand and sing whichever rousing or sentimental song our one-eyed Internatsdirektor, Herr Kautz, had selected. Remarkably few of these songs were in praise of Peace, Freedom, and Friendship among the Peoples, or attacked the Fascists, or celebrated our eternal friendship with the Soviet Union. Herr Kautz clearly preferred songs from the nineteenth century—songs about wanderlust, about driving in an unstoppable stagecoach with Death as the bugle-blowing coachman, about treacherous sirens, about life being a crap game with quaffs of beer between throws of the dice, about the lonely well and the linden tree before the old town gate. The food was bad, girls and boys were kept from seeing very much of one another, Herr Kautz was a secret Nazi; but the singing of these old songs, twice a day, two hundred voices strong, at least refreshed the heart, though most students agreed it was a silly, superfluous ritual. Actually, it was the only halfway sane one we engaged in.

Herr Kautz was a passionate but ineffectual disciplinarian. Given a cane to supplement his voice and distrustful nature, he might have succeeded, but those days were gone. Every morning at five-thirty he would sound a shrill electric bell and rush through the boys' rooms as if his pants were on fire, shattering our ears with "*Aufstehn! Raus!*" while his timid wife woke the girls inaudibly. Room by room and floor by floor, we heard his shouts receding, and many of us used that interval to pull the blankets back over our heads and relish ten more minutes of slumber. Gradually, like a pendulum on the backswing, his shouts approached again, and when they were a few doors away we would climb out of bed and proceed toward the washroom, enduring his last gratuitous "*Raus!*" as we stepped through the door. Occasionally a lurid touch was added by his oversleeping, in which case he didn't take the time to get dressed and insert his glass eye but came storming through our rooms in a nightshirt, with that gruesome socket gaping through a shock of black, disheveled hair.

The washroom was in the cellar, a huge cold echoing box of damp concrete, filled with long tub-like sinks with rows of faucets that spurted furious jets of icy water into our hands. Herr Kautz was always there to supervise our washing: armpits were important items on his agenda, as were the bottoms of feet.

Then came the morning exercises, coeducational. Following the rhythmic screech of his whistle, we flapped our arms and jogged about on the lawn in skimpy training suits, rain or shine, summer or winter. And if there were complaints, Herr Kautz would remind us of Friedrich Ludwig Jahn: clad in bearskin, armed with just a heavy wooden cudgel, he had defied Napoleon's troops, daring them to test their mettle against his, abusing them day after day with nationalistic insults from the mouth of his cave, rain or shine, summer or winter, in hills much like these.

After the morning song and breakfast, we left Kautz's domain and trudged uphill toward the school building, joining up with hundreds of students who were approaching from the nearby town (some of them on skis, if it was winter). Everyone assembled in front of the school for the matutinal flag raising. This was very serious business, and any excessive stirring of frivolity was countered immediately and firmly with ocular cross fire from all the assembled teachers and their "functionary" stooges of the FDJ. Peter and I were particularly vulnerable to attacks of giggling, which, with all good will and respect for the national anthem, we were sometimes unable to stifle. One blisteringly cold winter morning, for example, the flag, perhaps due to the frost, refused to climb higher than half-mast, and a muscular member of the school's track team attempted to shin his way up the ice-glazed pole. It was impossible; even several pairs of hands supporting his buttocks could reach only so high—then he'd slowly, reluctantly, come sliding down again. A sharp wind was howling among the pines and around the rafters of the school, whipping flurries of fine stinging snow in our faces. Herr Kautz was pressing his fingers against his glass eye, which tended to fall out when he got upset. A phalanx of five teachers, an FDJ chief, and Herr Luedke, the stocky, wheat-blond school principal, stood shoulder to shoulder, tense faces turned sideward and upward, hair flying in parallel motion. ("Goddamned cold," someone whispered behind us.) Herr Luedke stepped forward and ordered the ludicrous rescue operation suspended, but the athlete on the mast had made some progress and was loath to give up. He argued; Herr Luedke insisted and pointed imperiously at the ground. The boy slid down and rejoined the grinning student body with a sportsman's self-absolving shrug. Peter and I kept our jaws clamped and our faces averted from one another—we couldn't afford

to crack so much as a smile. Then the last straw arrived
in the person of Herr Brohm ("Bromus," he was called,
a Latin reference to his extraordinarily bad breath), a
very thin and ill man who, when road conditions permitted, came to school in a taxi and always entered the
classroom late and with a deep bronchial cough, totter-
ing from exhaustion, but seizing hold of the edge of his
desk and hoisting himself into a rigidly upright position,
from which he would face us with a look of titanic defiance, as if to say: Hm! You thought old Brohm wouldn't
make it today! This paragon of tenacity could now be
heard retching his very soul out among the howling of
the elements as he dragged himself uphill toward his
place of duty. The laughing demon would not be contained any longer: out popped the cork of self-restraint.
We shook and gasped; the best we could do was strive to
keep the convulsions voiceless. But even that vestige of
control abandoned us when the music teacher's quavering soprano launched the first bars of the national anthem: "*Auferstanden aus Ruinen*," "Resurrected out of
ruins." We staggered, wheeled, collapsed in a helplessly
hooting and—we admitted this to one another later—
urinating mess in the snow.

Memory has punished most of my teachers with oblivion. The only survivors from the Friedrich Ludwig
Jahn school are the above-mentioned Herr Brohm and
Professor Müller (Promü), a teacher of French who
had learned the language as a prisoner in the First
World War and who had an endearing habit of occasionally burlesquing his own authoritarian pedantry—
for example, by underlining a word on the blackboard
not two or three but *fifteen* times. Both these men harbored a kind of exasperated affection for Peter. Maybe
his porcelain-blue eyes and charming smile gave them
the deceptive impression of moldable human clay. Herr
Brohm often detained him after class—seized him, literally, by the collar, and badgered and urged him to

please, finally, pull, your, self, together, a *boy* of such *ability*—while Peter rolled his head away to escape the infamous breath and fine spray of quite possibly tubercular spittle. Promü, more resigned to life's disappointments than Bromus, contented himself with waspish attacks *en passant*, like breezing into class in a great hurry and obviating the usual *"Bonjour!"* *"Bonjour, Monsieur le Professeur!"* with a curt *"Vogel—raus!"* Or else he'd explicate a French word of negative meaning by referring to Peter: *"Qu'est-ce que ça veut dire: irritant? Peter Vogel est irritant."*

As for me—they ignored me almost totally; or maybe I was invisible. I might just as well have been absent. But playing hooky was out of the question there. An overwhelming torpor enveloped me nearly every day. Sometimes the struggle of trying to keep my eyes open was too much for me; my head would sink down to the table and I would start to snore. As before, in Potsdam, I wasn't considered the brightest fellow. Intermittently I'd wake up; for instance, when, through Herr Brohm's enthusiastic spittle-spewing intermediation, I heard the voice of Walther von der Vogelweide ringing bell-clear all the way over to my bench in the Friedrich Ludwig Jahn school from the twelfth-century rock upon which he was sitting, one leg crossed over the other, his elbow propped on his thigh, his chin and one cheek cradled in his palm, pondering how one might harbor wealth, honor, and the grace of God all at once in the shrine of a human heart. Or when Promü in all apparent seriousness dashed into class, frowning, and gave us the following riddle as a written test—marked and graded it, too:

The philosopher Voltaire was a guest at Frederick the Great's well-known palace in Potsdam. One day the Kaiser sent a dinner invitation to all his friends:

$$\frac{p}{grand} \; à \; \frac{ci}{sans}$$

Voltaire sent an immediate reply:

G a

Decipher the messages. Both are in French.*

But such epiphanies were rare. The lord of the classroom, as of the surrounding adult world, remained Duty
—*Pflicht*—and the little devils it sent out to torment us,
or at least me, had names like gerund, hypotenuse, metab-
olism, $CaCO_3$, and negation of the negation.

The second half of the day provided some compen-
sations. Peter and I went to the movies, or spent our
allowance on a meal in Zum Goldenen Löwen, a bar-and-
grill, or played pool in a Freie Deutsche Jugend club-
house. During the winter session we skied—if such a
term may be used to describe anything so inept as our
anxious slipping and sliding among swarms of screaming pre-school children on sleds, down a gently sloping
hill that was commonly referred to as the *"Idioten-
wiese"* (idiot's meadow). We did this in the belief that
we were training for the midterm winter sports exami-
nation, never suspecting that the test would consist of a
headlong precipitation, practically a free fall, down a
horrendously steep and curvy ravine that had served to
prepare Thuringian skiers for the 1936 Olympics.

I seem to have forgotten or rejected, in Thuringia, the
pleasure I had once taken in walking in the woods. By
far the greatest part of Peter's and my free time was
spent, or killed, in the dormitory. Very often we played
table tennis. Sometimes we read; but the lack of privacy
made it difficult to concentrate. For a short while *The
Brothers Karamazov* managed to pull me into an absorption so deep I could just barely hear the din and
commotion of the dorm, like a distant rim of sounding
foam. According to Peter, I assumed, successively, the
personalities of Alyosha, Ivan, and Dmitri during that

---

* The solution: *"Grand souper à Sans-souci." "J'ai grand appétit."*

period, so that he worried for my sanity. Ivan's scowling nihilism alarmed him especially, until he divined its source.

Peter took to naps as if to opium. It seems we were both slightly narcoleptic, I during class, he shortly after; the main difference was that he *lived* in his sleep. His dreams were in color, rich in incident, always satisfying—even to those of us who listened when, thick-tongued but enthusiastic, Peter sat up in bed to report on what he had witnessed and done: sexual conquests, bizarre metamorphoses (like dreaming of being a turtle when a few of us amused ourselves by bouncing an eraser off his imperturbably snoring skull); artistic accomplishments (the most unusual of these was a painting consisting of two panels, one of which went to Bulganin in Moscow, the other to Eisenhower in Washington, compelling both statesmen to reach out to one another across oceans and ideologies, inspired by a sudden longing to restore the broken world to its wholeness); exciting encounters with corrupt, famous, brilliant, strong, dangerous, funny people; and over and over again, feats of sportsmanship of which, in waking life, he was conspicuously incapable. Constant successes, never a nightmare—at worst, a narrow escape from some peril.

We would have liked to spend more time with the girls, but we were forbidden to cross the boundary between their dormitory and ours except for two hours during the afternoon. There were rules, not of Herr Kautz's making, that guaranteed us a coeducational clubroom and occasional dances, but he was always around in a silently obstructionary manner, operating the turntable, serving the punch, watching. After sunset he sometimes searched the shrubs behind the school with a flashlight, and a ridiculous, pathetic sight it was to watch him hunting his sexual phantoms; from our fourth-story window we could plainly see he was the only one there. We heard that he grilled certain girls about their virginity. And more than once, during the usual hysterical reveille, he whipped the blanket off a sluggish body and proceeded to *slap down* an erection. Such energetic restraints combined with such tempting proximity couldn't fail to produce an accumulation of sexual tension in both dormitories. And since its normal expression through individual relationships remained blocked for most of us (mainly by the undeclared threat of scandalous public disclosure), it had to discharge itself in other ways—the usual epidemic fits of laughter, for one. An undercurrent of homosexuality made itself felt. Love affairs were rumored among a group of weightlifting buffs in the twelfth grade. In our own room, a strange ritual took place almost nightly: one or another of us would leap out of bed to thump his prick upon the table in a resonant, bongo-like tattoo.

Herr Luedke, the school principal, must have caught wind of this development. He began to pay us creepily intense visits shortly after the lights were out. Unlike Kautz, he didn't have to threaten and shout to make us respect his presence. An untrustworthy air of authority hung about him even when he emerged from his office to chat with us during recess, smiling a disarming smile, one hand in his pocket as a sign of relaxed confraternity with his students. So, when he stepped into our room and walked from bed to bed with a flashlight, talking to each of us, we fell silent and attended every shade of innuendo in his words. "Vogel? Have you acclimatized yourself yet? Learning how to slalom? Good . . . Uhse? How are *you* today? I hope not too tired? Good. I hear you are failing in physics, Russian, chemistry, and mathematics. Will you promise me to buckle down? Good . . . Krause, don't you ever wear pajamas? I see, underwear. I hope you don't wear the same shorts you sleep in. *Verstehst du recht?* D'you understand? Good . . . Radke? Come now, I know you can't be asleep already. Well, good night anyway . . . Mohr . . ." When he reached Karl-Heinz Mohr he sat down on the bed and

spoke longer and much more quietly than he had with
us—almost a whisper. Mohr, too, kept his voice low.
Once, when the moon was full, Radke claimed to have
seen Luedke stroking Mohr's hair. Mohr denied the al-
legation indignantly, but I believed it, because Mohr
had beautiful curly black hair and I had felt Luedke's
fingers running through my hair one night and withdrawing in distaste when they met with a tangle. He
scolded me quietly then: "You really should brush your
hair more often, Uhse. You are altogether too slovenly.
Verstehst du recht?" There was never any real danger,
as I had feared at first, that he would offer me tutorial
assistance in his home, as he did Mohr and several
other neat, long-lashed, well-groomed boys. He wasn't
very taken with Peter's appearance either. "You really
should brush your hair, both of you," he told us once,
"and keep your shirts tucked in your pants. *Versteht ihr
recht?* You especially, Vogel, ought to polish your
shoes. I'd like to see you hang *them* from a nail on the
wall, put a frame around them, nicely polished, instead
of those sloppy paintings you make. *Then* I'd be impressed. *Versteht ihr recht?*" "We're not really trying to
impress you, Herr Luedke," Peter said. "Of course not,"
Herr Luedke said, "you are merely trying to be different. Well, I promise you, you will not impress *any*one
that way—least of all the girls, if that's what you're
trying to do. Take my word for it: girls, at least nice
girls, don't like the bohemian look in a man." If he was
right, so much the worse for me; I seemed to be congenitally bohemian.

We didn't clash openly with Herr Luedke until the
day after the *Jugendweihe*—a sort of socialist First
Communion. Since I never attended the ceremony, I
can't say how it's conducted. All I know is that the can-
didates assemble wearing their very finest clothes, and
that their names are called one by one. At least that's
how it was done at our school's Jugendweihe on a
sunny March Sunday in 1956. The names of Joel Uhse

and his immediate alphabetical successor, Peter Vogel, were called out, but the young men thus summoned into maturity were eating Holstein steak at Zum Goldenen Löwen and trying to stave off the laughing attack that was about to be set off by several stimuli at once: to wit, a perfectly bald and nearly perfectly round man at one table, and an extremely crooked old woman at another; the sound of their combined slurping and smatching; the sight of the woman's rapidly chomping jaw; the rhythmic squeaking of Peter's chair as he salted his meal; the thought of the analogous squeaking of Klaus Radke's bed when he presumed everyone to be sleeping; the wrathful looks we got from the waiter and his guests when the laughter began to break loose and we sputtered into our beers; the accelerated and fortified squeaking of both our chairs as we shook with suppressed laughter.

Our mirth abruptly ceased when, on the way home, we ran into some festively dressed boys and girls carrying bouquets and holding what looked like diplomas rolled up and tied with ribbons. It seemed we had mistaken the date of the Jugendweihe. How to explain this one? What kind of punishment would there be? Was there any precedent for what we'd done?

Karl-Heinz Mohr conveyed a message from Herr Luedke: We were to come to his office during recess the next day. Luedke was furious, Mohr said. He'd never seen him like this.

Peter and I conferred in the yard behind the dorm.

"What'll we tell him, Peter?"

"I could limp and say I hurt my leg skiing and you had to help me home."

"That's no good. Mohr knows you're all right. I think we'll just have to tell him the truth."

"You know, if he says '*Versteht ihr recht*,' I don't think I'll be able to keep a straight face."

"Don't say that, Peter, we *have* to keep a straight face."

"That's true. Forget what I said. Maybe he won't say it anyway."

"But he *will* say it, Peter, he always does. Just don't laugh. *Verstehst du recht?*"

He laughed.

He laughed in Herr Luedke's office as well. We both did. We howled, we drooled on his rug. Herr Luedke had withheld his dangerous phrase for a while, but then it came, suddenly, like a shot from the hip. He was pacing back and forth before us, gesticulating: "Two people were absent from the Jugendweihe yesterday. Jugendfreund Uhse and Jugendfreund Vogel. That is bad enough, since it undermines our effort to give our youth something dignified, meaningful, elevating. People laugh when they hear your names called and you're not there. *Ach ja,* Uhse and Vogel, the heroes of the winter-sports test, the clowns from Berlin, here they go again. What troubles me most is that these clowns are the only ones here whose parents are in the Party." He snapped his head around to pierce us with his eyes. "*Versteht ihr recht?*"

What could the poor man do, once we were laughing, but send us out of his room, shouting: "I will bring this matter up with your parents! And with the FDJ! And Herr Kautz! *Versteht ihr recht!* There will be repercussions!"

There were no repercussions. There were too many more pressing things to attend to. The school year was drawing to a close. Herr Luedke broke an arm while wrestling with some boys in the gymnasium. A new national youth organization was founded, the paramilitary and deceptively misnamed Gesellschaft für Sport und Technik; Herr Kautz volunteered, and was officially appointed, to drill some fifteen boys and one girl in the art of goosestepping, saluting, presenting arms, et cetera, in the courtyard. Some kids sent swooping squadrons of paper doves down upon them from the window, but it was hard to distract them. Never had we seen Kautz so

enthusiastic. Clearly his heart was in soldiery, not peda-
gogy. He walked lightly, struttingly, with a gleam in his
remaining eye. He even felt emboldened, one day, to
join us in our clubroom and boast about his glorious
days in the Wehrmacht, how they'd put those Czechs to
rout, almost in no time. It occurred to some of us that if
we cared to, we could tell Luedke or the school board
about that, and Kautz would be in trouble; but no one
disliked him enough to do that.

Herr Brohm discovered a smoldering spark of intelligence in an essay I wrote, and scolded me for having
kept it hidden most of the year. He took me by the
collar and shook me and wafted his awful breath into
my face, imploring me to "wake, up, study, learn! If you
hate school so much, why not at least get, it, over, with!
Do you really want to repeat the tenth grade?"

Peter set the sights of his ambition on the gold Medal
for Good Knowledge. I don't recall whether participation in this contest was compulsory; in any case, I did
feel compelled to study for it. Halfheartedly, though; I
remember the revulsion I felt at the mere sight of the
study guides with their lists of dates and formulas. Still,
I did manage to win the bronze medal. Peter worked
hard and won the gold. But at the award ceremony he
discovered his medal was actually made of tin. He
asked Herr Brohm about that. "*Ach, das ist doch symbolisch mit dem Gold,*" Brohm said. That was Peter's
catch phrase after that, whenever one of us suffered a
disappointment: "*Ach, das ist doch symbolisch mit dem
Gold.*" For example, when the long overdue orgy took
place, shortly before the end of the term.

Kautz and his wife were attending a conference
somewhere. There must have been several conspirators,
both male and female, who arranged to put every light
in the building out of commission, lead some two hundred boys and girls into an empty pitch-black attic I
had never known existed, and barricade the door. A soft
damp hand grasped mine, after a shy mutual explora-

tion of hair and clothes to make sure of each other's gender, and for a long time we just sat holding hands, bestowing upon one another the most chaste and generous affection by the mere involuntary pressure of our palms, while all around us a lascivious commotion swarmed and slithered, giggled and breathed. To ask one another's name would have been to exchange this seamless communion for the risk and give-and-take of a relationship; to bring our bodies into play, even anonymously, might have been to give up this nostalgic affection for pleasure. It seemed safer and more beautiful to renounce everything, even desire, in that moment of possible fulfillment. And it was Kautz who sealed our pact by bursting noisily through the barricade and dispersing everyone with his flashlight. I caught a glimpse of curly yellow hair, and thought at various times later—during the morning exercises, on the way to school, in the clubroom—that a blond, not very attractive girl was watching me with a shy and wondering look. We never exchanged a word. But when Peter asked me how I'd made out in the attic, I told him of a fabulously passionate creature who had been about to welcome me with open thighs, unfortunately at the precise moment when Kautz showed up. "_Das ist doch symbolisch mit dem Gold,_" Peter said.

I passed the tenth grade by the skin of my teeth, much to my surprise and Herr Brohm's satisfaction. Only my studies for the Medal for Good Knowledge can account for this turnabout. Peter, too, passed, but that was expected.

([Peter and I spent three weeks of the summer of 1956 in Ahrenshoop, a seaside village resort favored by the intelligentsia, and there we met Gudrun and Gisela, two charming and extraordinarily pretty sisters. Their comeliness derived entirely from their mother, a soft-spoken,

pleasant-faced woman with green eyes and a nearly perpetual half smile of contentment. Their father, while not
exactly repulsive, looked as if someone had briefly struggled to carve him out of a gnarled root and had given up
before finishing the job. He was an organist at some West
German cathedral, a noted interpreter of Bach, and he
built organs as well. I have no idea why these wealthy
people from the West were spending their summer vacation in East Germany; they weren't socialists. My
parents and they kept the kind of respectfully friendly
distance from one another to which the unlucky word
"cordial" is frequently applied.

Peter's and my parents were more compatible. Bodo
and Peter's father, Kurt, had both fought in the Thäl-
mann Brigade in Spain some seventeen years previously.
Whether they met then or not I don't know, but they
became good friends in Ahrenshoop. Alma and Kurt's
firm-jawed wife, Ilse, struck somewhat less responsive
chords in one another, since Ilse had none of the bohemian in her and Alma none of the political cadre;
they too made do with "cordial" civilities, and it was up
to Kurt to distract them from their discomfort. Not that
he had any difficulty doing that. He was extraordinarily
able to make people feel at ease, and to coax them into
forgetting the seriousness of life for a while. Even
Bodo's somewhat bitter and sorrowful gravity gave way
to laughter during those sessions over beer and schnaps
in the *Kurhaus*—some of which I had the good luck to
attend.

Kurt told spellbinding stories, mostly about his past,
and perhaps about the past of others as well, for it was
hard to believe that one man could have experienced so
much. Sometimes one got the impression that he was
boasting; for example, when he told of being employed,
long ago, as tutor to the daughter of a wealthy Berlin
widow, and sleeping with both women, whose social
standing imposed the necessity of pretending a high vir-
tuousness, not just to the world, but to each other. Each

would have been horrified to learn of the other's con-
cupiscence; but this did not prevent either from giving
free rein to her own. Thus, thanks to so much morality,
Kurt was able to entertain two passionate and, to a degree, sincere love affairs simultaneously. No wonder
Peter spoke of his father with pride. But were his stories
true?

What, for example, was one to think of the Beer
March to San Mateo? Supposedly, this had really happened, during the Spanish Civil War. Kurt received
multiple wounds during an attack on some castle. Because the field hospital was overcrowded and in danger
of being shelled, several hundred of the most severely
wounded, Kurt among them, were carted by freight
train toward Madrid. The train was attacked by Stuka
fighters—the locomotive smashed, more than half the
men killed, including the troops sent along as escorts.
Also, the food and water supply was destroyed. A long,
torturous trek then across the Sierra, under the burning
sun, "the half dead supporting the half alive," the one-
armed leading the one-legged, the blind hanging on to
the lame, everyone dragging crutches and splints and
bloody bandages, and also a few guns. Those completely incapable of walking had to be left behind; others collapsed along the way. After several hours, thirst
became a severe torment. At long last, a village emerged
on the horizon, quavering like a mirage. But it was
real. How many of those "wrecks," as Kurt called them,
limped and crawled into San Mateo? There must have
been at least twenty or thirty, otherwise what followed
would be completely incredible. San Mateo was deserted,
not a living being was there, except for flies. The flies
were feasting on butchered animals that were beginning
to rot—mules, goats, chickens, cats—and each of these
corpses was inside a well. Every well in San Mateo had
thus been systematically polluted. Nor was there any
food to be found. Had the townspeople, knowing the
Fascists were coming, fled and destroyed all that could

be useful to their enemies? In that case, why not burn the houses? Perhaps they hoped to regain them after a Republican victory. Or had the Fascists ordered them evacuated? And were the slaughtered beasts an act of sabotage?

I don't remember the explanation, but what I'm not likely to ever forget is Kurt's account of the beer battle itself. It began with the discovery of a keg of unpolluted, indeed excellent, beer in the village tavern. Since just a few mugs could be found, a trough was hauled in and the tap was opened over it, and then the wounded men crouched and lay down and sucked and slurped and all but drowned themselves in the good beer until their thirst was slaked and, needless to say, they were drunk. Shortly after, a truck came rolling into town and pulled up right in front of the tavern. Inside the truck were four casually chatting Fascist soldiers—just for a moment. The next moment they were dead. Even drunk amputees can shoot an enemy at close range, particularly when he is too surprised to reach for his gun. In the back of the truck were two machine guns and a number of submachine guns, rifles, hand grenades, what have you. Mysterious alchemy that makes unconquerable heroes of a band of cripples: a fortuitous victory, the gift of an arsenal, exhaustive acquaintance with death and with pain, passionate camaraderie, political idealism, acute danger, and lots of beer. That danger was approaching was written plainly on a sheet of paper found on one of the dead Fascists. Troops were scheduled to arrive at this and that time. Herculean labor of hauling the machine guns into position, of dragging furniture, boxes, mattresses, barrels, and the Fascists' truck into the semblance of a barricade. (Note that the truck wasn't used to escape.) The Fascists came, a slow convoy of trucks, jeeps, and motorcycles down the long, curving road. The machine guns opened fire.

Kurt shoved glasses, matchboxes, ashtrays about: this is where we were, here was the road, here was where they tried to encircle us . . . and so forth. The Fascists were put to rout. A few hours later, a Republican plane flew past; the pilot spotted the bandaged men celebrating their victory, and flew off to fetch a rescue team. They were flown to Madrid, and a number of them died in a hospital there. San Mateo fell, of course, to the Fascists, along with the rest of Spain.

A strange story, a not quite believable story. Yet it was true. Professor P. in Dresden had fought together with Kurt in San Mateo, and so had that guy with the game leg, Max So-and-so of the foreign ministry. They could attest to it; indeed, Bodo had already heard partial corroboration of everything Kurt had told us. Years later we discovered that Kurt, far from boasting, had modestly withheld information that would have singled him out as a hero.

There were two beaches in Ahrenshoop: the regular beach, used by people in bathing suits, and the *Nacktstrand*, officially reserved, by whatever agency held responsibility in such matters, for the enjoyment of nudity, or, as the statutes euphemized it, Free Body Culture: *Freikörperkultur* (FKK). On both beaches (really one beach, since no clear demarcation divided them) people shoveled up *Burgen* (burgs), circular ramparts of sand for protection against the wind; swam and played volleyball; helped their children build sand castles; walked about in discussion with their hands behind their backs . . . the only difference being the absence of swimsuits, in one case, and their presence in the other—a surprisingly unexciting distinction. Everyone except Johannes R. Becher knew this. Johannes R. Becher was an enemy of FKK, calling it a vile and disgusting practice fit for the cesspools of capitalist decadence, declaring it a heaven-stinking scandal that such goings-on were permitted in the First German Workers and Peasants State. Had he only consulted Peter and Gudrun and Gisela and me (which he could have, since we ate at a table adjoining his in the Kurhaus), he wouldn't have made an ass of himself saying things like that. But chances are that he never suspected the masses, both clothed and naked, of laughing at his ful- minations. After all (he must have thought), if anyone was qualified to be the judge of any kind of *Kultur*, it was he, Johannes R. Becher.

"Who is Johannes R. Becher?" asked Gudrun and Gisela, in their West German simplicity.

"Johannes R. Becher is the Kulturminister," Peter ex- plained.

"You've seen him," I said. "He's the guy who comes into the Kurhaus and seems to fill the entire dining room."

"Fat?"

"Not extremely. But important."

"Oh," said Gudrun, "you mean that bald man whose glasses are shaped like a spread eagle?"

"That's the one."

"Is he really going to make everyone wear bathing suits?"

"Nobody knows."

Johannes R. Becher was, of course, dead wrong. The indispensable condition of public nudity, in East Ger- many as elsewhere, is a kind of Edenic neutrality be- tween the sexes. Chastity is the price for being permitted to dispense with shame. People's movements take on a frolicsome, healthful, prophylactic expressiveness. The penis is required to hang slack; any responsive stirring on its part would be universally noticed and disapproved. Add to this, in our case, the stamp of government sanc- tion, complete with occasional coast-guard patrols, and the constant presence of one or another set of parents . . . the most stringent morality could not devise a more in- hibiting atmosphere. It extended even into my fantasies, urging them to roam far from the only locale where they might have come to fruition, away to exotic settings where plump women in transparent pantaloons awaited me, oozing with lust, batting eyelids like palm fronds. Peter, however, fantasized frankly about getting into bed with Gudrun and Gisela, and used me as a sounding board. Naturally, this awakened my interest. He liked to review things that the girls had done and said—thoroughly innocent things, as far as I could see—and give them a sexual interpretation. It excited him greatly, for example, that, far from being naked, they wore tiny crucifixes that dangled between their breasts. This detail, he explained, this rudimentary garment, this gossamer-frail chain binding them to their parents' religion with its injunctions to chastity and virginity—on bodies like theirs, all this was of undeniable erotic significance, whether the girls were conscious of it or not. Very dimly I felt I could see what he meant. I had noticed before, but never so clearly as now, that Peter was very smart and worldly-wise, and also that his imagination was at least as lecherously inclined as my own—and this without stimulus from Fuchs's *Sittengeschichte*. Where did it come from, then? Just from growing up? It came from *his* father's collection of erotica, it turned out, from old Chinese novels and from Balzac's *Droll Stories*, and from Casanova. On the beach, though, in immediate proximity to the girls' breasts and crucifixes, all of Peter's bookish savoir-faire abandoned him. It became painfully obvious to both of us that he and I were in the same boat, caught in the same dilemma of shame and excitable flesh, in a place that militated against both.

If the girls fantasized about us, it certainly wasn't apparent. Their eyes, sky-blue in radiant contrast to their tanned skin and abundant sun-bleached flax-blond hair, were clear and smilingly bright. They laughed like children, high liquidous bubbling peals. They straddled our shoulders with athletic zeal, clamping their feet behind our backs, to wrestle with one another, laughing happily, while Peter and I staggered and grimaced underneath, gripping their thighs. I remember them one morning waving eagerly and jumping up and down with pleasure as I approached them on the beach—a morning, it so happened, a good part of which I had spent masturbating, with them in mind, since the pantalooned ladies were beginning to fade. The experience had already left me feeling faintly vile, as if I'd polluted something clean and lovely, but seeing the girls brought forth an instant self-purifying judgment: never again! Never. I vowed to be chaste and pure as they were, yes, immaculate. I would wait for the day when love, like an angel, would gently usher me and the girl who loved me into one another's arms.

No such angel came, not that summer or the next, but a strange awkward faunlike creature named Kasimir showed up almost immediately, as if in answer to my prayer, and supplied the much needed catalysis—for flirtation, if not for love. It was on an excursion to the clothed part of the beach in search of ice cream that we were introduced to him: a boy with completely untamable thick black hair, acne on his forehead, eyebrows that converged over the bridge of a beaklike nose, very peculiar ears that came to a point at the top, a pair of widely set, black, moist, somewhat shifty eyes, lips of an amorphous thickness, and a general expression of shy brooding sullenness which was erased endearingly, but at odd moments, by a broad gummy smile. (Why does memory, fickle memory, think nothing of discarding whole months and years with all the faces that crowded them, and retain all the features of a face I saw just for a few hours?)

I had already heard of Kasimir from his parents, a Czech playwright and his Polish wife, a journalist, who had joined Peter's and my parents at their evening get-togethers, and who shared with them all their views and values except for the choice of a beach. Kasimir was a problem child. He was not only failing in school, but had so far, in the course of his fifteen years, completely failed to repay his progenitors in the only coin that held any

value for them: talent or intellectual acuity, those were
its two sides. He was a genuine dunce. "All he's interested
in," his father complained, "is mopeds." "And before he
reached puberty," Bodo asked, "what did he like then?"
"Bicycles." This was Kasimir's first forced separation
from his beloved machines. "Are you saying he's interested in *nothing* else?" Alma asked incredulously,
frowning in commiseration.

"Nothing."

But Peter and the girls and I could tell right away
that Kasimir's interests ranged further than mopeds. He
was awestruck when he learned that we came from the
Nacktstrand. After the girls had gone off to buy the ice
cream, he whispered, in his halting Czech German:
"How can you be *there*—" (thumbing in the direction
of the naked beach) "with *them*—" (tipping his head to
where they were climbing the boardwalk across the
dunes, their white dresses blown by the wind) "—and
not get a *giraffe?*"

"A giraffe? Oh, a giraffe." Czech terminology, evidently.

"You learn to control it," Peter said, with the suave
smile he had picked up from his father.

"I can't control it."

"Why don't you try?" I suggested. "Come back with
us. You'll see, you'll be too embarrassed to get a giraffe."

"I can't control it," Kasimir said glumly.

"You don't *have* to be naked there, you know," I said.
"It's up to you."

"Really?" Kasimir's eyes unfocused and swam in reverie. "All right, let's go," he said, "but I'll keep my swim-
suit on." He was as eager, suddenly, as he had been
reluctant just a moment ago. He could hardly wait for
the girls to return so we could set off on his guided
tour.

I soon began to regret that we'd ever teamed up with
this Kasimir, and that I'd persuaded him to join us,
against his own well-founded scruples. He was an em-

barrassment. As the first naked bodies came into view, he began to peek and turn his head and point and comment behind his hand: "Did you see *her?* Take a look at *that!*" And he had the audacity to ask the girls when *they* would take off their clothes. And this giraffe of his was really and noticeably uncontrollable. I felt as if I'd created a monster. But the girls, to my surprise and great relief, broke out laughing at the sight of Kasimir's anxious efforts to camouflage the tentlike bulge in his bathing suit with a towel Peter handed him. For his sake, we all sat down on the sand. Gudrun very kindly suggested to Kasimir that he go for a swim. "I've heard cold water helps," she said. "Thank you!" he cried out, already sprinting into the surf. "He calls it his giraffe," Peter said. I gasped inwardly—how could he talk to them like that! The girls' laughter pealed out as brightly and clearly as always. Kasimir's large feet and hands were splashing in a headlong clumsy crawl stroke away from the shore. I could feel Gudrun's long hair blowing against my neck and shoulder. An extraordinary contentment and languorous relaxation flooded my body. My breath flowed deeply into the bottom of my lungs, tarried there for a moment as if stretching luxuriantly, flowed out with a sigh of comfort. I looked around. Everything seemed suffused with happiness and a kind of sensuous splendor I hadn't noticed before. Everything: hot sand, shells and pebbles . . . the compact shining bodies of small children playing in the water . . . their high-pitched squeals mingling with the quarrelsome exclamations of gulls circling and swooping for fish . . . the surf's constant booming and soughing . . . volleyball players with bouncing breasts and leaping penises . . . Kasimir's knobby elbows rising and dropping, rising and dropping, as he progressed toward a white bathing cap that was, in turn, bobbing in his direction, propelled by a sturdy breast stroke . . . Gisela turning to say something to Gudrun and leaning her warm arm against my leg, giving rise to a giraffe of my own (happily concealed beneath a bathrobe) . . . the exquisite shape of that arm—it caught my breath. For the first time, I noticed a spray of minute golden hairs on her shoulders. My hand rose to touch them and then, as if of its own accord, changed course and came to rest on the nape of her neck. She looked at me with a puzzled expression, smiled, gave my shin a brisk friendly rub with her palm, and turned away again, disengaging my hand with the pivoting of her torso. The hand slid dreamily down her back, drinking in its warmth and tender smoothness; paused in regret when it reached the edge of her low-cut dress, then brushed along the cloth and cupped itself firmly, deliciously around a buttock— *What was I doing!* I yanked back the impertinent hand, fully expecting a punishing shock of anger or ridicule from Gisela, perhaps from Gudrun as well, for she had surely seen it. Neither girl gave any sign. Peter was too engrossed in attempting to excavate an ingrown toenail to have noticed anything. I just sat there rooted in shame, hoping absurdly that maybe Gisela hadn't noticed anything either, and that if she had, she had liked it—but I hardly dared hope for that.

Kasimir's black mane, meanwhile, and the white bathing cap were approaching each other inexorably, until they were just a few meters apart, at which point the cap rose straight up in the air, followed by the head and torso of a large naked middle-aged woman. Evidently there was a shoal out there. Kasimir froze, treading water. Gisela laughed and clapped her hands. Kasimir turned and started swimming back toward us with flailing limbs. Gudrun and Peter were laughing now, too, and I gratefully joined in.

Kasimir emerged from the sea detumefied and penitent. "I shouldn't have come here," he said. "I can't control it." Maternal Gudrun tried to encourage him to stay, but he shook his head firmly and left us with a wistful wave (and with Peter's towel slung around his

neck). He drove off to Prague the next day, together
with his disappointed parents.

I was still stunned by what I had done, as we walked
on toward our family burgs. Peter, walking before me
with Gisela, playfully put his arm around her waist. So
he, too, had caught the bug from magical Kasimir. For a
few steps they walked like lovers, with their hips touching, until she laughed and pushed him away. I followed
behind them, smoldering, brooding, while Gudrun next
to me talked about her hopes for a teaching career.
When we reached our parents, we found a discussion in
full swing, engaging neighbors who normally didn't
have much to say to one another. Once again, Johannes
R. Becher's displeasure was rumbling across the Nacktstrand like distant thunder. A naked man with a handkerchief on his head—he was an artist whose work had
suffered official disfavor for several years—exclaimed,
in a tone of anguished exasperation, that this time the
Kulturminister did seem to be making his threats in
earnest, otherwise why would he bother, now that the
season was ending.

A young man wearing spectacles and a shirt ventured
a political justification for nudity. "It has a democratiz-
ing effect, don't you think? If Becher were here among
us without his clothes on, how many people would
know he's a big shot? I mean people who don't already
know who he is?"

"They could tell by his glasses," said the man with
the handkerchief.

"Well, forget about the glasses, let's say we took them
away. Why, no one would even recognize him."

"I would. I'd recognize him better here than in a
bathing suit. I'd see a pompous old man without balls.
I'd say: That's Johannes R. Becher."

What did I care about the fate of nudism in Ahrenshoop. The season was ending. Peter had now put a hand
on Gisela's shoulder. I hated him. But on further observation, he seemed indiscriminate in his fawning and

tentative touching . . . Gisela's shoulder, Gudrun's knee, it made no difference to him. I spent the rest of the afternoon trying to determine whether Gisela had received the full message of my somnambulant palm, whether she had noticed it at all after it had left her neck. Little signs—subtle, intoxicating signals in her movements, in her eyes—told me she had indeed noticed, and that she was not averse to it, or to me. Ambivalent maybe, but not averse. In fact, I concluded, we had all noticed something. Other people were noticing it, too. Our foursome was turning into an oasis of budding carnality on the otherwise counter-erotic Nacktstrand.

Under Peter's and my unbelievably cautious two-pronged attack, the girls were becoming giddily voluptuous, voluptuously giddy, as if drunk. Especially Gisela. (Or was it that I paid attention only to her? Years later, Peter told me that Gudrun had been in love with me. "Really?" "Didn't you see? Couldn't you tell?" I wished it had been Gisela.) To get away from the eyes of others (not that this was our conscious motive—we didn't dare be too conscious), we went to the girls' cottage, where, fully dressed, without risk of being compromised by the obviousness of giraffes, we could play at being men and women who found each other desirable: by turning on the radio, for instance, and making up comical, always comical dances, in the course of which it was permissible, as part of the fun, to pull the sleeves of the girls' jerseys down with a yank, so that, with some luck, the tops of their breasts were laid bare. (As if we hadn't had an unobstructed view of their breasts for the past three weeks; but there was a difference between nudity and denudation, a difference that made one's heart leap into one's throat.) Or else amorous gestures would be exchanged in the guise of inane jokes, masking the unacknowledgeable urgency of our wanting with a parody of it—as when Gisela with mock lewdness showed me a minute rip in the crotch of her slacks

("Look where it tore! I wonder why") and stuck her finger in it, and I exorcized my bewilderment and impotence with a clever and amusing (I hoped) impersonation of slavering lechery. Time was running out, and Peter and Gudrun, Gisela and I were gesticulating and circling around one another, at moments meeting, then drawing away, helpless, smiling, like mechanical dolls in a courtly dance, each new gesture unfolding with aching protraction, as in those nightmares where it's impossible to flee. Except in this case we were fleeing toward one another. Everything had to be veiled in frivolity. As soon as desire showed its face in earnest, fear was there to fend it off. Better to play, to embrace her in a mock wedding, to have her lay her head in your lap, as if absently, while telling jokes, and as if absently play with her hair. That is how we slipped through one another's fingers, like sand, like time itself.

❲I wonder what convinced my parents that it would be best for me to go to school in Berlin after all, and to live at home. Maybe my summer tan and the sight of me flirting with Gudrun and Gisela gave them the impression that a healthy maturation had taken place. Maybe the fact that I had stopped painting and writing poems altogether while I was in the boarding school in Thuringia convinced them the place was as constricting and philistine as I said it was. Or maybe I just melted their hearts with my pleading not to be sent back there.

Peter returned to the Friedrich Ludwig Jahn school and no doubt stood listening to Herr Luedke orating before the flag at the same early-morning hour of September 1, 1956, when I sat listening to a first-day speech in the auditorium of my new school. Named after the physicist and biologist Hermann von Helmholtz, author of *A Treatise on Physiological Optics*, this school had windows you couldn't see through—a massive four-

story building that ruthlessly united at least seven incompatible styles of architecture into one ugly bulwark
of brown brick. Once again I resigned myself to dozing
through physics and math and chemistry and history
and biology and French and Russian classes, and during
recess wandered pretty much friendless in the big dirt
courtyard, wistfully watching the girls.

At home, I spent a lot of time drawing and painting,
writing in my journal, listening to records. Often in the
evening, family friends would drop in or guests would
visit. There was a difference. In the case of friends, I
could walk back and forth between my room and the
adjacent living room, taking part in the conversation or
turning my back on it, as I pleased. But if guests were
there, and an atmosphere of politeness prevailed, I had
to be more discreet. Also, I had a horror of being grilled
about school and the FDJ, two subjects I couldn't possibly admit to caring as little about as I did. To avoid
this discomfort and still satisfy my curiosity, I'd sit on
the floor of my room near the living-room door, reading
or painting, and wait for some word to catch my attention. It could be a loaded word like "love," "sex,"
"work," "war," "art," or "religion"; or a quarrelsome
word like "*Formalismus*," a bitterly debated cultural-
political category; or the closely associated "Kurella,"
which was the name of the new Minister of Culture. Talk
of a play, poem, novel, film, or story would always do it;
or, simply, the sound of people having a good time, or dis-
agreeing; and of course any mention of my name. Any
of these would lead me to press my ear to the door, and
if that test sustained my interest, I'd saunter into the
living room with an indifferent look on my face, sit
down on the rug, at some distance from the speakers,
lean against the bookcase, and pretend to be leafing
through a book on my lap.

Pretty soon I'd be burning to inject my two cents'
worth into the conversation. Someone was saying Otto
Dix had never painted so well as he did after 1945—

what nonsense! I had been to the same exhibition, and anyone with eyes in his head could see that the man who painted those brilliant surrealist portraits of World War I casualties and syphilitic whores, or those grand-masterly parodies of Nazi art, had *died* in 1945, and that someone else, someone mellow and dull, had taken to painting flowers and young children in his name, with a muted palette and in exemplary DDR-realist style, even though he lived in the West—only the signature could convince you that the same hand was wielding the brush! So how could this nincompoop say something like that? Kissing Alfred Kurella's ass in absentia, that's what he was doing! Otto Dix discovers Socialist Realism in his old age, like a sinner embracing the cross! The prodigal son returns to his philistine father! And there was Bodo wagging his head and coughing and evading the issue. Come on, man, defend yourself—it's *you* that's being attacked here. If you can't stand up for art, well, neither can I. I'm not supposed to have strong opinions, it always comes off as arrogance.

I liked to think I was being kept down on account of my youth. There was a small grain of truth in that, and no more. Actually, the suppression, in almost all instances, came from myself. Crippled by self-consciousness and self-doubt, I could have no idea of how willing most adults might be to hear me out. The grain of truth involved two or three men who didn't expect me to be anything but deferential to their experience and worldly wisdom—if they paid me any more than the most perfunctory attention, that is. That made me want to challenge them. Unfortunately, they *did* know more than I did, and had earned a right to the indulgent smile that appeared on their faces whenever I ventured to question their views instead of humbly inquiring about them. This smile—which was friendly, if condescending—invariably filled me with a deep feeling of illegitimacy, as if I were merely pretending to a fully

formed intelligence and had better do my homework;
but it also made me feel cheated, like a boxer listening
stupefied to the knockout count and trying to remember
what it was that had somehow felt different from an
ordinary blow with a glove, and doubting his own suspicion. I blushed, I lost my line of reasoning. My interlocutor would then either kindly reach out and help me
get my feet back on logical ground, or else he'd shrug in
genuine incomprehension; in either case, I'd retreat,
gritting my teeth, to the obscure periphery of adult dis-
course—eavesdropping by the door, in other words, and
coming in to listen, perhaps to ask questions, and talking only if I could be sure of not having to meet with
that patient, amused, and forbearing look.

Once Fania Fénelon, the French chanteuse, came to a
party at our house. I had heard she had terminal cancer
and wasn't expected to live more than a few months,
but it was hard to believe that this stout, impassioned
woman in her thirties was about to die. She sang throughout most of the evening with full-chested vigor, accompanying herself on the piano. There were always a
few people who welcomed with happy nods whatever
political chanson or cabaret ditty she sang—perhaps
they had passed through France on their odyssey of
exile. But many of her songs were known to most of us
from records or from Yves Montand's recent, enormously popular tour of the DDR. Bodo, I remember,
made a request: "*Il n'y a pas d'amour heureux*," a song
we had listened to many times on a record he had
brought back from a trip to Paris. Probably he liked this
song especially because his friend Louis Aragon had
written the words. Alma and I liked it for its melody.
"*Non*," Fania said, firmly shaking her head, "this is one
song I will not sing." "But why not?" several people
asked, with a note of petulance—apparently they liked
the song as much as we did. "*Absolument pas!*" And she
threw up an arm with a violently peremptory gesture

that caused her wide sleeve to fall below her elbow and reveal a row of blue numbers (which after several seconds I realized, with a shock, must be a concentration-camp tattoo). *"J'adore le poème!"* she exclaimed, *"mais je déteste la musique!"* The words *"je déteste"* were spat out with acidy contempt, while *"j'adore"* came out like a shower of gold. Between these burning poles of adoration and detestation could there be any coolly neutral or even ambiguous territory?

After a while Fania withdrew from the piano (against protest) and sat down in an armchair. I must have gotten bored with the conversation that followed or tired of the strain of trying to understand rapid exchanges in French, for I was startled when Fania suddenly jerked around in her chair to face Peter's father, and said: *"Toi?"* Kurt nodded, smiling. *"Mais c'est pas possible!"* she then said to the man with whom she had just been disputing a political issue. "But it's true," the man said. "Kurt is the person we've been talking about. And it's only because of his extreme, his immoderate, modesty that I'm probably the only one here besides him who knows that."

Fania looked back at Kurt—she had a hand on her cheek and was shaking her head, and Kurt was smiling at her—and then she jumped up and ran to where he was sitting and threw her arms around him. Kurt stood up, and they stood hugging and laughing, and Fania kept saying *"C'est pas possible!"* and finally Kurt said, *"Mais cependant c'est vrai"* ("It's true nonetheless"). *"Mais tu es allemand!"* ("But you're German!"), and she stepped back for a moment as if in sudden mistrust, or else to see his features more distinctly. Kurt shrugged apologetically, and everyone laughed. Then Fania took Kurt's hand and faced us all and said with great forcefulness: "He was my hero. Yes, when I was a young girl, he was my hero, my dream. But not just *my* hero, he was a hero for all free French people, for all anti-Fascists. He did wonderful things, extraordinary. And

only a few people ever laid eyes on him. Almost a legend
—but we knew he really existed."

Later Peter told me of one of his father's legendary
feats. He had marched into the Nazi General Head-
quarters in Paris, dressed in the uniform of a high German officer, and demanded a complete list of the names
and addresses of people who were to be arrested and
held as hostages to be shot in reprisal for acts of resistance. I suppose some Resistance fighters may have
guessed from that incident that their mysterious general
might not be a Frenchman.

I also learned the precise origin of the numbers on
Fania's arm. She was a survivor of Birkenau, part of the
Auschwitz complex, and she survived thanks to the grotesque circumstance that the camp's directors had organized an orchestra composed entirely of women prisoners to accompany the daily work of extermination with
musical tributes to *Hochkultur*. On the day Fania arrived in the camp, a request was issued for someone
who could sing the part of Madame Butterfly. Dazed,
bloody, covered with filth, her head shaved, Fania responded; she had, in fact, been trained as an opera singer
and knew the role. In the course of her audition, she
revealed her skill as a pianist, and was made a permanent member of the ensemble.

Often the topics that lured me out of my room were
the very ones that bored Alma. Since she couldn't drift
in and out of the living room as I did, she had to invent
ruses of her own. One of these was to put on some
bouncy New Orleans jazz record. If the fog wasn't dis-
pelled by that, she'd urge everyone to dance, sometimes
literally pulling them off their seats by their arms; and if
the mood permitted, she'd show them how to dance in
the "open" (and at that time forbidden) American style.
Most people had fun doing it, even if they felt a little
silly flinging each other about and twirling and bop-
ping. Only once did someone object. But this wasn't at

home, it was in the Kurhaus in Ahrenshoop. Alma was jitterbugging with the long-legged wife of a composer of revolutionary oratorios. The sight of two pretty women, the spouses of prominent "cultural workers" and Party members, flaunting not only this disgusting American dance decadence but their bodies as well, leaping about in sensual abandonment, barefoot, long hair in carefree disarray . . . this was too much for one lady, whose influential husband (off to some conference abroad) could have made life unpleasant for Bodo and the composer if their wives hadn't stopped their frivolity right away and without argument.

One day a very tall and humble member of the People's Chamber came to visit. He was almost immobilized by respect for Bodo, he hardly dared walk about or lean back in his chair. At the dinner table, someone dropped the word "*Selbstkritik*." I had seen one example of "criticism and self-criticism," in the FDJ in Potsdam. Emboldened by the visitor's almost juvenile timidity, I said: "In my opinion, self-criticism is just hypocrisy." A pained silence followed, which I took to be an unspoken request for further elaboration. "I mean, no one can possibly *want* to prosecute him*self*. It's just not something you can do with sincerity." Everyone seemed to be pondering the truth of what I'd said. "I think it's a disgusting practice all around," I added. I felt very pleased that for once I hadn't suppressed my opinion. Let someone disagree with me, as no doubt everyone here does, to judge by their shocked silence and that venomous look Alma's giving me—I can hold my own. But no one disagreed. Bodo had a brief coughing fit, and Alma broached some unrelated topic. Later I was told I had committed an awful faux pas: our guest had still been reeling from the criticism he had hurled against himself in front of colleagues and Party members just a week ago. And who did I think I was, making pompous pronouncements like that?

I generally didn't feel qualified to converse with adults as an equal, let alone spar with them. Or rather, I did feel qualified, in a deep-down, potential sort of way, but felt also that I lacked the necessary credentials of maturity—the solid physical presence, for example, that comes with pride of achievement. I was a skinny kid with perpetually ink-stained hands and a shirt that refused to stay tucked in his trousers. I could hardly blame people for failing to probe beneath this unpromising surface, and clearly I wasn't exactly demanding their attention; but it rankled anyway to be invisible so much of the time. Someday I would show them. Someday I would avenge myself with some blazing accomplishment, and they would write about me the way Nikolai Gogol's teachers did about him (I'd just read his biography): "A pity we did not sense what was there. But, then, who knows? Maybe it was better that way."

I worked at my painting, wrote poems, attempted a play. One of my most ambitious efforts was a prose poem about a spider web. Though writing in German, I tried to imitate the style of certain passages in *Let Us Now Praise Famous Men* (which I had been browsing around in ever since I could remember), where my father had lavished some gorgeously baroque and luminous sentences on seemingly plain things like floorboards, blue jeans, and an oil lamp. Contrary to Jim, though, I never actually observed my subject. I suspended it between two imaginary beams in an imaginary attic and proceeded gradually, carefully, day by day, to embroider it with more and more word-music, load it with more and more metaphysical debris. In the end it was hard to believe in this cobweb's frailty or even remember its arachnid origin, since the very destiny of man was entangled in it. Still, of all the things I had written, that page and a half seemed at least to approach a professional standard of competency. I showed it to Bodo. He returned it to me with a negative verdict: "Try something less complicated." Yet when he read a journal I'd kept during a potato-gathering expedition with the Friedrich Ludwig Jahn school—something I hadn't put the least effort into—he seemed genuinely pleased and encouraged me to continue taking notes. Notes! Some fat chance I'd have of becoming the talk of Berlin on account of the notes I took.

Nor did my paintings come anywhere near to meeting the exorbitant standards I set myself. One day, though, Fritz Cremer, the sculptor, saw something I'd done in oils (a bricklayer on his scaffold, with an interestingly geometric mess of boards, ladders, and tools lying around), raised his eyebrows significantly, and said: "There's a talent here. But without work he'll never develop it." Bodo relayed this heartening news to me. It felt good to have done something that made him feel proud of me. (I knew it must please him, because he respected Fritz Cremer enormously, and even spoke of him as a "giant.") Some time later, Alma and I were visiting Fritz in his studio. He handed us some clay and suggested we try our hand at sculpting while he finished draping wet rags around the nude he was working on. Alma tried to capture Fritz's powerful taurean frame, but she was having trouble getting the proportions right. I was aiming at something that would resemble the mask that lies at the feet of Michelangelo's *La Notte* (it was reproduced in a book we had at home). "How are you doing?" Fritz asked after a while. "Not very well," Alma said. "Keep trying," Fritz said. Then, spontaneously, Alma bent her little figure's recalcitrant legs into a ridiculous squat and made its arms reach out in a lunging sort of way. I laughed and gave my mask, which wasn't succeeding too well either, a walrus mustache and cavernous nostrils. Fritz approached us in time to notice we were effacing what had begun as a serious effort. He got angry at both of us, and especially at me: "You should

never, never do that! You have to respect your work,
even when it's no good! *Especially* then!"

The discomfort of being reprimanded was very slight
compared to the pleasure I felt at being taken at all
seriously. If Fritz demanded that I respect my own
efforts, *he* must respect them as well!

I craved recognition. To hear that someone had
spoken with appreciation of something I'd done or said
invariably moved me to tears of gratitude and inspired
me to vows of lifelong devotion to the perfection of
whatever it was I'd been praised for. I filled my journals
with passionate resolutions. Tomorrow, always tomorrow! I was always projecting a glamorously successful
future as a promise of redemption from the ignominious
present. At times, the thought of this future became a
serenely confident anticipation of it. My day would
come, the fruit would ripen. Like a demiurge, I would
burst upon the world with creations of unrivaled
beauty, profundity, splendor. At other times, the actual-
ity of a poem wilting under my labored, perhaps too
labored pruning and retouching filled me with such self-
disgust I would bang my head against the wall.

How much more fortunate Stefan seemed to me, despite his asthma. Ten years old, precocious and gifted,
he attracted everyone's attention, despite the fact that
he was even more timid than I. People were passing
around parodies of hyper-Prussian pseudo-socialist
complaint letters he'd written for Alma: *"Sehr geehrte
hochwohlgeborene Frau Genossin Uhse!!!* It has come
to our attention that while vacationing in the Red Beet
Hotel in Kleinwanzleben you have been consistently
pocketing public property in the form of cutlery, in particular *forks*. We politely request that you return said
silverware right away. Otherwise we shall have to bring
the matter up with the Ministry of Consumption and Re-
duction, Subdivision Unpleasantness. *Mit sozialistischem
Gruss*, Wilhelm Gustav Kartoffelblitz, Manager." That

was very good, especially for a ten-year-old, and a hell of a lot more entertaining than the odes to frogs and sunsets I used to compose when I was his age.

I no longer begrudged Stefan his success. There was precious little else for him to enjoy, sick as he was so much of the time, cut off from school and from friends. Indeed, I was proud of him. He showed me everything he wrote, and I usually liked his writing and told him so, which of course spurred him on to more ambitious projects: intricate correspondences between irate officials and befuddled members of the public; several chapters of a novel about a ghost who wants to serve the people instead of haunting them but finds it difficult to get anyone to believe him; comic verse, some of it as clever and poignantly witty as anything by Christian Morgenstern:

> *Kleiner Mann im Ohr,*
> *Hast du denn kein Rohr*
> *Für die Wasserleitung*
> *und für Brief und Zeitung,*
> *kleiner Mann im Ohr?*

(It's untranslatable, but the words mean: "Little man inside the ear,/Don't you have a tube/for the conduction of water/and letters and newspapers,/little man in the ear?")

The ghost story was something of a premonition. One day Stefan conceived the idea of publishing a school newspaper. He would solicit articles from other students and write some himself; there would be reports, poems, short stories, announcements, jokes, photographs, drawings, cartoons. He could start with the school's mimeograph machine, and if the newspaper's quality warranted a more professional presentation, maybe Bodo could arrange to have it printed, just like *Aufbau*, the magazine he edited. Stefan brought the idea up with his teachers. Their response was ambivalent: the plan of having a school newspaper was splendid, and Stefan's initiative in proposing it was commendable, and warmly appreciated; but it wasn't appropriate for a student to simply start such a project on his own, as an act of private enterprise, as it were, even though there was clearly no profit motive and the outcome would almost certainly constitute a public service. Perhaps he could bring it up with the Young Pioneers? Why not issue it under their auspices, as their official organ in the school?

So Stefan submitted his proposal to the Young Pioneers. The following is a very brief synopsis of an episode that took weeks to unfold.

The children were enthusiastic and immediately came up with imaginative suggestions. The two adult leaders were interested, too, but they looked troubled. If this was to be an organ of the Young Pioneers, it would have to have a certain *line*, a definite cultural and political profile. It would have to be educational as well as entertaining and informative, as was the case with all publications in the DDR, even humorous journals. To this Stefan agreed somewhat grudgingly; he had already worked out the whole format, and frankly it wasn't intended to be educational, since there was plenty of that in school— though politics weren't excluded. But he would try to amend his concept to the leadership's specifications. Perhaps a teacher could contribute the missing ingredients.

No, that wouldn't do. It wasn't a matter of missing Parts that could be supplemented but of the Whole. The whole newspaper. If the Young Pioneers were to issue a newspaper, it would have to truly represent the Young Pioneers, and not the idiosyncratic views of one or some of its members. Therefore, though Stefan's proposal was welcomed and his collaboration as editor was warmly invited, the editorial *policy* as such would have to be determined by the leadership of the Young Pioneers. "But," said Stefan, suppressing his tears, "then it won't be my newspaper, the way I wanted to make it!" "That is true," said the leaders. "We're sorry, but there's no other way."

Stefan wrote a detailed report on this ordeal of frustration—from the excitement of the original conception, and the joy and pride he took in the typewritten draft of the first issue, through the long string of meetings with teachers and Young Pioneer officials, the painful revisions, renewed proposals, prayers, tears, to the final heartbreaking moment of resigned sobriety: "So finally I realized that what I wanted to do can't be done." He didn't show this report to anyone—after all, we all knew what had happened; he put it in the drawer of his desk. Without Stefan's knowledge, Bodo and Alma showed it to their friends. I was present when it was discussed one evening. One man, a professor at the university, was deeply moved and said: "You know, this story is prototypical of a thousand others. It's really a terrible indictment of the way things are mismanaged in our country." Bodo and Alma and the other guests sadly nodded. "Wouldn't it be marvelous if you could publish this piece in *Aufbau?*" the professor said, smiling wistfully. Bodo, too, smiled, shaking his head. "Why can't you?" I asked. The professor answered for Bodo: "It would be used against us." "By the West?" "Of course." "But it could help change things for the better here, couldn't it?" Now there was headshaking on all sides. "It can't be done," they said, "it's too complicated. It's really impossible." Some of the voices sounded annoyed. Intimidated, I swallowed the "Why?" I had on my lips. The professor's wife said: "Maybe Otto Grotewohl should at least see it." (Otto Grotewohl was the Prime Minister.) "That's a good idea," someone acknowledged. Others agreed, but without conviction. There seemed to be some unmentionable hitch to that option, too. Bodo wagged his head. Everyone fell silent. It was late and very quiet, we could hear a streetcar screeching four blocks away on Kurt Fischerplatz. Then the professor said something that must have been on everyone's mind: "We're all in the same position as Stefan."

❨[There was at least one solid reason for going to school every day. That was Herr Scholz, our history teacher, totally inexperienced and handicapped by a Saxonian accent, always a liability in Berlin. He was given the fancy nickname Hermes, just a few days after school started. Eventually it contracted to Hermi. I don't know why he was called that, but the name stuck to him like a burr, so that after a while he responded to it as if it were his own. He stammered and committed Freudian slips with gratifying frequency, and he was manifestly unlucky in having chosen teaching as his profession; so there was nothing in his nature that should have attracted to him the name of the god of luck and eloquence. Conceivably, "Hermes" referred to his hurried and springy gait, which might have suggested wings on his heels; but that sounds too sophisticated for a group of sixteen-year-olds. Most probably his first name was Hermann.

Herr Scholz brought us comic relief, and more than that. Never again have I seen cliques and lone wolves, the clever and the dull, the unattractive and the good-looking united in such fellow feeling; and not just for the moment either: it spilled over into the long noon recess, and even into weekend outings to youth hostels outside Berlin—all thanks to the merrymaking that prevailed in history class. It's too bad, I think now, that a defenseless and gentle man had to be the source and the butt of our amusement. But we had little pity then. After all, who pitied the boredom and anxiety inflicted on us in ten years of schooling?

He comes bouncing into the classroom as if on extremely elastic shoes, and is welcomed by a shrill chorus of mostly feminine screams and raucous male laughter. A salvo of bunched sheets of paper stops him short. He looks around, frowning, pretending annoyance and surprise, even though this has happened many times before. One corner of his mouth betrays him by curling into a nervously twitching smile. A blush floods his face, the shrieking intensifies. He opens and closes his mouth, smiling foolishly, but no one can hear what he says. He proceeds toward the teacher's table in the front of the room and dumps his bag on it with an authoritative thud that is accompanied by the precisely simultaneous thunderous deposition of dozens of heavy fists, schoolbags, and elbows on as many desk tops: BOOM. The girls scream like demons. Hermi turns to the blackboard and demands instant quiet with large firm letters: R U H E ! But the chalk breaks off as he slashes the exclamation mark, and that sets off a new wave of hysteria. There's no need to feel sorry for Hermi—look, he thinks it's funny himself. He sits facing us with the textbook open before him, blood-red from the roots of his hair down to his collar, grinning. Gradually the noise subsides. People take out their lunch, begin to play chess, set themselves to doing homework for other teachers. "Open your books!" Hermi shouts, and announces a page number. Those who have nothing better to do read along with him, out loud, as he recites the textbook to us. Someone declaims from another page or another book. Hermi pretends not to notice. A grape bounces off his head. Now Hermi feels it beholden upon him to leap up and search for the perpetrator. He paces between the benches, red-faced and bedeviled by that idiot half smile; he holds his hands behind his back, stooping a little, and fingers a piece of chalk. "Who eats grapes here? Everyone show your lunches!" One boy sticks his finger in his throat and makes retching sounds, others initiate a jurisprudential inquest into one another's lunch boxes. The girls scream. Hermi hitches up his jacket—always the same tweed *Sakko*—with a high shrug and peers at his watch. There's still plenty of time. For once there's a teacher yearning and sweating for the clock to release him. "Pull yourself together, Hermi," someone suggests. "Why don't you teach us about Essex, Wessex, and Sussex. We're supposed to be learning history, remember?" "But we went over that yesterday," Hermi says plaintively, "and the day before." "Yes, but we still don't know the difference, they all sound the same." He refuses, suspecting some trick. Now the girls wheedle him: "*Please*, Herr Scholz? *Bitte, bitte? Please* show us again?" He blushes and melts. We wait while he sketches a map of England on the blackboard. He steps back and says: "You remember I told you about *Caedwalla* . . ." We pound our desks with our fists and shout the name like a battle cry: "CAEDWALLA!" "Quite right. Caedwalla was, as you know . . ." (he lunges to point at the appropriate place on the map) ". . . the King of . . ." and a militant chorus joins his voice: "WESSEX!" again accompanied by pounding fists. "Very good!" Hermi says. "Caedwalla, the King of . . ." (pointing again to Caedwalla's kingdom) "WESSEX!" ". . . conquered the kingdom of . . ." "SUSSEX!" This is all leading up to a final insane roaring avalanche of "ES!-SEX! ES!-SEX! ES!-SEX! ES!-SEX!" that rends our ears and reaches through every thick wall of the Helmholtz school to its remotest classrooms and storage bins, on and on. Caedwalla's men couldn't have sounded fiercer.

I took advantage of Herr Scholz to make my rather shadowy presence in class really count—*ruthlessly*, as I noted in my journal with sad self-disgust; but that was an exaggeration. The furthest I went, aside from teasing Hermi in class along with the others, was to impersonate him in his absence; nothing so cruel as the heap of junk some other class piled on his desk as a birthday present, or as violent as the steel ball someone slammed against the blackboard near his head, causing his knees to buckle from the sudden shock of fear. He called in

sick one day and I quietly left the classroom with my
schoolbag and someone's tweed Sakko I'd taken off the
rack on the wall, and came back in with springy steps,
wearing the jacket and swinging the door shut with an
authoritative bang, dumped my bag on the table, and
bade the class a loud *"Guten Morgen!"* with my hands
behind my back and a smile curling up on one side of
my face. The resulting hysteria encouraged me greatly.
I stalked between the rows of benches and grilled my
classmates on the subject of Essex, Wessex, and Sussex,
stooping a little and pulverizing a piece of chalk behind
my back. I hitched the Sakko up with a jerking shrug,
punched the air with my left fist to shorten the sleeve,
brought my wristwatch close to my eyes. I could feel it:
I *was* Hermi. If I hadn't known it, the screaming of the
girls would have told me so. One of the more prestigious
boys did me the inestimable honor of sliding off his
bench onto the floor, holding his belly and gasping for
air. A deep blush lent my performance the crowning
touch of authenticity.

After that, I ventured into other imitations: Herr
Fisch, with his habit of rubbing his chalky fingers on his
bifocals, as if he really preferred not seeing our faces
too clearly; Herr Kahlau, who liked to do things with a
ruler—point it, smack the table with it, drag it along
the ribs of the radiator, scratch his neck with it, tap his
shoes (it was easy to think up variations on this theme);
our immense, overbearing, sarcastic, terrifying chemistry teacher, whose marvelously apt name was Frau
Domin and who sometimes scratched herself in the
pubic region; Fräulein Bartel, who taught Latin with a
simpering Saxonian accent; Herr Kunze, who often dove
into a bar during the long recess, after which he would
come into our classroom, close the door with meticulous
precision, stride across the room in an absolutely
straight line, make a 180-degree turn, grasp hold of the
radiator behind him, and greet us, chin up, chest out,
with military crispness. (He'd make similar beelines for

the table, the blackboard, and back to the radiator in the course of the lesson, always with the same determined linearity.) That was the beginning of my brief career as clown and stand-up comic, which in a high-school class amounts to a kind of kingship. I ceded that high place willingly to Ralle Wenzel when he arrived two or three months later; it would have been folly to compete with him for it.

But I'm jumping ahead. Let me savor the memory of that sudden upsurge of popularity, and of my grateful astonishment at feeling myself buoyed up and borne aloft on its crest. "Nothing succeeds like success," as the capitalists say: the populace, raising its hero high on a cushioned palanquin, encourages him to fresh deeds of valor; the touch of laurels on the poet's temples inspires him to more enthusiastic song; the Hero of Labor, receiving a medal and the Prime Minister's handshake, overfulfills the plan once again. In the same way, I shone with redoubled brightness in the glow of my new friends' appreciation. Before my first day at the Helmholtz school, I had rehearsed in front of a mirror the precise arrangement of furrows on my forehead that would make me appear *intelligent* and at the same time *handsome*. They weren't needed. Even the teachers seemed to like me. Everything began to improve. Pitted against a much stronger boy in a boxing match during gym, in retreat from his expert jabs and hooks and prancing footwork, I suddenly walloped him off his feet, startling myself at least as much as I did him. When the music teacher asked for volunteers to sing in front of the class, I stepped forward and sang *"Die Lorelei,"* triumphing over the shameful memory of the day, years previously in Gross-Glienicke, when I pretended illness —in the face of universal disbelief—to avoid having to attend a parents' evening where I was scheduled to sing that same song. After cramming during recess to memorize Goethe's ecstatic *"Ganymed,"* I was called to recite it, needed two or three promptings, but reached the end of the poem, sat down with a breath of relief, expecting a slightly better than middling grade, and found myself surrounded by smiling faces and even a hint of applause: apparently I had given a performance. Success brought female admiration in its wake. Unbeknownst to me, a slightly wall-eyed girl with Gretchen-like braids slowly encircled me over a period of months, with a perseverance that is nothing less than amazing, considering my lack of response. Her name was Monika Mietke. Even more amazing is the innocence with which, in my journal, among commemorations of Ping-Pong scores and of raptures induced by music, I recorded the unfolding pattern of her advance without recognizing it: "Monika Mietke wants me to look at a painting in her home and tell her if I think it's valuable. I told her I'm not an expert, but she keeps insisting I should at least see it. I don't want to hurt her feelings, but I really don't care to go all the way to Karlshorst to look at this painting—especially after learning it's of ducks flying over a lake at sunset, and that the colors are bright." "Monika Mietke asked me to help her with Russian grammar after school. I tell her I know next to nothing about Russian grammar, and she gets annoyed. I find her a little weird. I wish she didn't keep asking me for favors." "Mietke wants me to take her to see a midnight showing of Cocteau's *Orphée* in the West. I don't want to go, mainly because she gets absurdly irritated when I don't do her bidding, and it annoys me to be pushed like that. Also, it seems to me it's the guy who should ask the girl out." "Monika Mietke has organized another weekend at a Youth Hostel in Münchehofe. This is the second time she's booked a space for me without consulting me first. I don't really mind, but . . ." "Playing *Schnipseljagd* near the Youth Hostel, Mietke practically lay on top of me in a sniper's trench where we were hiding. She seems to be totally unaware of sex."

I wonder what can account for such persistent (or

should I say stubborn?) unawareness on my part. Was
it vanity (since she wasn't beautiful)? Or was I too
fearful to notice? But I was fairly observant of other
matters, and aspired to be conscious of my motives. I
think I would have stumbled over my true feelings at
some point, if I had been hiding them from myself.
Most likely, it was ignorance and inexperience that kept
me from seeing.

But probably I was also distracted by Ulla Mehlhausen, the buxom, somewhat snippy, and extremely
spoiled daughter of an eminent brain surgeon. (Ulla
was spoiled, incidentally, because the state spoiled her
parents: they owned a Mercedes, their back yard was a
small park, their villa could have housed two families
twice their size, and they had another house near the
Baltic Sea, and a sailboat. How else to keep an eminent
brain surgeon from going to the West to get rich? Someone had heard Ulla say to her father: "Vati, can I have
ten marks? I want to buy a bockwurst." A bockwurst
cost twenty pfennigs. Dr. Mehlhausen was as vastly
overfed as he was overpaid, and so were his wife and
Ulla's younger brother, and also their maid and even
their dachshund. Only Ulla had so far escaped the family curse of obesity, and what intimations of it were
present, beneath her chin and in her breasts and hips,
were appealing.)

Ironically, Ulla, among all the girls in our class, was
the only one who seemed to feel something akin to contempt for me. Two or three were indifferent, most liked
me, Monika pestered me with her requests—only Ulla
refused to show that she so much as noticed me. And
when I asked her one day, after weeks of deliberation, if
she'd like to go to the theater with me (gulping with
anxiety), she didn't deign to answer, just tossed her
brown curls and shrugged one shoulder as if to say:
"Why should someone as pretty as I have to consider
the likes of you?"—quite a ridiculous gesture, but I
found it attractive; not *likable*, but . . . provocative, that

was it. I resolved I would make love to Ulla before the year's end.

It's probably just as well Monika didn't succeed in capturing me. Look at how differently she and I went about the business of wooing—we must have been incompatible. Where she deployed her forces coolly, deliberately, like a field marshal in a war of attrition, I resorted to the shamanic device of invoking spiritual forces. I prayed. I had learned this in Mexico, when I was six, from a Catholic housemaid who supplemented the crucifix on her bedside altar with Aztec *ídolos*; so I was deeply imbued with the belief that every manner of occult aid can be brought to bear on one's affairs, provided one calls for it with sufficient intensity and constancy. I prayed to God for an opportunity to get closer to Ulla.

The Supreme Being promptly arranged for a showing of Chaplin's *Great Dictator* at the Film Institute, by special invitation only. My parents received several complimentary tickets, and I was told I could bring four friends. I chose Piesel Winckelmann, Willi Klawitter, Monika Mietke (in return for her inviting me to the Youth Hostel), and Ulla Mehlhausen. This time Ulla did not shrug disdainfully. She threw her arms around me, explaining that she simply *loved* Charlie Chaplin, that she'd seen the same collection of silent short films of his at least six times, and that she'd *heard* about this screening and was *dying* to see it and had tried to find a way, and gave up in despair when she found out that her only contact at the Film Institute, an apprentice director, was off on location somewhere . . . and now this! I was the answer to her prayers! "Does it have subtitles?" she asked hopefully. "No, it's in English, but I can translate." She hugged me again.

On the big night, after the lights went out, she hooked her arm under mine and leaned close against me to make sure she caught every word. Never had my attention been more divided—between the happenings on the screen, the task of rapid interpretation, Ulla's voluptuous body pressed against me, giggling, then breathing serenely until shaken again, my lips virtually kissing her ear as I whispered my translation, the unfastened top two buttons of her blouse and the pale glimmering light illuminating the place where her breasts began to swell into prominence and, alas, immediately vanished under the cloth, the dizzying perfume rising out of her hair into my nostrils, Monika's finger poking me in the back and her irritating voice: "Would you *please* lean over to the left? I can't see. And speak a little more loudly, *I'd* like to know what they're saying, too!" Fortunately, someone hissed her down.

After the show I helped Ulla into her coat. Struggling to disregard the inhibiting presence of parents and friends, I ushered her toward the exit, one hand welded to the small of her back, on my face a debonair smile of which I became unpleasantly conscious a moment after she quickened her steps (leaving the hand and the smile behind in a state of suspension) toward a good-looking young man who stepped toward her and handed her a bouquet of roses. They exchanged an intimate kiss, during which Ulla raised one foot up behind her.

Naturally, I was disheartened and felt I had been made a fool of. The next day, in school, Ulla raised my spirits somewhat by thanking me for having invited her to the show. But it seemed an obligatory sort of graciousness, and as the days passed it diminished. Soon I found it once again impossible to so much as catch her eye for a moment. No question—she was avoiding me. When I put some perfectly neutral, school-related question to her, she bluntly answered with a question of her own: "Why do you ask *me?*" "Why *not* ask you?" She looked at my lips and my eyes—as if to unmask me—shrugged, and turned away. Willi Klawitter noticed my troubled absorption and put a counselor's hand on my shoulder: "Forget about Ulla. She thinks she's too good for us. She only goes out with older guys, and every one of them's some kind of big shot." *"Bonze"* was the word he used. He was forgetting, in his friendship for me, that I came from *Bonzen* circles myself. I felt grateful for that.

I abandoned my plan to conquer Ulla Mehlhausen. Seen from a distance, and especially from the eminence provided by the classical records I began listening to once again, it seemed not only futile but unworthy. If Mozart's Clarinet Quintet could make me feel like embracing the world, if the nuance of a grace note or the majestic evolution of a fugue could ignite such exquisite pleasure, shouldn't the girl I sleep with inspire me with some equivalent fullness of feeling and generosity? Shouldn't sex be allied with love? I didn't even *like* Ulla. Maybe Providence had withheld her from me for a good reason. My day would come, I would meet my girl, my future wife, face to face and heart to heart, her loveliness would flood my being, no force on earth could deflect the sureness and purity of that love. It would be like music. (Meanwhile, Providence did nothing to stem the recurring tide of lust—blind craving for the soft flesh of woman, as loveless and urgent as hunger.)

¶[One morning in November or December, the principal stepped into our classroom, leading by the hand a tall, thin, blond, blue-eyed boy with a gulping Adam's apple. It was Peter Vogel. "I must say I'm pleased," I wrote in my journal, and by that I meant a sense of triumph, in addition to the renewed pleasure of Peter's company. His father had given in to a series of desperate letters detailing the boredom and spiritual deadness Peter was feeling at the Friedrich Ludwig Jahn school, its philistine atmosphere, the lack of privacy—in short, all my own complaints, which, when *I'd* made them, many adults, and especially Peter's father, had dismissed as the evasionary tactics of one who needed his flaccid spine firmed up by some old-fashioned discipline.

Peter's presence also emboldened me in what some teachers were beginning to complain were the signs of a growing indiscipline and disrespect. I had developed a habit, before his arrival, of showing up every morning exactly five minutes late. Now my excuses ceased to be shamefaced repetitions of the usual "I overslept" or "I missed the streetcar" and became ever more elaborate inventions, which the class began to look forward to—a new installment, dependable as the morning news on the radio, five minutes after eight each day: "The neighbor's goat broke loose and was standing in front of our door, and I was afraid to go out, and when I tried the front window it was stuck"; "The streetcar bumped into an apple cart and tipped over all the apples and everybody had to help pile the apples back into the cart before the streetcar could move on." It was fun to think up a new story each day on the way to school, and see the expectant smiles as I stepped into class. After a while the teachers stopped asking me to excuse myself and complained to my parents instead.

Because I knew from experience the anxious discomfort that was making Peter's Adam's apple bob up and down all the time, I wanted to help him feel at home. Who or what is it that binds together "what convention stern divides," according to Schiller's famous ode? Joy. And since no greater source of joy existed in our school than Herr Scholz, I encouraged Peter to drive poor Hermi to distraction in some novel way that would endear him to the hearts of his new classmates. So Peter introduced to the Helmholtz school a certain sound that had rung in chorus and ad nauseam through our Thuringian dormitory for a while, a loud, forcefully expelled farting noise that is produced by the pneumatic interaction of a palm and an armpit.

Moderately unruly though we were in school, Peter and I always defended the political status quo against "reactionaries" among our peers. (Had the FDJ only known about this, we might have been spared the degrading criticism heaped on us later that year.) Peter usually argued as a good Marxist should, with philosophic patience and an impressive arsenal of scientific information (he had definitely earned that gold Medal for Good Knowledge). I, on the other hand, made use of a sort of Ulbrichtian sledgehammer rhetoric combined with a style of argumentation which my mother sometimes adopted to good effect: it consisted of simply blowing dry facts away with a strong gust of emotion. (I had developed a dogmatic contempt for facts anyway, in the course of four years of resistance to school.) *So what* if the Soviet Union appropriates X percent of the DDR's gross national product: didn't Germany ransack the Soviet Union and take in human lives alone more than could ever be paid back in saltpeter and soft coal? What? Hungary, Poland, and Czechoslovakia, too? Well, I just don't believe that. Why would one socialist country exploit another? That's precisely what socialist countries *don't* do!

This earnest "progressiveness" of ours had developed in response and in direct proportion to the perceptible faltering of our parents' faith ever since the Twentieth Party Congress in Moscow, earlier that year. We were still in Thuringia at the time, so we could only guess how it might be affecting our parents. That something extremely unusual had happened was immediately obvious when we saw the front page of *Neues Deutschland*, the official Party newspaper, being read with avidity all over the school; and then there were the rectangular discolorations on various walls where Stalin's portrait had hung until recently. The spectacular nature of the news itself took a little longer to sink in: Joseph Vissarionovich Stalin, "the immortal glorious son of the working class," a mass murderer . . . concentration camps in the Soviet Union, the motherland of social justice . . . It was shocking and a little frightening. Just three years ago everyone had been weeping over the death of "the Father of Nations"; five, six weeks of mourning, enough private and official sorrow to make you think no greater tragedy had ever befallen the human race—and now this sordid mess of numbers: numbers of prisoners, numbers of corpses.

The Politbureau must have sent identical directives to teachers and newspaper editors. The discussion of Khrushchev's revelations in classrooms and editorials took the form of self-congratulation: what capitalist government could boast of such candid, courageous self-criticism? Mistakes had been made, grievous, terrible mistakes, but now, thanks to Comrade Nikita Sergeevich Khrushchev, First Secretary of the Communist Party of the Union of Soviet Socialist Republics, the cult of personality belonged to a bygone era. Most of us, teachers and students alike, were perfectly content to be lulled into security. I don't remember anyone voicing any questions once the official answers had been handed down and repeated with emphatic frequency.

But when Peter and I came home to Berlin, we found that, for our parents and their friends, Stalin's crimes weren't a settled matter at all. Bodo told me of a good friend, Otto Katz—I had known him, too, in Mexico, when I was little—who was executed in Czechoslovakia, a self-accused imperialist agent. Bodo had never been quite able to believe Otto's confession, though he recognized his friend's personal style in the words reprinted in *Neues Deutschland*; and he was disturbed, too, by the number of Jews among Otto's alleged co-conspirators. But he had silenced his misgivings. Who was he to criticize the Party? Now he was certain Otto had done nothing wrong. I remember Bodo groaning one evening, over his eighth or tenth beer, bent double with contrition, that his life was in ruins, that he had wasted his talent, that he had given over his soul to that bastard, Stalin. Of course he was drunk, and got sober again, but I was shaken; and my response was to grasp hold of what Bodo and Alma had taught me were the essential and incorruptible values of Communism—that man is basically good, and his deformations perfectible; that all human beings have an equal birthright to a good life; that it is better to cooperate than to compete, more ennobling to serve others than to enrich oneself; that no one should own what others need for their existence and happiness—and to fashion all these ideas into a poem. Bodo was moved to tears, by its sentiment more than its beauty, I think, because he advised me a little later to stay away from agitprop, it just wasn't the right genre for me.

Friends of our family suffered crises similar to Bodo's. A neighbor who had written one of the most famous of the many heroic odes to Stalin declared in a fit of self-loathing that what he wished to be more than anything else now was a lumberjack in some remote country like Norway. Very shortly after that, he was introduced to a Norwegian lumberjack who wanted nothing more than to leave his backwoods existence and be a poet engaged in the battles of the day. It must have been a relief, at least for the moment, to see one's despair reflected in the distorting mirror of a comical coincidence.

Bodo had always been of delicate and somewhat morbid temperament, easily unsettled; but this time he seemed to have lost all assurance of there being any solid ground beneath his feet. He listened more than he talked when his friends were over, often with a pessimistic look on his face. From time to time he'd sink into a morose depression, the corners of his mouth pulled down, a strand of hair falling over his eyes, nursing a beer and a tall glass of vodka. Gradually, though, as everyone else made their adjustments, he made his. I heard of a new kind of hero—from Bodo's lips more than from anyone else's: a victim of Stalinism, a Communist, unjustly imprisoned for years, is reprieved, returns to society, and humbly, without bitterness or recrimination, devotes himself to the Party work he was forced to abandon long ago. These weren't just inspirational tales (though they did serve that purpose); there really were such saints, and not just in the Soviet Union but in our neighborhood. I regarded them with a respect approaching awe. How contemptible, in comparison, seemed Alfred Kantorowicz, our onetime neighbor in Gross-Glienicke, who was now hurling diatribes against us from West Germany, in books, articles, and on the radio. What had *he* suffered? Just disgust and frustration; no jail, no exile. What a venomous, small-minded man—how could he forget, beneath the merely human errors of well-meaning bureaucrats, politicians, judges, and journalists, the noble foundations of a new and more humane society? How could he, a Jew, join forces with former Nazis, unpunished and still in power in West Germany? Why didn't he keep his mouth shut, or at least say what he had to say in Switzerland or somewhere like that? These were the judgments generally made of him by people I knew, and I saw no reason to contradict them. Especially not after the revolution (or counter-revolution, as the case may be) broke out in Hungary.

On November 4, 1956, the handwriting in my journal grew jagged and agitated: "For days now I've been making notes on almost exclusively trivial and personal happenings—at a time when bombs are falling on Cairo, when statesmen forged terrible plans in deliberate disregard of the danger of a new world war, just for the sake of profit. Yesterday Fascist terror was still raging in Hungary. 21 men who were keeping watch before the CP building in Budapest were hanged from lamp posts. Communists are being beaten to death, or drenched with gasoline and set on fire. *It could happen here!* Everything seemed about to topple in Hungary, everything new . . . the state that wanted to build socialism, that strove toward this noble and glorious goal, the government that had made so many mistakes along the way, and had made so many enemies that the return of the aristocrats and great landowners seemed imminent. This evening the Soviet Union made an armed attack on Budapest, after Kadar formed a counter-government contesting the government of Imre Nagy. How sad Chancellor Adenauer was about that, what crocodile tears he wept for the poor Hungarian people. He didn't waste a word about the Egyptian people, who experienced a trial at least as heavy in recent days. But at least, in the West, the news about Cairo came promptly. Our own radio stations attempted, idiotically, to pretend all was well and peacefully progressing as usual in the socialist camp, till the Western radio forced them out of their silence. And they're still keeping their reports five hours late, presumably because the truth has to first pass muster with the Central Committee or the Politbureau. Meanwhile, the West broadcasts dramatic and, I suspect, invented appeals from alleged rebel radio stations in Hungary. Who to believe in? One side lies, the other keeps silent. *Is our silence not deception as well?* This evening at 10:00 p.m. the UN General Assembly will convene to vote on the appeal of Imre Nagy for an armed defense of his government. Bodo and Ludwig Renn don't believe there will be a UN intervention, but I'm not so sure. I'm afraid the West might see its chance here to deliver a decisive blow against the suddenly vulnerable Soviet Union. But that would mean a world war. God protect us!"

Rummaging through Bodo's desk one of those troubled days (I was looking for an eraser), I discovered a large bottle of chloroform and a plastic bag full of cotton. I knew Bodo was unhappy, that was plain to see, but I'd never heard of chloroform being used against this kind of pain. I poured some on a wad of cotton and sniffed it. It made me feel sick. Was it for Stefan? But why would they give him chloroform if he had trouble breathing? And why was the bottle so hidden away? I asked Alma about it. She was as surprised as I was. No doubt she questioned Bodo about it that same day, but she didn't tell me his answer until a few years later. He had bought the chloroform with the idea of painlessly killing us and himself in case of a Fascist takeover: he was afraid we would be tortured. Alma's immediate reaction was horrified disbelief, followed by contempt: "Can you really be such a coward? You'd kill your own children—out of fear?" Bodo hung his head low and said nothing. Then Alma proposed the much more sensible plan that we all leave the country and live in the United States, at least until peace was assured in the DDR. But Bodo wouldn't dream of asking a capitalist country for refuge—not from an uprising against the socialist Germany that had been the passion of his life, however marred and frustrated the dream had become in reality. He would go down with the ship if it sank; but he begged Alma's forgiveness for having been so selfish as to want to take us down with him, and to mistake that for protectiveness. Alma chose to stay then, out of loyalty to Bodo more than for any other reason. He said he needed her. He was afraid. If there was to be a civil war, she would ship Stefan and me off to the West, but she'd stay with Bodo and face whatever came.

As is well known, the Soviet Union suppressed the Hungarian revolt, and the UN chose not to intervene, thus obviating any need for drastic decisions on the part of my parents. Radio DDR caught up with its five-hour lag and gave prompt reports on the restoration of order in Budapest. American journalism, more than Communist propaganda, convinced me that the Soviet invasion was justified. East German dailies published double-page spreads (in the manner of Western tabloids) of _Life_ magazine's horrible photographs of burned, hanged, and shot human beings, and of their murderers dancing around them with expressions of fiendish gaiety and hatred. The question of whether this was revolution or counter-revolution, Communist or Fascist, dissolved in the face of such inhumanity: let it be stopped by all means and as soon as possible. Thank God for the Soviet tanks.

Bodo, who was floundering in the most anguished irresolution, told his friends—I learned about this decades later—that I had helped him see the light, that he felt so proud of my calm strength and political maturity. That was wishful thinking. No one was showing much political or any other sort of maturity those days. Not much calm strength either. Who could be calm on the brink of Armageddon? At the end of that hastily scribbled diary entry of November 4, with its measured sentences leaning against the vertiginous pull of hysteria, I copied out the last words of an article by Stefan Hermlin, a poet who was a close friend of Bodo's:

Hungary and Egypt must be saved so that we will not be struck tomorrow by plagues beside which all the biblical plagues will seem harmless.
    Stop them!
    Stand together!
    Murderers, murderers, murderers above you!

This was followed by a plaintive and simple statement of my own: "I'm afraid I don't believe in anything anymore."

On November 6, we attended a performance of *Mother Courage* by the Berliner Ensemble, in memory of Bertolt Brecht. "At the end of the last act," I wrote, "waves of shudders went up my back, watching Helene Weigel as the old Courage, skeletal, burned out, dragging her wagon across the desolate land, almost touching the ground with her face, directionless, everything valuable destroyed by war. But still she believes in war, follows it like a lodestar. Then, after the show, as we

stepped into the foyer, we saw a woman wandering
about among the crowds before the buffet and by the
cloakroom, weeping and embracing all kinds of people,
including Bodo, including doddering old Arnold Zweig;
no one seemed to know who she was. From a loudspeaker mounted on a car that was slowly passing by on
the street, a man's voice shouted: 'Citizens of the DDR!
Egyptian cities are being carpet bombed at this moment!
Help the Egyptians any way you can! Prevent a third
world war!' This message was repeated over and over.
After that we went to the Presseklub with the L.'s and a
fat, long-haired man whom I don't know and who was
accompanied by an extremely stupid and conceited
woman. The fat man said he wouldn't believe any
news from the East, including the report of the carpet
bombing in Cairo, until he heard it confirmed by the
West, and vice versa. Nothing interesting was said after
that. When we got home, I turned on Radio Freies Berlin—it's true, they've been bombing Cairo. But the West
isn't worried about a world war, they're paying much
more attention to Budapest. Sometimes I get the terrifying feeling everyone, East and West, is being led around
by the nose—but by people who themselves don't know
where they're going. Like Brueghel's blind men, heading
for the ditch."

I prayed a lot during those days, and I believed I was
answered in the language of music. Or was it the other
way around, that music revealed itself as a language of
prayer? The imp of coincidence had arranged, in the
planning of the curriculum for eleventh-graders, that
we should begin practicing the canon *"Dona Nobis
Pacem"* at the same time that war would break out over
Cairo and Budapest. Never had the harmonious unison
of human voices seemed such a miracle, nor, listening to
my records at home, had I ever heard music sound so
urgently beautiful.

[After the noise and panic abated, we discovered again how truly boring the peace of normalcy could be. And then Ralle Wenzel arrived.

Why he was taken out of his school and transferred to ours so late in the term the teachers didn't explain. Ralle himself bashfully answered our questions with evasive generalities. But our feeling was that his delinquency must have been considerable. For one thing, he was introduced to the class with a good deal less than the warm endorsement Peter had received—not exactly coldly, but with a touch of suppressed apprehension in the teacher's glance and tone of voice, as if she were thinking, Let's hope for the best. And there was the hoodlum-like swagger and sneer he affected, and he wore jackets with oversized shoulder pads, and his hair was oiled and slicked back in the Entenschwanz fashion— clearly a hood, clearly someone to stay on the good side of. Actually he was a self-effacing, awkward, rather melancholy boy, no real menace to anyone, just a misfit to his very bones. And a born comedian. By that I mean someone who can't help being funny, as distinguished from lesser talents, like myself, who must sweat and strive for the reward of laughter, and who can be serious, or look serious, without being funny. I had not dared to inflict my clowning on teachers other than Hermi. Most teachers commanded at least that minimal degree of respect that showed in our falling silent and rising to our feet when they entered the room. But Ralle respected no one; or at least he lacked the necessary reflex of subordination, and seemed incapable of simulating it convincingly—not even in the face of such massive authority as was personified in Frau Domin, our Goliath of a chemistry teacher. To give an idea of just how overwhelming she was: the first twenty minutes of her first day with us were devoted to a sort of physiognomical inspection. Striding from bench to bench, she briefly examined each face and then with Delphic assurance delivered pocket-size character analyses: "You are proud"; "You have a soft heart and thick skin"; "You are courageous and narrow-minded"; "You are invidious" (What was "invidious"? We had to look it up); "You're not as bright as you think you are." She called this "getting acquainted."

Frau Domin sprang a surprise test on us shortly after Ralle arrived. He pleaded illness, melodramatically and without the slightest pretense of sincerity. We didn't laugh; we held our breath waiting for the annihilating flash of sarcasm from Frau Domin. She chose to defer her rebuttal. She seemed intrigued by this unknown quantity that had risen up among her subjects. She cocked her head, placed her fists on her hips, and asked to know precisely what was the nature of his alleged discomfort. With his fingers peculiarly interlaced (like a zipper), Ralle stroked a vague area comprising the upper part of a thigh, a hip, and a kidney, and exclaimed, with a pained, effeminate groan: *"Diese ganze Partie"* (this entire section here). For one moment—just enough of a breach in her armor to let a few damaging snickers penetrate—Frau Domin stood open-mouthed and blinking incredulously. Ralle packed his books and started to walk out. Frau Domin, noticeably unsettled, demanded to know who had given him permission to leave. "No one. It's just too boring," he said with a shrug, and closed the door behind him. The news spread to other classes. By the time Ralle returned, a few days later, he had become a celebrity.

I was proud to be Ralle's friend—his only friend, you might say, since no one else came close to matching his reckless will to fail. Others were admirers and followers, not really friends—Peter, for instance (though his respect for Ralle was not unmixed; I remember him speaking a little uneasily of Ralle's "petit-bourgeois" tendencies, whatever that meant); tough weasel-swift

little Piesel Winckelmann; chubby Willi Klawitter with
his gap-toothed smile; even Jürgen Stoltz, an FDJ functionary with a vise-like handshake, an impressive athlete who would surely have been voted "most likely to
succeed" if such contests were held in the DDR. They
all fell under Ralle's spell, imitating him, each in his
own sphere of preference or competence. Stoltz, for example, in leaping off trains. The doors of the S-Bahn
could be yanked open before the train stopped, and
Ralle always leaped out onto the very first square meter
of platform available, while the train was still going
fast. I can still see him scampering frantically in pursuit
of his own momentum from one end of the platform to
the other and up the stairs, past whatever uniform—
police or stationmaster—was there to stop him, chin
thrust forward, legs flailing, his broad-shouldered
jacket, always fastened by the lowest button only, filling
up with air behind him, like Quasimodo's hunchback.

Willi Klawitter, on the other hand, apprenticed himself to Ralle as a thief. If theft can be considered the
poetry of the marketplace, Ralle was a bard, a rhap-
sodist of the highest order. His bedroom was furnished
with extraordinary trophies: hundreds of marks' worth
of books; enough stylish haberdashery to attire a small
army of fops (he rarely wore these clothes, but kept on
stealing them); a sizable record collection, containing
the near-complete works of Little Richard, Chuck
Berry, Fats Domino, Elvis Presley, and Bill Haley; a
lovely rococo mirror; an original Matisse watercolor; an
ever-fresh supply of Swiss chocolate; who knows what
else.

Only Peter and I were allowed to witness a few of
Ralle's major heists (most of which he carried out in
West Berlin, where the better merchandise could be
found). But during recess he frequently gave demonstrations to anyone who cared to come along for the
show. In small private bakeries, for example, of which

there were several in the school's neighborhood. These stores were designed to thwart thieves; most of the goods were stacked on shelves behind the counter, and others were displayed on the counter itself, but were shielded from the customer's grasp by a high pane of glass. The weak spot in all this defense was the fact that only one person, usually the proprietor himself, worked there. Ralle would politely ask for some fancy item on one of the higher shelves. This required his usually elderly and slow-moving victim to put up a ladder and climb a few rungs, leaving Ralle just enough time to reach over the glass and hastily gather up the day's goodies, with the indispensable help of Willi Klawitter, who was lifting him up by the waist. When the salesman or -woman, still unsuspecting, came down with the pie, Ralle would ask the price, make a face and a sound expressive of shocked incredulity, and declare in a regretful tone that he simply could not afford to spend that much money on cake, even though it looked and smelled wonderful, that much he would grant. He'd apologize for having caused so much trouble; to which the mechanical reply would usually be: "That's all right," or "It's my job." Eventually word must have spread among the local bakers, for one of them suddenly turned around halfway up his ladder and caught Ralle in flagrante delicto, hoisted off his toes by a puffing Willi Klawitter, his right arm straining to reach over the glass and down to the counter—an icy, fatal moment. I think almost anyone other than Ralle would have fled or else frozen, immobilized by guilt. He pointed at the cake he had been about to seize and said: "Not up there, silly—*this* is the one I want."

That was the end of the bakery circuit, though there were still variety stores and some fruit-and-vegetable stands to steal from. Rather than waste his talent on anything so unchallenging, Ralle treated us to pure exercises in legerdemain, not for loot, but simply for the art of it, or to win a bet: removing, with infinite care, the most inaccessible, central one of several dozen tin cans stacked in a pyramid, and simultaneously substituting for it another object of equal size, while shopkeepers and customers went about their business all around him; or the day he carried some ten or twelve chairs out of a bar-and-grill on the Luisenstrasse, setting them up in a row on the sidewalk. The trick—leaving aside the sheer luck that, according to Goethe, comes to the assistance of genius—consisted in a fearless conviction that most people are virtually asleep most of the time, and in an almost uncanny adaptation to the atmosphere of the place in his gestures and pacing and even his facial expression.

Only in the classroom did he seem at all times grotesquely misplaced, hence unable, as a rule, to·act in concealment. He did seem to *try* to adapt: by wearing glasses, for instance. Several times a day, whenever he was called on to recite, he extracted from his breast pocket a pair of steel-rimmed spectacles and, having carefully wrapped their slightly wavy wires around his ears with a curiously pedantic earnestness, was suddenly transformed into the image of a myopic dreamer pretending, for some farfetched reason, to doctor-like intellectuality (with the ducktail and shoulder pads absurdly appended). He didn't need his glasses for reading; when one day a lens fell out and shattered, he took two months to replace it, without, however, missing a single occasion to repeat his strange routine. After a while, any time a teacher put a question to Ralle, the class would perk up, all faces animated with sly expectancy. Ralle would reach for his glasses and install them with the usual fumbling pedantry, clear his throat, and address himself to the question with beetle-browed deliberation, tracing vague explanatory diagrams in the air with his fingers, orating at length and with an incredible paucity of factual information, until ordered to sit down again.

It was around this time that rock-'n'-roll began announcing itself in TV news spots of Elvis Presley in silver-studded denim standing high on a crude wooden platform with his glittering guitar, surrounded by a whirling tide of screaming girls, hundreds of necks, arms, and fingers stretched and yearning toward the unambiguously thrusting hips and the soft sneering smile. More and more often, turning the radio's dial, I'd come across the new thumping beat, and blues sung too fast for blues by men with twangy names like Duane Eddy or zippy ones like Conway Twitty and Jerry Lee Lewis. *Neues Deutschland* and *BZ am Abend* came out with diatribes against this newest *Kulturbarbarei* from the U.S.A.: how it was infecting youth throughout the Western world, sweeping across nations and continents like a huge horrible sewage tide of vicious venal subhuman impulses. I couldn't see what all the furor was about. The music was a little more exciting than the standard corny pop songs, but nothing compared to that hoarse-sounding black gospel singer you could hear every Friday on the American Forces Network hollering YOU BETTER GET READY! (echoed by the chorus: *You better get ready!*) uh-YOU BETTER GET uh-READY! JESUS GONNA COME! (*Jesus! Jesus!*) JESUS GONNA COME BY 'N' BY! or that other one about the train to heaven: It won't be,—*too! late!* It won't be,—*too! late!* It won't be,—*too! late! toolaytoolayate!* Now that was something that could make you want to leap straight out of your body!

One evening, at 7 p.m., the American Forces Network began to play the ten most popular American songs—as usual. "Tutti Frutti" was up there (in Pat Boone's rendition) and "Be-Bop-A-Lula," all okay stuff to do your homework by. Then the disc jockey slowed down his rapid-fire patter and adopted a momentous tone of voice: "Here's a brand-new record that's sweeping folks off their feet all over the Yew-Nighted States, and boy, is it a bombshell. Maybe your sweethearts have already written you about it. The name is Chuck Berry, and the song's called 'Roll Over, Beethoven'! Hold on to your seats now, 'cause *Here It Comes!*" That's when the evil virus infected my soul, and what an exhilarating disease it was. A joyful rage invaded my body. I started laughing. I turned up the sound as high as it would go.

You know my temperature's risin', the jukebox blowin' a fuse!
My heart's beatin' rhythm and my soul keeps a-singin' the blues!
Roll over, Beethoven, and tell Tchai-kowsky the news!

My God . . . tears were streaming down my face and I was laughing soundlessly. What to do with this? Run? Jump? My God . . .

I got the rockin' pneumonia, I need a shot of rhythm-'n'-blues!

I writhed, bent double, mouth wide open, eyes clenched shut. It didn't occur to me to dance. I wanted to explode.

Apparently the G.I.'s were similarly affected, because the following Friday, instead of playing the usual top ten, the D.J. reeled off "Roll Over, Beethoven" ten times in a row, so great was the volume of letters requesting it. "Okay-all-you-folks-out-there-you-asked-for-it-you're-gonna-get-it, turn-up-your-sound-and-hang-on-to-the-steering-wheel-if-you're-driving: *Roll Over, Beethoven! I gotta hear it again today!*" Ecstasy. Over and over. Ralle was listening, too; we called one another on the phone when it was over. "Wasn't that incredible? *Unheimlich! Dufte!* Fantastic!" Ralle started coming to school with a little Soviet transistor radio pressed to his ear. "What does Tubah-*tu* mean?" "Tubah-*tu?*" "You know, Chuck Berry, heyrahkennin Tubah-*tu.*" "Oh, two by two! They rockin' in two by two—it means two

at a time, *zu zweit*." "Sounds better in English: Tubah-
tu!" Pretty soon, he had a phonetic version of all
the lyrics memorized, once in a while a recognizable
English word, the rest a close imitation of the *sound*
of Chuck Berry's voice belting out those marvelous
lyrics:

Ahgotderahkenyuhmownyah, ahneedashahdawivvimen blues!

We were both obsessed, Ralle probably worse than I.
He came to school after several days' absence, wearing
a beret which he refused to take off when the teachers
told him to. He had a skin disease, he said, and it was an
ugly sight, and frankly, he'd be embarrassed. During
recess people tried to snatch it off, but he defended
himself with kicks and karate chops.

After school we went to his house, and he let me see
the round bald patch where the doctor had shaved the
top of his head in order to tend to a large multicolored
bump and some cut skin. Ralle had been to a now legendary Bill Haley concert in the West Berlin Sports
Palace. Some music lovers had started off the evening
by ripping up seats and floorboards and throwing them
down from the balcony. When the music started, bottles
and pieces of furniture came sailing from all directions.
Bill Haley and the Comets took shelter under the stage.
The police came, wielding nightsticks, and started to hus-
tle the crowd of thousands into the street. Ralle picked
up a board that had landed near him and, holding it
over his head for protection from the flying debris,
made his way toward the exit. A policeman, thinking he
was being attacked, banged his nightstick against the
board and the board against Ralle's head. Ralle dropped
the board and was whacked again in the same spot, this
time directly with the nightstick. Among the throng
that was fleeing toward the trains and subways were
five or six girls trotting in a row with their arms linked,
their skirts so absurdly tight it was impossible for them

to run. Half the guys who passed them took a moment
to give one or two of them a kick in the ass.

That was Ralle's story. It could easily have enhanced
his celebrity in school, but he asked me not to tell anyone. It wouldn't be fun if the teachers started thinking
of him as one of those *Halbstarke*—"half-strong" van-
dals and hoodlums, punks. The government was starting
to show real signs of alarm; you'd see news stories like:
"Hans P. and Anneliese H. were ejected from a dance at
the FDJ Clubhouse in X, after receiving a thorough
going-over by workers' fists. They had insisted on dancing 'open' despite repeated prohibition by the club directors. Bravo, Comrades of X! That is the way to deal
with *Halbstarke* and *Bürstenbubis!*" (*Bürstenbubis* referred to people with crew cuts.) Also, stories started
circulating about people being summoned to court for
listening to Western radio stations in disregard of a law
that ordinarily was never enforced. The threat, it
seemed, was rock-'n'-roll.

School, meanwhile, was becoming more stale by the
day. We cut classes a good deal—Ralle and Peter and I
especially, and somewhat less frequently, Piesel Winckelmann and Willi Klawitter. Often we went to the
movies in West Berlin, or listened to music in record
shops there. Piesel, who was half my size and could
have passed for twelve years old, liked to hold my hand
when we walked into a store, making believe he was my
son. He'd gaze up at me with an expression of innocent
wonder (while the others looked on, suppressing their
smiles) and ask, "*Vati*, may I have an apple?" "They
don't *have* apples here, Piesel, this is an *ice*-cream store."
"But I *want* an apple!" "Do you have apples, sir?" I ask
the proprietor, with a smile that solicits indulgence. He
shakes his head, half-amused, half-disturbed. "You see,
Piesel, the man doesn't sell apples. How about some ice
cream?" Piesel nods meekly, but as if on the verge of
tears. "Vanilla or chocolate?" the proprietor asks Piesel.

"Apple." If Piesel and I didn't break down laughing as this went on, one of the others would sooner or later. Sometimes we went to the East Berlin zoo, or rented boats on the Spree. There was a startlingly bucolic spot right in the heart of town, where the Friedrichstrasse gently buckled across the Spree on the Weidendammer Brücke. There was almost always someone angling there, as oblivious to clock time as any bunch of kids playing hooky. Gulls were constantly wheeling and dipping into the smoothly flowing gray-green water. There were ducks, too, pushing against the stream a bit and then letting themselves float back with it. Once in a while a broad black barge would come and slide soundlessly underneath the bridge; all you would hear was the steady rumble of traffic, the screech of streetcars grinding around a curve, an occasional quarrelsome cry from a gull. Whenever I played hooky by myself, I liked to go there, usually after visiting the several museums in the neighborhood. It was my favorite spot. Sometimes I brought my friends along. Nearby was a vendor's stand where you could buy a deliciously greasy knackwurst in a crisp bun, or thick pea soup with pieces of pink bockwurst swimming in it—it tasted good after a day's bumming around, especially with cold lemonade. If the salesman was in a good mood, he'd even let us buy some bottles of beer, despite the law prohibiting him from selling it to minors. We'd take the food and drink down to the edge of the river, feed the birds, try to grab fish that came close to the bank.

Sometimes Ralle and I would sneak through a window into Ralle's room while his father, a psychologist, sat with a client in the room next door. Through the wall we could hear the alternate mumbling of the patient's uncertain or querulous or angry voice, and Dr. Wenzel's somehow muffled voice, subdued rather than calm, and with a predatory edge to it. There was little danger of being discovered so long as we kept quiet. So we read. Ralle's relationship to books was twofold. In his capacity as thief he was a genuine bibliophile, and showed a discriminating and wide-ranging taste. As a reader, on the other hand, his focus of interest was decidedly narrow: no book could hold his attention unless it dealt with faraway places and exotic cultures. As a result, Ralle was somewhat of an expert in anthropology. Maybe that's a little exaggerated; but it was impressive to hear him expose the nonsense Karl May had written about the Apaches—that Winnetou lived in a forest, for example, that he went paddling about in a birch-bark canoe, straddled a white mustang to hunt buffalo on the prairie, went on the war path wearing a long feathered headdress like a Plains Indian, and never killed his enemies. Ralle was an expert, too, on the customs of several African and South American tribes. Even their more bizarre or cruel practices, such as the chest-pounding duels of a certain tribe in Brazil, or another tribe's custom of spitting phlegm into their soup, or the ancient Eskimo practice (I believe it was Eskimo) of strangling feeble old men and women, had an unimpeachable dignity and respectability in his eyes—quite a contrast to the contempt he felt for nearly everything people around him took seriously. Someday, he said, he would go to one of the places he had read about, and live with those people, learn their legends, their wisdom, their medicine, become one of them, if possible. Then maybe he'd come back someday and tell what he'd seen and heard. "How will you get there?" I asked. "I don't know. Maybe I'll get a job on a ship. There are places where you can make lots of money, like in the Sahara, drilling for oil. And with money you can travel." "You mean you're actually thinking of fleeing the Republic?" I asked, pretending to gasp with horror.

❡[Peter, meanwhile, had taken a fancy to Ulla Mehlhausen, and was attending classes regularly so as to be

near her. I was filled with disquiet at the thought that
he might succeed where I had failed. I became even
more jealous when Peter claimed Ulla was showing
signs of responding. I observed Ulla closely and saw
nothing, at first, to substantiate this boast. She sprawled
about with her customary display of provocative lethargy, and unfastened the top two buttons of her dress,
but that wasn't for Peter's benefit, it was for all. Let him
try his luck with her, I thought, he'll get the same
snippy shrug she gave me.

But I was mistaken. Peter asked Ulla to help him
make an outline for a history assignment, explaining his
helplessness with the blatant lie that he'd never had to
make outlines in the school he came from. I had a mind
(but not the heart) to expose him on the spot. Ulla
graciously, patiently, kindly agreed to help him. She
even looked a little flushed and flattered. How could she
refuse those angelic blue eyes, the soft touch of his
hand on her arm, at once respectful and proprietary, as
if sweetly asking her indulgence and conveying at the
same time a message of tenderness and desire? How did
he do it? He had once told me in a letter that he had
shed his virginity in the woods behind the Friedrich
Ludwig Jahn school, with a girl from the twelfth grade
—now I believed him. I had never seen him flirt with
this kind of assurance. The way he talked about Ulla,
too, and the wandering glance of appraisal with which
he followed her as she walked by, had the suave touch
of connoisseurship. "What a body . . ." he murmured,
"she must really be something in bed . . ." What did he
have that I lacked? An extra dose of inborn masculinity? It seemed I had more courage than he, though, at
least when it came to physical danger; and he was
childishly weak—I could probably wrestle him to the
ground with one hand behind my back. Nevertheless . . .
Alma had once told me there were three kinds of homosexuals: "open" homosexuals; those who pretend to be
heterosexual; and, finally, unconscious homosexuals.

Might it not be that I belonged to the last group? The possibility had to be faced.

My journal began to overflow with morbid psychoanalytic self-exploration, and, worse, with speculations that I might be crippled by some genetic imbalance. Once or twice I thought of putting an end to my anguish by asking my mother to tell me outright what was her perception of me as a male; but I thought better of it. Even if she thought me an unconscious homosexual, would she tell me, would she pronounce judgment on me like that? Of course not. So I still wouldn't know.

That Alma was an authority on these matters I didn't doubt for a moment. She generally seemed keenly observant of the ways men and women responded to one another. At least she often commented on their behavior: So-and-so had been showing off her legs; So-and-so had been obviously attracted to So-and-so. So-and-so, contrary to appearances, was not really a man. How could she tell? What was a man? Or, more importantly, what was an only apparently real man? What were the indications? She spoke of subtle habits, an indefinably feminine way of moving, a manner of bending down to pick something up . . . And there was an even subtler phenomenon: the fact that she, a woman, did not feel the stimulating current of sexuality emanating from So-and-so, an apparent male; that she sensed a telltale neutrality instead.

All this raised serious questions about my own manhood. Did any of the girls I met feel and respond to my masculinity? I could think of no one. And wasn't Ulla Mehlhausen responding to Peter, after having snubbed me? Most definitely. She liked him.

Maybe his advantage is environmental, I thought, and not genetic. In that case there was hope, since conditions could, after all, be changed for the better. What is there in Peter's home, I asked myself, that favors the development of masculinity? The answer was as obvious as it was startling: his father! Did Kurt coach him? Probably! At least to the extent that they spoke together about love and sex, casually, without embarrassment. Peter was always coming out with the sort of gallant figures of speech that could only have come from Kurt. Of what help was Bodo to me when it came to learning about women? None at all—he hid his erotic books from me, while Kurt warmly recommended his to his son. In Kurt's bedroom was a large round bed which he referred to as *"meine Lustwiese"*—"my lust-meadow"— and which he shared with his secretary, an attractive woman who was just a few years older than Peter and I. (Ilse, Peter's mother, had moved to another part of town.) Bodo rarely commented on the charm of women, at least not in my presence; and the closer they were to my age, the more aesthetic was his point of view, just as art lovers will squint and step back from a painting. Old-fashioned corkscrew locks on the head of a young girl being taken to church; a tall blushing bosomless brunette making mistakes playing Beethoven's *"Wut über den verlorenen Groschen"* at a school recital; the pair of dimples dancing above the buttocks of a stunningly proportioned girl striding into the surf on the naked beach—just the dimples, not the girl—these were the sorts of things he noticed in women, or that he spoke about—details to admire, not touch and caress. How different from Kurt, who, when the subject of Ulla Mehlhausen's beauty came up, said: "I've seen her—she's certainly got lovely eyes," illustrating that with cupped hands molding an imagined pair of breasts.

Fortunately Peter lost interest in Ulla rather quickly. He'd gotten so far as to kiss her, he said, and to feel her breasts for a moment (precious moment—and how indifferently he spoke of it!); but she became cold, and when he persisted, she slapped him and told him with a ridiculous air of outraged virtue that she wasn't that kind of girl and that she was as good as engaged to some asshole who was helping to restore a bombed-out church in Potsdam, and to whom she'd vowed to be faithful.

I felt deeply relieved. I chastised myself briefly in my journal for having been jealous of a good friend, and happily dropped the subject of my psychosexual development. Back to the world and its happenings! (The next entry in my journal reports on an event at the dinner table: Stefan had playfully pronounced the word "*Rohkost*," "raw treat"—the fancy restaurant term for the grated raw carrots Bodo was eating—as "*Rohkotz*," "raw vomit," which sent Bodo hurrying out of the room with a hand cupped over his mouth.)

⟨[One day, during Latin class, several giggling people followed Ralle out the window, single file, onto a scaffolding where masons were restoring the school's hideous façade and down the narrow ladders from floor to floor, knocking on each window as we passed, beckoning hundreds of gaping faces to join us in a general revolt (nobody did). Another time, Ralle got the son of a watchmaker to bring a gallon of phosphorescent paint to school, and someone else to bring a pulley and a rope. The school's skeleton was carefully painted and concealed behind a cabinet in a corner of the classroom. (The idea, as the reader may remember, came from Herbert Gessner, the radio commentator.)

We were about to be shown an educational film about revolutionary Soviet methods of farming. As soon as the lights went out, the loose end of the rope was hastily conveyed from hand to hand until it reached Ralle. Slowly, majestically, like a ghostly moon, the top of the skull rose over the top of the cabinet, accompanied by the screams and laughter of the class, and was followed by the rest of the head, the neck, the shoulders, and a few ribs, at which point the skeleton noisily dropped back into darkness as Ralle threw the rope away.

East German law prohibits the expulsion of grade-school and high-school students (though reform schools, of course, are available). Imprisonment and corporal punishment have been scrapped along with most of the detritus of traditional Prussian education—all of it except the principle of pedagogic authority itself. This principle is hard to maintain without its most effective means of suppression; at least in our case it was. The most the teachers could do was threaten to fail us, and the one weapon they had to that end, other than giving vent to personal anger or wagging their fingers at us, was handing out *Tadel*—official demerits—which were entered in a little black book of records each of us had to keep, and which our parents had to sign weekly. A certain number of Tadel could ensure one's failing the class, no matter what one's grades were. But since, under Ralle's leadership, Tadel had become medals of honor, the burden of pedagogical responsibility passed from the teachers to the parents. The school did its utmost to enlist their support. Wage war on absenteeism! Enforce the production of homework! If coming home with one's black book full of Tadel could be made sufficiently unpleasant, the scales might tip back in favor of progress and order. This, I believe, is what happened to most of our classmates. From one week to the next, they became unnaturally compliant. They were no longer with us. Peter anxiously wavered, and suffered, unable to join either camp wholeheartedly. Only Ralle and I remained thoroughly unreformed.

In the end—who would have suspected it?—the Party took action. Peter and I were put on trial before a tribunal of Party members that was made up of several teachers from our school and an official of the Board of

Education of the Democratic Sector of Greater Berlin.
The reasoning behind this was simple: our fathers were
highly regarded public figures, so what we did reflected
not just on our parents but on the Party. We were being
charged with something frighteningly close to political
subversion.

Ralle protested: "Why wasn't I invited?"

"Your father is not a Communist," the teachers explained.

"Oh, you just don't like me," he said, with a mock
pout.

On the day of the trial, he waited on a bench outside
the classroom where we were to be questioned.

First, Peter was called. After a while he came out
wiping traces of tears from his eyes and cheeks. He
walked past us, sniffing, without saying a word.

"Uhse!" It was my turn. Ralle squeezed his thumb as
a sign of good luck.

I was offered a seat at an isolated desk in the middle
of the room, opposite seven men and women, all wearing
Party membership pins, who had arranged themselves in
a semicircular bloc, also behind desks. Directly facing
me, at the center of their group, sat a beefy man in a black
suit who had to be the official from the Board of Education. To his left were two teachers whom I knew. (I
also knew that they had nothing against me.) The four
others I didn't know, though I had seen them often at
school.

The proceedings were opened by one of the latter, a
man with wavy hair and a corduroy suit. I felt an immediate and passionate dislike for him. He seemed to be
having a good time. While he spoke, he kept gesturing
in my direction, without once turning his face toward
me. As the trial continued, I was struck by the fact that
I was not expected, let alone allowed, to defend myself
—it was taken for granted that my actions were inde-
fensible. I was to deliver facts, not explanations. "Who

was the ringleader in your group?" "Where did you go when you played hooky?" "Did you ever go to the West?" "Did you make any purchases there?" "Why Ping-Pong balls—couldn't you buy them here?" "Do you consider the kind of activity you were engaged in compatible with your membership in the Freie Deutsche Jugend?" Rhetorical questions like the last one were easy to answer, but it was impossible to answer some of the others truthfully. I certainly couldn't tell them about Ralle's crimes or about my humble participation in them. So when asked where we went, and what we did, I answered, with a flash of malice, "We went around corners." Seven pairs of eyebrows shot up in astonishment, and there was an appalled silence. The only sound was the pounding of my heart.

The man with the wavy hair rose to his feet and exclaimed: "*Ich plädiere für Rausschmiss.*" That means, in English words that express none of the crude pomposity of the original, "I propose that we throw him out of school." The man from the Board of Education reminded him that this was impossible; and that even if it were possible, it would not serve to enlighten me. The wavy-haired man exclaimed that no educational facilities existed to reform such corruption as sat before them in my person. Facing me for the first time, he pointed out the disheveled state of my hair as a sign of a typically bourgeois, bohemian disregard for the ideals of the working class; my chewed-off fingernails, the pimple on my neck did not attest to clean and productive aspirations; the fact that I was simultaneously wearing tennis shoes and a winter sweater made one wonder whether I lived in the present at all. "Perhaps," he suggested, "our Chinese comrades have shown superior wisdom in dealing with the bourgeois element in human nature. I am referring to their programs of reeducation. But we have nothing of the sort in our society, and I am afraid that keeping this young man and his like in our schools, without such efforts to change their mentality, will continue to infect

the student body with the virus of bourgeois individual-
ism and the kind of provocative behavior we have witnessed today."

Years later, telling friends about this trial, I was
ashamed to admit, each time I arrived at this juncture—
the wavy-haired man's speech—that I hadn't defended
myself in some manner. To make up for that, I· lied. I
professed to have stood up, propelled by an instinctual
spasm of righteous fury, and to have tipped over my
desk, kicked away the chair I'd been sitting on, and
stalked out of the room. With repetition, this fabrica-
tion came to feel more plausible than the unpalatable
truth, and eventually what should have been very
nearly supplanted what was, even in my own mind. It's
time to set the record straight. I did not stand up, I did
not kick a chair. My blood boiled, that is true, and my
hands, which had been lying on my lap, pressed against
the desk from below, tilting it and causing ink to trickle
from its porcelain well onto the floor. That was the extent of my revolt.

Conferences with our parents followed, apologies and
promises were exacted. I was reprimanded with particular sternness for my behavior at the trial; and I was
spared "further steps" (whatever those might have been)
only because several teachers stepped forward to testify
that I was ordinarily a model of peaceableness and good
manners. Peter and I both felt sorry for having caused
our parents so much worry and embarrassment, and for
having, perhaps, really brought discredit to their good
cause, as our judges contended.

Just as the tension-laden air seemed to be clearing,
Peter and I were called to submit to an after-school investigation by a court of FDJ functionaries, who, possibly
on orders from the Party, wished to determine our right
to continued membership in their organization. (Since
Ralle was not a member, he was, again, not invited.)
Peter put on his blue FDJ shirt for the occasion—a ges-

ture of good will which I might have been well advised
to imitate, if I hadn't torn my own uniform shirt while
playing soccer. Peter was the first to be questioned, and
as at the first trial, he was dismissed after only a short
while. This time he wasn't crying, though. He had a
satisfied look on his face, like someone who has done
something he can be proud of. "It's not so bad," he said
to me as I rose from my bench in response to a summon-
ing motion from a blue-shirted girl at the door, a girl
who, whenever she passed me on the stairway or in the
courtyard, excited me and made me long for the knowledge of how to charm women. "Just be honest," Peter
said. What he must have meant by that was sincere
repentance, for repentance was what was required—I
recognized this right away as I stepped into the room.
And no doubt it was an emotion Peter was able to express without difficulty and in all sincerity: he felt it.
Unfortunately, what I felt as I took the seat assigned to
me, confronted by a jury of kids my own age, was a
mixture of disgust and fear. How self-important they
looked! The way they pulled the corners of their
mouths down and leaned toward each other in a huddle
to discuss my case, like the grotesques in a Daumier
tribunal! I despised them. But at the same time they
filled me with fear. These weren't old men and women
whose judgment I could shrug off in secret pride as
irrelevant to the law of my being. They were my own
kind. Their probing questions, the disapproval accumu-
lating behind their knitted brows, the glances they exchanged, all these signs carried a deep threat of ostra-
cism, not just from the FDJ (that would have been
merely a scandal), but from the community of my
peers, a community which, while it lived by stern laws
of its own and imposed its own implacable judgments,
could ordinarily be relied on to protect all its members
with a shield of neutrality against condemnation from
the adult world. Now these boys and girls were assess-
ing the strength and dependability of my moral fiber,

testing it against the ethical statutes of the Free German Youth; and the test found me wanting. Later, looking back, I could dismiss them as traitors and ambitious
lackeys, and most of what they said lost its cutting edge.
But face to face with them, hearing them use the same
cynical, witty argot my friends and I favored, watching
them chew their pencils and doodle in their notebooks,
I felt afraid.

The attractive girl who had motioned me in seemed
to take pleasure in expatiating on my deficiencies: "We
should recognize that he is not acting from outright opposition. If he were, it might be appropriate for us to
get him into a friendly discussion, argue with him, persuade him of the right way. Or question him and find
out what is the influence motivating his antagonism. It
could be reactionary literature, or an ideological con-
flict between his parents, who knows. But I don't think
the problem is a rational one. My impression is that
we're simply dealing with a labile character."

Ein labiler Charakter (nominative case). I had never
heard this expression before, but I could guess at its
import, especially since it was accompanied by a gesture of her hand that seemed to suggest something val-
ueless being tossed aside.* For a moment, a cold sorrowful guilt invaded my heart—the awful guilt that consists,
simply, of being without inner or outer defense against
a hostile intelligence. Once again, anger came to my defense—fury, rage—and again I choked it back; prudently,
I think now; but for a long time after, I was ashamed at
having cowered so meekly when I ought to have demol-
ished this whole farcical inquest with one impatient brush
of the hand, like Alice the pack of cards.

* Just recently, more than twenty years later, I came across the same
word again, in *The New York Times*, of all places, reporting on
"Restive Youth in East Germany"; *"labil,"* it says, is the term applied
by officialdom, on both sides of the border, to unassimilable but not
particularly militant personalities.

The meeting continued, virtually without my participation. I felt sleepy, limp. Labile. "Let me ask you something, Uhse," said the chairman. "Do you actually *want* to be in the FDJ?" "Of course I do, yes." They looked at one another, agreed silently that I sounded sincere, nodded. "Will you promise us, then, to change your attitude toward school?" "Yes." "Being a member of the FDJ imposes on you the obligation of setting an example. As you know." "I know." "I propose," said the chairman, "that we take a vote. Who is in favor of allowing Jugendfreund Uhse to remain a member, but on a probationary basis. At the slightest sign of recidivism, he will have to leave our ranks." He raised his hand. All others followed suit. "The meeting is closed." The chairman shook my hand, smiling. I made a grateful face. The others, too, shook my hand. It seemed they were congratulating me.

The teachers made a decision—it seemed almost insultingly lenient at first—to judge Peter and me by our grade average at the year's end, just like any other students. That way, one of them explained to me, if we failed, we'd have only ourselves to blame; for if we felt unjustly punished, it might drive us deeper into "contradiction" with the school, and ultimately with the state. ("And you don't want to become a criminal, do you?") On the other hand, if we passed, it would have to be due to a heartfelt conversion to homework and constant attendance. It was an invitation to maturity. It was up to us.

We stopped cutting classes, and we applied ourselves to homework—Peter wholeheartedly, I fitfully, almost painfully; something like the teeth-grinding, half-disoriented effort of those heroic stragglers in a marathon race who plod on, not hoping to win, just to finish, separated by miles and miles from the stadium where the crowd's jubilation is already welcoming the victor. I was so far behind that I found most of my schoolbooks impenetrable, the very texture of the writing as opaque as if I were trying to read a foreign language.

Ralle alone continued to carry the torch of rebellion, all by himself. He stayed away from school more and more, and no longer even bothered to type out written excuses on his father's stationery with its fancy letterhead. His black book had nearly as many Tadel as it had pages.

The final exams approached, and all my classmates went into a frenzy of cramming. One day I spontaneously and definitively gave up the struggle—tossed my notebook into a corner, filled my schoolbag with books of my own choosing, took a three-day vacation from school with Ralle, helped him steal a book about some Frenchman's exploration of the Amazon, went paddling on the Spree River. What freedom, what exquisite indifference to time, to fate. We found a secluded spot on the riverbank where he could read about El Dorado and I could follow Musil's "Man Without Qualities" on his quest for "the other condition":

A thrilling sense of being predestined to something or other is the beautiful and only certain thing for one whose gaze examines the world for the first time. If he keeps a careful watch over his emotions he cannot say yes to anything without reservation; he seeks the possible beloved but does not know whether she is the right one; he is capable of killing, without being sure that he must do it. His own nature's will to develop forbids him to believe there can be anything fulfilled and complete; yet everything coming his way pretends to be perfect. He has a presentiment: this order is not as solid as it claims to be, no thing, no ego, no form, no principle is safe, everything is in a process of invisible but ceaseless change, there is more of the future in the unsolid than in the solid, and the present is but an as yet unsurpassed hypothesis. What better can he do than keep the world at arm's length, with the good sense exemplified by a scientist faced with facts that want to seduce him into believing in them prematurely?! That is why he hesitates to make something of himself; a character, a profession, a definite temperament—for him these are notions through which he can already discern the shape of the skeleton that will remain of him in the end. He seeks a different understanding of himself; with an inclination toward everything that inwardly increases him, even if it is morally or intellectually forbidden, he feels himself to be like a stride that could be taken in any direction, but which leads from one equilibrium to the next and always onward. And if at some point it seems to him that he has struck on the right idea, he notices that a drop of unspeakable radiance has fallen into the world, and that its glow makes the earth look different.

What a magnificent excuse! I failed the eleventh grade. So did Ralle. There were a few horrified reactions from students who would have gotten the hiding of their lives or died of shame if they'd had to go home with our report cards—mostly 4's and 5's, except for a solitary 1 for German, in my case; Ralle didn't even have that. Ralle and I shrugged nonchalantly, with an air of quiet disdain—as if, having *chosen* to fail, we had in fact, in some fundamental sense, really succeeded. Everyone else passed. Peter too.

⟨[Monika Mietke made a last-ditch all-out effort to clinch her year-long pursuit of me. She invited me and Piesel Winckelmann and Anita Schröder, her closest friend, to the Youth Hostel in Münchehofe. She had only three days to carry out her plan. On the fourth, Bodo would pick me up on his way to Ahrenshoop (Alma and Stefan were already there). And over the summer, Monika and her family would be moving away from Berlin. It was now or never. This time, to make sure I'd notice, she dispensed with all subtlety. And I

noticed. I noticed the extravagant admiration she professed for my playing of Bach's Prelude in C on the
hostel's tinny upright; I noticed the way she hovered
close to me during the walks our little group took
through the countryside, how she pretended to be unable to cross a puddle, so she could lean on my arm; I
certainly couldn't fail to notice her bare foot stroking
my calf under the table while, above it, I ingested the
dish she'd insisted on preparing for me—fried potatoes
neatly surrounding a fried egg and lovingly garnished
with slices of tomato. I noticed all this, felt flattered and
touched by it, but not aroused. Somehow, to be seduced
by this aggressive, short-tempered, rather homely girl,
who still braided her hair like a child, who was, in fact,
slightly wall-eyed; to be pursued, *period*, instead of
being the pursuer . . . it seemed incompatible with self-
esteem.

On the night of the second day, Monika and Anita
came into the room where Piesel and I lay in bed, talking, by the light of a candle. They were wearing night-
gowns. They hadn't been able to sleep, they said, and
they'd heard our voices through the wall, so they decided to join us. They sat down on our beds near our
feet, Monika on my bed, Anita on Piesel's. We had to
keep our voices low, so as not to arouse the suspicion of
the hostel's director, for the girls had broken a rule by
visiting us after midnight. This atmosphere of secret
intimacy, combined with the candlelight and the still-
ness of the late hour, had an aphrodisiacal effect. So did
Monika's legs when she put them under the blanket,
next to my legs ("It's warmer that way," she said). If
only she was less pushy, I thought to myself. I feel as if
I'm under siege. Is this what it's like being a girl? How
awful!

Piesel was casting about for distractions: teasing
Monika, telling about our German teacher's dog, who
had fallen from a window, and foolishly insisting it
must have been suicide . . . and why hadn't we brought

playing cards? Did anyone hear that owl hooting before? No? There's an owl near here. There must be
mice, too. Anyone here scared of mice? No? My mother's scared of mice . . . He kept babbling until he ended
up telling us the dead-serious story of his father, a construction worker who'd played a leading role in the
strike that led to the riots on June 17, 1953. "He was in
the Party then, and he believed in it, too, wasn't just an
opportunist like some. After June 17 he was criticized,
and they asked him to criticize himself if he honestly
felt he had done something wrong. But he honestly felt
what he'd done was right. The Party said no, he was
wrong, because this is a Workers and Peasants State,
and you can strike only against your Class Enemy, so by
going on strike he was denying this is a socialist state. It
went back and forth. Finally he just left the Party. They
were really upset about that, they kept coming to our
house to try and talk him out of it, but in the end he just
threw them out. He's got a really bad temper, a lot
worse than you, Monika. And then he started drinking,
and getting arrested. For getting into fights, disturbing
the peace, things like that. Once for vandalism. He
claims the cops are trying to get him into trouble, and
keep an eye on him. But I think he gets himself into
trouble. Sometimes my mother talks of divorcing him.
He keeps saying he has nothing to live for."

"Why doesn't he leave?" Anita asked. "Construction
workers make good money in the West."

"It's not the money. He makes enough here. It's just
something he believed in. Now he's lost that."

"Does he think the state shouldn't have put down the
uprising?" I asked.

"No, he thinks they had to, otherwise we would have
gotten a capitalist state, and that's no good for workers
either. That's what he says. But he says if workers really
owned the means of production and all that, there
wouldn't have been an uprising in the first place."

"I think people should stay away from politics," Mon-

ika said, seeing I was about to launch into a defense of
the First German Workers and Peasants State. "It just
leads to bad feelings. I think people should just try and be
nice and gentle and not get angry about everything."

"Look who's talking," Anita said, laughing.

"Well, I think it's *true*," Monika said crossly. "I think
you have to try and do something to make someone
happy each day. That's what *I* believe."

"*Every day a good deed for socialism!*" Piesel said,
quoting the most recent slogan and pointing upward
and onward at a forty-five-degree angle.

"No, not socialism, *people*," Anita said.

"Not people," I said, "just *someone*."

"You could start with someone you really like," Monika said. "It's easiest that way."

"Or someone you *love*," Piesel said. "How about that
food you've been cooking for Joel?"

"*That's different!*" Monika exclaimed hotly, much too
loudly. We all put our fingers to our lips and said,
"Shhh."

"*Liebe geht durch den Magen*," Piesel said, "Love
goes through the stomach," and made kissy sounds with
his lips.

Monika grabbed a pillow and threw it at him.

"There she goes again," Anita said.

"Choleric," Piesel said. (We'd learned about the clas-
sic temperaments in school.) Monika was blushing; and
strangely, for someone ordinarily so brazen, she avoided
looking at me. Then and there I desired her without
reserve. How charming she was in her long shift with
the red flowers embroidered on the collar, and the red
almost as deep burning on her face, her ears, her throat.
Even her braids were charming. She raised her head
and, still blushing, looked at me without flinching.
There was a strange melting luster in her dark asym-
metrical eyes—they were beautiful. Was it the candlelight? She suddenly looked very, very pretty. It was
surprising. And that we were gazing at one another

without discomfort or shyness, as if Piesel and Anita weren't there—that was even more surprising. Where to proceed from here? This question must have been on everyone's mind.

Piesel began talking again. I averted my gaze. I, too, was blushing now. Monika and Anita laughed—at me, I thought at first, but it was at something Piesel had said. He kept talking, talking, I was no longer listening. She must love me, I thought to myself: otherwise why would she look at me like that. Her leg lay hot against mine. I looked at her. She was looking at Piesel and smiling. Then she looked at me. I must have looked troubled, because a pitying expression appeared in her eyes. She reached under the blanket and squeezed my foot. That did it. It was such a comforting and friendly gesture. I was overcome by a rush of tenderness for her and gratitude for this gift from heaven, a friend, a girl-friend, knocking on my door so patiently—no, not at all patiently, so *insistently!* How could I have been so blind, proud, stubborn, cold, afraid—afraid of love! Oh, I have to talk to her somewhere alone, I'll just go to her room with her, leave Anita here with Piesel. But how to get out of bed with an erection and not have it be obvious? "Monika," I whispered, sitting up, and waved for her to come near me so I could say something in her ear—what, I didn't know yet. She moved toward me, but instead of her ear, she presented her puckered lips to me and closed her eyes. Very carefully, I placed my lips on hers. She reached out to hold my head in place, anticipating, perhaps, that it might start back, and then, to my intense astonishment—I had never, in all my erotic readings, come across a mention of this delicious practice—her tongue darted in and out of my mouth. My heart leaped like a startled rabbit. Was this an emblematic invitation to coitus? What else could it be? I must try it myself. This time I slid my tongue in and out of her mouth, and cautiously reached for her breast. She gently pushed my hand away.

"Monika." It was Anita's voice, with a tone of auntish reproof. Piesel had long stopped his monologue. "I'm not going to sit here while you . . ."

Monika shrugged. "Why don't you leave, then," she said.

"I'm not going to do that. Remember what your father said."

Another peevish shrug from Monika. "I don't care."

"Well, *I* care," Anita said. "He told us to watch out for each other, remember?"

"We're only kissing," I interjected.

"You can kiss all day tomorrow," Anita said. "Come on, Monika. It's late. I'm sleepy. Come. I'm not going back alone."

"We just got here," Monika said.

"I'm sleepy, too," Piesel said timidly.

"Why don't you two go to sleep in the other room, and leave us here," I said.

Anita got out of bed and put on her slippers. "Monika," she said, looking her friend firmly in the eye, "if you don't come with me, I'll go tell the director. And I'll tell your father on you, too."

"All right, I'm coming, I'm coming," Monika said, frowning, and got out of bed. At the door, she turned around and bade me a good night.

"Sleep well," I said.

"You too," she said. "Have a nice dream."

Then she just stood there, smiling, in her long white shift, one hand on the doorpost, her head tilted to one side, looking at me. Once again, my heart overflowed with affection and thankfulness. My eyes blurred.

"For God's sake, *come on!*" Anita pulled Monika's sleeve.

"Wait— When's your father coming?" Monika asked me. Anita walked out.

"Day after tomorrow."

"I mean, in the morning or later?"

"Maybe later."

"Good night, Joel."

"Good night, Monika. See you in the morning."

Monika turned and floated away in her long shift.

"Good *night*, Monika," Piesel called after her ironically.

"Oh—good night, Piesel." Then she came back to shut the door, and blew me a kiss. Was this the same girl who marked all her belongings with a neat *M.M.* and scolded people for not wiping the crumbs off the table?

"Mietke's in love with you," Piesel said after he blew out the candle.

"I know."

"I'll try to keep Schröder away from her tomorrow. If you want."

"Yes. Please do. Thanks a lot, Piesel."

Long after Piesel was snoring, I lay awake, shivering with happiness and anticipation. I imagined her lying in the room next door feeling the same way. Why did Anita have to be so protective and domineering? Was she just being a spoilsport, was she jealous, or what? Such a nice evening, and suddenly the alarm goes off because we're kissing, or because we're kissing on a bed, or who knows why. It made no sense. Maybe by now Anita would be sleeping, just like Piesel, while Monika tossed in her bed, longing for me. I tiptoed out of our room and listened through the girls' door. No sound of restless insomnia. Distinctly I heard instead the sound of two pairs of lungs breathing in counterpoint. I tapped the wood. There was no response. After much trepidation, I pressed down the handle and pushed. The door was locked.

Bodo didn't come when we thought he would. He came the next morning. Monika, Anita, and Piesel had gone to pick berries. They'd left a note behind; they had decided to let me sleep. Bodo said there had been a change of plans, and no one had answered the phone at the hostel when he called, so he'd been unable to send

me a message. Stefan was having bad asthma attacks in
Ahrenshoop, and Bodo and Alma thought that possibly
if we were all back together again, he'd feel better. I
went upstairs to pack my bags. I didn't want to go. I'd
had such an extraordinary dream about Monika. I was
sitting in the lunchroom of the Friedrich Ludwig Jahn
Internat. Peter was at my table, too, and some others.
They were eating soup, but I was waiting for something. Then Monika came toward me with a small dish.
She looked happy in anticipation of the pleasure it
would give me. It was a special dessert she had prepared just for me. It smelled of almonds and looked like
custard. As she put the plate down before me, she
leaned over, and then her breast was in my hand. The
breast was exquisitely round and warm, and it was
swelling from inside, like a balloon, filling my palm. I
woke up with a feeling of intense pleasure, which was
followed by a vague sweet faintness, a need to suck in
large amounts of air, and an almost unbearable unease.
I remembered having had the same feeling four years
ago, when I couldn't stop thinking about Uschi Tunger . . . Did Monika feel that way, too? I wanted desperately to see her, and dreaded it at the same time. Maybe it
was for the best that I was leaving without seeing her
again. But I didn't want to go. Numbly, mechanically, I
went through the motions of packing. I stopped to write
a note, explaining the reason for my sudden departure
and wishing everybody a nice summer. Then I lingered
over a separate message to Monika. "I love you," I wrote
after a while, and immediately tore that up. In a few
days that statement would no longer be true—what was
the use of saying such a thing? It would only upset
her. It wasn't love anyway, it was just the possibility of
it, the promise. I lay down on the bed and wept into the
mattress. Then Bodo called my name from downstairs.
"I'll be right there," I said and resolutely washed and
dried my face. What to say to Monika? Maybe nothing.
No, that would seem cold. I took a clean sheet of paper

and wrote: "I dreamed about you. It was a beautiful dream." I folded the paper, and wrote "For Monika" on the back. Then I carried my bag down to the car. The chauffeur helped me put it in the trunk. Suddenly it occurred to me that I didn't *have* to leave with Bodo. I could stay a few more days, until Monika left, and go to Ahrenshoop by train or by bus or however people without cars got there. But then what? We would never see each other again. If leaving now was painful, what would it be like then? I got into the car and we drove off. I sat in the back with Bodo. We didn't talk. I was thinking to myself that Monika probably didn't feel about me the way I did about her, otherwise she couldn't have started something so precious knowing that it would be over in a day or two.

"You seem sad," Bodo said after a while. I nodded. "A girl?" I nodded again. "I'm sorry," he said. "It's not your fault," I said. "No. I'm just sorry." He took my hand in his. "You lose and you win and you lose," he said. "And you lose, and you win and you lose and you lose." I went over that for a while. Two to five. Those were lousy odds. It couldn't be *that* bad!

❨That summer, in Ahrenshoop, my parents began fighting again: long arguments and bitter emotions behind closed doors, premonitory rumblings heralding the final thunderbolt that was to cleave our family so wide asunder—wide as the ocean's span—just three years later.

Once again, Peter Vogel was there (Gudrun and Gisela, unfortunately, had gone somewhere else for their summer vacation). We painted—from postcards, not from nature. At first I resisted this approach as somehow smacking of dilettantism, but Peter informed me that some of the Impressionists had worked from postcards, so it was okay. We thought more highly than ever of our critical discernment, if not of our work, which would

have to ripen with time and the acquisition of technical
skills—that just couldn't be helped; it was one of the
drawbacks of being young. Who'd ever heard of a child-
prodigy painter? The indispensable thing was to show
signs of talent and true inspiration. What, if not inspiration, would hurl Peter out of a sound sleep and send him
staggering back to his canvas, fired by the thought of
adding a touch of carmine or yellow to it? (At least
that's what he told me.) I, too, had attacks of sublime
excitement. No question but that we had talent. I think
if someone had proven to us that we had no talent, for
painting or for anything else, one or the other of us might
have killed himself, so sharp was the scorn we felt for
those hopelessly ordinary landscapes exhibited in the
town's art gallery or in the Bunte Stube, together with
amber pendants, swimsuits, straw hats, boats in bottles.
What an awful fate!

When we weren't painting or cultivating our snob-
bery, we swam and played volleyball on the beach; and
when we weren't doing that, we ran. It was five years
after Emil Zatopek won the 5,000-meter, 10,000-meter,
and marathon races at the Olympic Games, but the spectacle was still vivid in our minds, remembered from magazines and newsreels: the weak asthmatic body yoked and
driven to triumph by a hypertrophied will; the mask of
gasping agony, the twisted neck, the piston-like whirling
of bulbous knees and elbows as "the Czech locomotive"
cleared the curve of the track. Sports reportage in East
Germany has taken a self-consciously political and nationalistic turn, I've been told, but at that time the chief
radio sportscaster lent his nimble tongue to the sensuous
evocation of atmosphere. Invariably, bicycle tires *susur-*
rated (the German word was *"surren"*) on wet asphalt as
they whizzed past, and the cigarette smoke above the expectantly buzzing crowd was *diaphanous*; and when it
came to celebrating certain great athletes, of whatever
nation, he'd wax eloquent indeed and give virtual ser-
mons on the romance and heroism of "sportsmanlike con-

test." Zatopek, especially, was portrayed in distinctly spiritual terms—a subvariant of the Christian martyr, a Beethoven among runners. There must have been thousands of kids emulating him all over the German Democratic Republic. I wonder how many were discouraged, as I was, by the rigors of "sportsmanlike contest." Having staked out a stretch of some 3,000 meters on an isolated dirt road, Peter and I scratched a line in the sand and assumed starting positions behind it; Peter said: "*Achtung . . . fertig . . . los!*" and we were off.

I took the lead. Like Zatopek, I was congenitally ill-equipped for long-distance running. (A couple of times, during the compulsory 1,000-meter race at school, I had stopped halfway for fear of vomiting on the track.) Unlike Zatopek, though, I was much too indolent and pleasure-loving to ever have much truck with will power. But as I took the lead that day, with long, springy strides, I imagined, or made believe, that I had discovered in the example of Zatopek the secret by which anyone may conquer the defects of his nature and achieve excellence in whatever field he desires. Today I would prove it by running, tomorrow I'd apply the method to more important objectives: catch up with the year's lag in my schooling, for example. The trick was simply to isolate the will to win from all other functions and considerations; identify with it completely; and ruthlessly press on. The mere thought of such transcendence lent wings to my heels. The sound of Peter's steps fell steadily behind. Don't feel sorry for him, I thought, he beats you at table tennis; and it's yourself you're conquering anyway. Run, run, run. Hard as steel, straight as an arrow, unflinching, unflagging. Never give up. The will triumphant. Run, run, run.

Before long, though, the flesh began to announce its weakness, and then the spirit lost its willingness, after the briefest of struggles. Peter's footsteps drew nearer. A Zatopek would have wrenched a final explosion of speed from some demonic reservoir of power in his guts.

I stopped, holding my side and limping. The pain in the side was real, but a disreputable reason for quitting; the limp was a pretense, and an acceptable excuse. Peter trotted past me, panting heavily. A group of masticating cows turned their heads slowly as he moved by. He collapsed at the telephone pole that marked the finish. There he sat facing me in a concave position with his mouth wide open, a worthier disciple of Zatopek than I was. I was still limping, to emphasize the reason for my defeat: not a failure of will, just a betrayal by the body. Maybe Peter believed me, but I couldn't deceive myself about the facts: *I* had stopped running, *I* had lost the race, *I* had betrayed my heroic intentions, none other than *I*—whoever that was. I limped up to my exhausted friend and told him about the bad cramp in my calf to which he owed his victory. Now I had betrayed him, too, and had compounded weakness with cowardice. I sat down with a grimace of pain and rubbed the afflicted leg; it was like rubbing salt on the wound of self-loathing. Wasn't I really, and simply, what that Russian teacher in Potsdam had called me: *Faul wie die Sünde*, lazy as sin itself? Who was I kidding? Wasn't I already stigmatized by failure? Didn't my gestures and posture proclaim it, against all efforts at concealment—especially when I was being introduced to adults who might have already heard about me? Stepping into the Kurhaus at dinnertime was like running a gauntlet of stares and judgments: *Look, there's the son of Bodo Uhse, he was left back twice; ungainly fellow, too, why doesn't he hold his head up . . .* that's what I imagined people were thinking and saying. I couldn't very well plead an indefinite "period of transition," as the state did to excuse its broken promises. In three years I'd be twenty. Then what?

"No more excuses!" I wrote in my journal. "As of September 1, first priority goes to my studies. With a lot of work and some coaching, and if they let me take the eleventh-grade finals in advance, I might be able to catch up. Who knows, maybe I'll be able to study in the Soviet Union!" As of September 1. That left a few weeks to do what I wanted.

Peter left on a trip to Prague with his mother. There was no getting away from the trouble in our family now—unless I were to build myself a separate burg on the beach. Stefan was having severe asthma attacks. Alma, after nursing him for hours in a room I wasn't permitted to enter, would emerge looking exhausted and grim. She had little patience with me at that time. I think she found it hard to forgive my failing in school, which must have caused her some embarrassment. Every once in a while she'd lash out at me verbally with a violence that was way out of proportion to the transgression it was supposed to punish.

All this tension relaxed somewhat when Wolfgang Harich, Professor of German History at Humboldt University, moved into a cottage near ours (together with a pretty young woman whose name I forget) and kept Bodo and Alma engaged in nearly incessant conversation. Harich had a dual reputation: some people considered him a young genius, others a chatterbox. I had no opinion one way or the other, but I liked him, and liked to listen to his brisk intelligence at play. No one else was likely to compare Thomas Mann's prose to beef stroganoff dished out on Meissen china, and Bert Brecht's to goat cheese, black bread, and a mug of Bavarian beer. Once, Harich did a very funny impersonation of several of the world's great conductors, each with his respective temperament and style, leading an orchestra through the first twenty or thirty bars of Beethoven's Fifth Symphony. I would always come out of my room to hear Wolfgang talk.

But maybe Wolfgang really did talk too much, because a year later he was put on trial for plotting to overthrow the government. He received a long jail sentence, and with him went several others, including Walter Janka, a man whom my parents liked and respected and who was generally believed to be innocent of any wrongdoing except lending an ear to Wolfgang's seditious talk. Harich, however, seemed to be in fact guilty of at least some of the charges against him, such as making contact with "the reactionary Petöfi circle" in Hungary; there were photographs, documents, witnesses, and also a confession. To this damning evidence the media added all sorts of extra-juridical invective. One newspaper article, for example, held up Harich's liking for foreign, exotic women as typically decadent, bourgeois-intellectual behavior. (A letter to the editors rebuked the writer of this article for raising the ugly head of racism in an otherwise perfectly justifiable attack on an enemy of the working class.) Frequently, Harich's subversive activities were compared to those of worms, pigs, and other animals of low repute. Someone on TV called him a hyena.

For a while, Bodo feared that he, too, might be brought to trial on account of all that talking in Ahrenshoop; but he wasn't so much as questioned.

I don't remember being particularly disturbed by this trial. Harich had evidently committed a crime, so there was nothing wrong in his being punished; and the way people talked, he had been given a rather light sentence —he could have been shot. Walter Janka was another matter. But none of my parents' friends spoke of Janka's imprisonment as if it was a scandal or an outrage—at least not while I was around; it seemed more in the nature of a great misfortune befalling a good man. He was legally culpable without being morally guilty, and no one could blame the government for that.

❡The teachers of the Helmholtz school had decided that Peter, Ralle, and I ought not to be allowed to go to the same school together. For this reason I was banished to the Oberschule Weissensee, named after the district of Berlin where it was situated.

September 1, 1957, the date I set for the commence-
ment of the arduous enterprise of catching up with
Peter and the rest of the twelfth grade (and the usual
date for the first day of school), happened to fall on
Sunday, the day of rest. "I'm a little upset," I wrote that
evening. "It's that I'm going to a new school, for reasons
that don't exactly commend me to either the students or
the teachers. I don't think I'll have the courage to tell
my classmates the whole truth. Actually it would be
stupid to do so." Then, without transition, the next sentence reports: "I've taken a whole bunch of books out
of Bodo's library, all works of criticism and literary
history, except for a treatise *Concerning Some Questions of Marxist Philosophy* and a biography of Beethoven." So much for my New Year's resolutions and the
priority of schoolwork ("No more excuses!").

I arrived at school forty-five minutes early the next
morning, having made triply sure I wouldn't start the
first day by coming late. I wanted to be as inconspicu-
ous as possible. These precautions were counterproduc-
tive. I was the first to arrive in front of the closed doors
of the auditorium, and had to endure a half hour of
extreme visibility as other early risers began to trickle
in. Gradually the crowd swelled and I receded into obscurity. Now I was able to make observations of my
own, uninhibited by the probing eyes of others. A revolution in men's hairstyles seemed to be in the making.
Over the summer, *Eulenspiegel*, the humor magazine, had
tried to nip this newest Western excrescence in the bud
—apparently to no avail: there they were, the infamous
haircuts, the "Brush," the "Macky," the "Ducktail," even
the arty "Roman," and they were no longer being worn
as an isolated gesture of defiance, as had been the case
the previous year, but appeared in sufficient numbers to
represent a sizable and confident minority. And many
of the boys were wearing clothes of the officially discouraged variety: studded denim pants, black camping

shirts, so-called bush jackets, extremely pointed Italian shoes.

At five to eight the doors opened and the crowd filed into the auditorium, a large shabby room decorated with portraits of Marx, Engels, Lenin, and Ulbricht. (After Stalin's fall from the pantheon, a problem of symbology had arisen: whether to continue with Marx, Engels, and Lenin as a sort of triune principle, or to maintain a quaternity, in which case some new hero of undisputed grandeur and orthodox purity had to be found. The choice was in favor of the number four, and of Walter Ulbricht as the only living German worthy of canonization.) On the podium was a lectern, and above the lectern a very large red banner with white cardboard letters affixed to it: *Fürs Vaterland ist keine Pflicht zu schwer, kein Opfer ist zu gross fürs Vaterland!* (For the fatherland no duty is too hard, no sacrifice is too great for the fatherland!). I sat down in one of the back rows, pulled out my journal, and wrote— in English, in case someone peeked: "I know the script for this ceremony by heart, and so does nearly everyone else here. The principal will step up to the podium and deliver greetings, welcomes, warnings, admonishments, and explanations concerning the coming school year. Then he'll talk about the political situation: revengists and neo-Nazis agitating in West Germany, sabotage and espionage against us on an increasingly savage scale, also defamation through the radio, leaflets, etc. What can high-school students do to contribute to the survival and progress of our Republic? Learn, learn, learn, and active social participation." After writing this, I felt confident and solid. I put the notebook away and sat up straight. I reread the slogan above the lectern. What a stupid pronouncement! Anyone could utter it with fervent conviction, wherever and for whatever purpose. I felt proud of this insight which raised me, the double repeater, above my educators. No doubt they thought they were being solid Marxists when they were settling for mere nationalism. Well, I was reading *Concerning Some Questions of Marxist Philosophy*, and I knew better. The principal acted out my scenario almost to the letter. What I had failed to anticipate, and should have known from experience, was that after the applause for the principal had died down, an FDJ functionary would step up and deliver virtually the same statement all over again. "This first day wasn't so bad after all," I wrote (in German) when I got home. "It helps to observe things and to name them. Remember Hohenweide."

That was a reference to an extraordinary afternoon I had spent with Bodo and Valentin Birkelbach, the poet, about two years previously. Valentin had taken us to Hohenweide, a village in the foothills of the Harz, in order to introduce us to the Bürgermeister, a collector and historian of antique glassware. (Valentin, too, was a collector, not of glass, but of rare and peculiar human beings; but this the Bürgermeister did not know.) Those five hours with the Bürgermeister of Hohenweide and his red, blue, and green jars and tumblers rank among the most tedious hours I have ever spent, and that includes roughly twelve years of school. Added to the desperate craving for release from that slow and murderously pedantic peroration on the history of glass in the Harz region was the painful thought of something I had found in the wastebasket of the hotel room I shared with Bodo: a draft of a letter to Alma in which Bodo expressed worry and bafflement over what he called my "extreme passivity and lack of focus, almost lifelessness." The judgment in those words had cut deeply, and began to rankle as the hours crawled along in the Bürgermeister's living room and I sat wrenching my sagging lids open and stifling the shout of protest within me: "Shut up! You're the ones who are dead! You're killing me with boredom!"

At long last—*extremely* long last—we left and drove back to the hotel in Valentin's car. I sat in the back. Valentin and Bodo looked tired, but agreed that, overall, it had been an interesting experience. I snorted with contempt. Extreme passivity—shit! Listening to that drone for five hours, if that's not an exercise in extreme passivity, I don't know what is. Going to the office every day, going to *school*—I suppose that's being focused. I'll show you focus . . . I began, in fact, to focus, in the optical sense of the word, on my surroundings. I was astonished by what I saw. The plowed fields were not brown, as one might have supposed them to be, but a color which, after some searching, I identified as mauve, with tinges of violet and even brick-red in places; and of these colors there was a surprising variety of hues. Green grass and shrubs burned against this red earth, and when I looked closely, I noticed there were as many shades of green as there were of red. Tumble-down wooden fences leaped up and dipped and rose again alongside the road as we drove past, and the contrast between their quick, discontinuous motion and the slow turning of distant hills was pleasing and even meaningful in an inexplicable way, like the counterpoint of two melodies. Not having pencil and paper with me, and not wanting to draw attention to myself by asking for them, I began to make mental notes: "Black-and-white cattle . . . three oaks, broad and squat . . . girls with sunburned legs and arms gathering hay, or something . . . a brownish-green stream shaped like a double S . . . long swirls of whitish-yellow foam like twisted dirty linen . . . willows alongside the river, deep holes in their trunks . . . a house with a rooster carved in the gable . . ." On and on. After a while, my mouth was watering from the pleasure of seeing things and naming them.

In this spirit of Hohenweide, and also, I think, in a spirit of ironic remove unconsciously adopted from Robert Musil's journals, I filled my journal with minute and not always kind observations about my teachers—all in order to counter the anxiety and embarrassment I felt at being the oldest (and hence, by logical inference, quite possibly one of the dullest) in the class.

Herr Gellert, our English teacher, a gentle, soft-spoken man with neatly parted blond hair, passed muster with something like a 2+ average. The worst fault I found in him was pedantry and Teutonic thoroughness; otherwise he impressed me as decent and sensitive—"and a good English teacher." Another exception was the sports teacher, a brawny, middle-aged man, thanks to whom our school produced the best athletes of any high school in the Democratic Sector of Greater Berlin. The rest, if I am to believe my judgments at that time, were either stupid, incompetent, or vicious.

My classmates received much more generous evaluations from me, maybe because there were two boys, not at all unintelligent fellows, who, like me, were repeating the grade. That must have put me at ease. There was also "a very eagerly studious little fellow in a confirmation suit who was kicked out of the Helmholtz school for some undisclosed reason and sent here, as I was." So I was in congenial company. My only reservation about my classmates seems to have been that they were younger than I, and hence lacking in seriousness and maturity. "But," I conceded, "I have myself to blame for that."

A note of humility, and of realism—but that's as far as it went. Every evening I'd open the thick hard-backed notebook that served as my journal, cock a supercilious eyebrow, and assume my customary stance of suave, flippant detachment from life and its silly demands. A curious journal. Instead of recording the day's events and my thoughts about them, I was dedicating everything—thoughts, facts, and the act of writing itself —to the perfection of a pose. Even my handwriting began to mutate: the capitals were growing larger, the loops of various lower-case letters preposterously calligraphic.

I did no schoolwork whatsoever. Instead, I listened to records, read in the pile of books I'd borrowed from Bodo on September 1, played the piano, watched TV, collaborated with Stefan on a comedy about a collectivized turkey farm. I also worked more assiduously than usual on my own writing, especially poems. On Saturday, September 7, just five days after the beginning of school, I cut my first class. A little later, when the school principal refused to authorize my taking an art course at an evening school for adults, arguing sensibly that someone with my school record simply couldn't afford to take time off from homework, I got hold of an official stamp saying "Oberschule Weissensee" and drew up an imposingly authoritative document. (I couldn't resist showing this creation to Stefan, that connoisseur of the comic pomp of Prusso-Socialist officialese.)

The arrogant tone that had begun to inform the style of my journal spilled over into an overt confrontation with our German teacher, Frau Kohl, who was reading *Macbeth* with us. (German class involved reading literature translated from various languages.) "She claims the three witches are 'merely' thoughts and desires rising from Macbeth's murky brain 'like bubbles,' " I wrote. "When I suggested that maybe they were really witches, she snapped at me: 'You can imagine whatever you want, I can't prescribe ideas to you.' But that's exactly what she's doing—she's afraid of allowing any discussion. And she's misinterpreting Macbeth. At one point, she asked me to read Macbeth's speech from the witches' scene: 'Two truths are told,' etc. She interrupted me and said I should read more gruffly and aggressively, more like someone who is about to commit a murder. I objected that he wasn't even thinking of murder yet, and that he was supposed to be full of the milk of human kindness, and that the words I was reading were noble and generous and not at all aggressive. 'Hm,' she says. 'Well . . . Hm. Well, I'd say that milk's got to be pretty damn curdled, considering what he's going to do.' I lost my patience and snapped back: 'The whole point of the play is that he's a good man to start out with—' 'Never mind, keep on reading, we don't have time for a debate.' So I continued reading in my own way."

It was impolitic of me to challenge Frau Kohl, who was known to wield considerable power among the teachers. She was supposed to be some kind of big wheel in the Party, too. The day after our disagreement over Macbeth—it was Friday, the thirteenth of September, I noted in my journal, with a quavering "*Meine Güte*" ("My goodness") that somehow failed to be quite convincingly lighthearted—Herr Gellert took it upon himself to enter all our final grades for the previous year into the class book, a ledger that contained our current grades, demerits, and records of attendance. ("I suppose he wants to bolster the unsteady judgment of people like Kohl," I wrote.) When Frau Kohl looked into the class book that day, she muttered: "My, my, what interesting background information have we here? Schmidt, Tauler, Tobias, Uhse. Hmmm . . . *Your* column doesn't look very nice, Uhse, *does* it? Not at all. Mathematics, 4 . . . Chemistry, 5 . . . Biology, 4 . . . German, 1?! How did you ever get a 1 in German? I hope that wasn't a reward for having a father named Bodo Uhse. Hmmmm . . . We'll have to look into that."

"My goodness," indeed. I was worried. The brink was near. I could sense it. Maybe I had already overstepped my bounds, and Frau Kohl was taking steps to have me sent "into the Production"—to work, that is, possibly in a factory or on a farm. But . . . but . . .What argument could I propose? That doing full-time physical work would take time and energy away from my writing?

"*What* writing?" asked the voice of the prosecution. "You have no experience, *that's* why you can't write. Go into the Production and you'll have something to write about."

"But . . . but I want to go to Moscow University . . . that palatial campus . . . students from all over the world, exotic girls . . ."

"Off limits for you, young man, you've had more than a fair chance, now it's time to make yourself useful. Or do you think you're too good for that, too fine a specimen? Millions of people your age work in factories. Why not you?"

The more I considered these unpalatable arguments, the more cogent they seemed and the less defensible my objections. I prayed for assistance.

Saturday morning in Frau Kohl's class I exhibited an alert and studious demeanor. Frau Kohl gave me an owlish glance from above her spectacles, after which she ignored me until the bell rang. Then she called me to her desk.

"Uhse, do you consider yourself a good actor?"

"I have no idea . . . I never really . . ."

"Maybe I should say *dissembler*. Well, making fine distinctions just isn't my forte. How would you like to act for real? On a stage?"

"I think I would like it."

"I thought so. I'm starting a theater group next month. We'll be doing Molière's *School for Wives*, and I need someone to play the role of Valère—you know, the young lover. You *don't* know? I thought you were so well-read. Do you consider yourself a young lover? Well, never mind. You can always dissemble. Do you want the part?"

I smiled and said yes, and sent a quick thank-you message to heaven. All I needed was another chance. Now I'd show them what was in me. I would dazzle them. I pictured myself on my knees in the spotlight, arms spread, declaiming my love to a girl in a crinoline.

On the way home, I passed by a large cartoon that had been mounted on the roof of an office building. It showed a green-faced, ghoulishly grinning Konrad Adenauer flanked by cannons, an aureole of fighter planes around his head, holding a slavering, helmeted, four-legged Nazi by a leash. The single word "VOR-SICHT!"—Caution!—burned in red letters beneath the poster. The news media, too, were striking a note of alarm. The West German elections were coming up, and our government was strongly favoring the socialist SPD against the conservative-reactionary CDU. My parents and their friends spoke of Adenauer as a dangerous, even malevolent man, a wolf in sheep's clothing who had not yet revealed his true nature. There was a tight fearfulness in the pauses between people's words, a breath held in apprehension of an as yet undeclared and un-specified menace.

Once again I took pen in hand, put on my hiero-phant's robe of elegant condescension, and tried to dis-miss this new threat with a quick rhetorical flourish. "You'd think the commentators had sighted a tidal wave, the way they're warning us with trembling voices: Woe to us, woe to Germany, woe to the world if the Christian Democrats win!" But I woke up from a nightmare the next morning—it was the day of the elections—and recorded all its details with care and without the faintest ironic remove:

I was fleeing from some officers who were pursuing me because of my Jewish blood. It was evening. I crept up to a building where I hoped to find temporary refuge. I opened a door, tapped my way through a dark passage, and suddenly stood in a brightly lit room. Ten or fifteen boys about my age sat on benches that lined the four walls. There was no other furniture, and no window. I sat down, too, sensing I had nothing to fear from them. Some quietly friendly remarks were made by them and by me, but no questions were asked, as if everything was understood. Later I learned they had been there for a week. They had run away from home for some reason, and were hiding. After sitting with them for a while, I saw through the half-open door (I must have forgotten to close it when I stepped in) a short, elderly gentleman in a gray suit. I had the impression he had seen me, so I stepped out of the room to avoid giving away the presence of the others. But it was only now that the man noticed me. He hurried into another room, apparently to make a phone call. I shouted after him: "Please wait! Don't call anyone! I am harmless and innocent!" He came back out. Now the other boys emerged from the room where they had been hiding, and the man looked very frightened by these visitors. But he pulled himself together and led us into a nicely furnished room and asked us to sit down at a large table. At this moment, officers appeared at the door, asked this and that, and began an investigation. I succeeded in passing myself off as one of the boys who had run away from home. I was saved!

I woke up then, wondered whether I should get out of bed or enjoy five or ten minutes of half sleep, and dozed off again.

This time I dreamed that I was on trial together with many hundreds of people. Nazi officers stood around. I remembered my escape in the house of the little man with the gray suit, and looked for a way out: there was no possibility of escape this time. Wherever I looked there were insurmountable barriers: walls, fences, armed guards. The condemned sat on benches outside. An officer was shouting orders to my right, while before me someone was giving a speech. A man was kicked and beaten by several men. A soldier went up to a large dirty building and checked the walls and the ceiling. Then the doors were opened wide and people were herded into the building. I felt a cold terror, but fought it off with the resolution to live through this final experience with open eyes. Since there was no escape, what sense was there in adding fear to my misfortune? Let me at least have as full and deep a sense as possible of my life and soul and the meaning of this existence and of death. Let me look, learn, understand, until my last breath. These were my thoughts as I stepped into the room. Many rows of benches stood there, like pews in a church. People sat down on them after being herded through the door.

Looking for a place to sit, I noticed a little girl clinging to her mother with a questioning look, already half comprehending that something terrible was about to happen. I didn't see tears anywhere, and no one screamed. All sat quietly on their benches and awaited the end. A soldier laid a small red hose across the threshold. Then the door was closed, and the gas began to hiss. Still no one cried out. On the contrary, there was an almost restful atmosphere in the room. I was astounded. I thought: What wisdom these people must have, to look death in the eye with such equanimity. But I was one of them. Then it simply seemed sensible to be quiet and embrace the inevitable. Suddenly I recognized someone sitting on the bench in front of me: Peter Vogel. He looked very grave and sad, and in his hand was a small black book. Without saying a word, I asked for the book. He handed it to me. It was a Bible. On the cover it said: "The Holy Writ. For all who are condemned to death." I recalled stories of people who became Christians immediately before dying, and I thought of the enormous relief, even joy, I would feel if I knew, at this moment, that I had a God, and that I could give myself to Him in the act of reading His book. I opened the book, rejecting the thought of God at the same time. At that moment, a terrible sorrow welled up in me. I looked up from the Bible, I looked at the people who were waiting for death with me, felt tears rising, no hatred for our murderers, no desperation, no rage, just an infinite sadness and longing. Then I woke up.

⟨The calligraphic loops disappeared from my handwriting after that dream, and the journal resumed its modest record-keeping function—modest but meticulously detailed, and in the present tense, as if I were literally trying to preserve that time for the future. All I need to do now is open the old notebook (some of whose pages are beginning to yellow around the edges), read a few lines, and the sights, sounds, and smells of a day twenty years past begin to revive.

Thursday, October 10, 1957
In the Ostbahnhof with Bodo, around midnight or later, waiting for a delayed train. An unendurably thick cloud of cigarette

smoke fills the cafeteria, and there is another, invisible, even more offensive cloud made of the combined smells of alcohol, sausage, sweat, and other body odors emitted by hundreds of people. Ill-tempered waiters in dirty white clothes perambulate among the tables, bumping into people and cursing. Every few minutes a loudspeaker bellows its announcements, drowning all conversation. We leave the room in search of fresh air and step into a hallway that smells of urine. People are sleeping on their feet, next to heavy trunks. Some hoodlums in the background are discussing the subject of pregnancy with their girls. A man passing by, not at all the well-read type, mutters something that makes Bodo smile with pleasure: "I feel like I'm in Gorky's flophouse."

At long last the train comes.* Bodo and I scarcely talk throughout the ride, but there's a sense of friendly communion in this. Part of the time we read, or doze, or else we just sit and watch the other passengers. We are sharing a first-class compartment with an elderly couple and an ancient wheezing dachshund that lies on the woman's lap. She strokes the dog's head continually and bends over from time to time to make solicitous sounds in its ear. The dog smacks its chops and responds with a faint stirring of its tail tip. The man reaches out to caress the dog's muzzle, and the dog licks his hand. This goes on for a long time: the woman's hand stroking the little grizzled head, the man holding out his palm, the dog licking it. Then the dog

---

* We were on our way to Oberhof, a ski resort in the Harz mountains. Not that there was any chance of skiing that time of the year. We were planning to join Alma and Stefan for a long weekend. Alma had taken Stefan to Oberhof in the hope that the altitude would help relieve his asthma. Then a flu epidemic broke out in Berlin, and all students who had been so much as touched by the disease were given a two-week vacation, while the healthy ones were enjoined to participate in a voluntary potato-picking expedition. (It *was* voluntary in a purely technical sense, but there was such pressure to participate—from peers as much as from teachers—that hardly anyone refused.) By lucky happenstance, I had feigned illness just a few days before, and my pretended symptoms fortuitously matched those of the actual disease when it made its appearance.

curls up on the woman's lap with a grunt, and falls asleep. The man pulls out his handkerchief and discreetly wipes his hand.

We arrive in Oberhof at 5 a.m. To our surprise, the hotel management has arranged for a car to pick us up.

One of the first things Stefan asks me after Bodo and I wake up later that morning is whether I have ever listened to—*really* listened to—Mozart's Clarinet Quintet. Indeed I have! It's a miraculous piece of music, I say—incomparable! We're both pleased by this agreement on something so dear to us. "Do you know Beethoven's Romance in F Major?" I ask in return. "No," he says, "but to tell you the truth, I have some reservations about Beethoven." "Oh?" "Well, he gets kind of bombastic sometimes, you know what I mean?" I do not. Beethoven falls just short of divinity in my scale of values, and to hear my eleven-year-old brother laying the measure of his half-formed mind against genius, against immortality—well, it makes my hair bristle. Stefan must have noticed a nervous reaction in me, because he reaches out to touch my arm and says: "Let's listen to this Romance in F Major together when I get home. I'm sure it's beautiful." Such delicacy and intelligence in someone so young. I love him for it, am proud of him, but I fear him, too. Someday he might eclipse me.

We go to the game room and play Ping-Pong, taking care not to step on any "children under the age of fourteen" who have sneaked in unattended despite prohibition. It's raining outside. Stefan shows me some caricatures he's made of the hotel's guests, each of whom, he explains, is either a dentist or a dentist's wife (they're here to attend a dental conference, which will begin on Sunday). What the guests are doing in Stefan's pictures is what they have been doing in the lounge all afternoon: playing cards, drinking, guffawing with wide-open mouths, swaying from side to side with linked arms, and singing along with some execrable music produced by three men with an accordion, a clarinet, and a piano. They are ugly, grotesque, bestially self-satisfied, in life as well as in the pictures. What Stefan doesn't capture (doesn't see?) is their sadness, and the inextinguishable spark of divinity.*

I wake up early on Saturday morning. It has stopped raining. I look out the window and see in a steaming meadow a group of oaks with bright-gold leaves, behind them a ski jump's semi-parabola among dark pines, and behind those the mountains, pale-gray-blue washes almost indistinguishable from the milky sky.

The four of us take a walk after breakfast. I have never seen such colors: radiant gold on the trees, moss a deep luminous green, and in the middle of this a strange crimson mushroom shaped like an antler, or coral. We stop at the Rennsteigklause, a log cabin decorated with broken ski tips. They are nailed all over the walls, one across the other, like X's, and each X has a name and a date written on it, commemorating the accident. There is even a lamp made entirely of broken skis. A blond woman with desiccated features plays the piano (she reminds me of a Toulouse-Lautrec poster), while a somnambulous-looking man operates the percussion with elegant arm movements and a lack of rhythmic sense that is nothing less than amazing, considering his function. There are so many people dancing that all attempts at "open" dancing are discouraged without any need for official discouragement. A soft-spoken young man and five lively young women are drinking beer at a table near ours, face to face with five old men and women who appear to be disapproving of the young folks' behavior, or perhaps of their youth. Generally, though, people are being exceptionally friendly to one another.

Sunday, October 13. An extraordinary announcement is made early in the morning on the hotel's intercom system and from loudspeakers driven past the hotel, and from radios and televisions: All Party members are to report to their places of work, and by nightfall each citizen of the DDR must exchange his

---

* The repeated mention of "divinity" betrays the nature of my reading at the time: Lessing's *Education of the Human Race*. Religious ideas were always slipping in through the back door as part of the "national cultural heritage," the preservation of which was one of the government's principal concerns.

money for the new currency: latecomers will not be reimbursed. Money in the bank will be automatically exchanged.

Hysteria develops in the hotel, people are running up and down stairs, there is lamentation and gnashing of, yes, teeth. The ordinance has made a shambles of the dental conference. I decide to go home with Bodo rather than stay on in Oberhof, despite the good time Stefan and I have been having together. He seems hurt, and I feel guilty. Bodo and I pack our bags immediately, but it's hard to get a taxi to the station, since the dentists are hurrying home, too. Bodo won't get to his office in time to obey the instructions for Party members, but there are several hundred marks in a drawer of his desk in Berlin, and if the trains aren't delayed, he'll be able to exchange them for the new currency.

Once again we sit quietly together. We have a compartment to ourselves this time. We read, look out the window, read again. We rise from our seats at the sound of the gong and worm our way through the massed bodies to the dining car, eat two small but tasty Holstein steaks, return to our seats more or less satiated, read, look out the window. It occurs to me that landscapes often remind one of paintings, but very rarely do paintings remind one of a landscape one has seen. When I mention this to Bodo, he looks intrigued, and I feel proud. I speculate out loud that maybe imagination precedes perception, at least the perception of beauty. Bodo shakes his head and says, "No, you've got it all wrong. Reality comes first, and ideas are a reflection of it. That's true of aesthetic ideas as well." "But," I say, "what about intuition? How did Democritus know about atoms? Was that just a lucky guess, or did he know?" Bodo smiles and says, "I really don't know." Hotly (because I feel he's not taking me seriously) I say: "I think there are things no one will ever know." "How can you know that?" he says. "I don't know, but I *feel* it," I say, with a tone of dogmatic certainty and a feeling of complete confusion. What was I getting at? I've lost track. "What is it that you believe is unknowable?" Bodo asks. Now I remember: "Beauty." But I'm far away from beauty; I'm annoyed that Bodo seems to think he knows that everything is knowable. Just as I think this, I notice he's not so self-assured at all—he's thinking about what I said. "I believe everything can be known," he says then. "How do you know?" I shoot back. "I *don't* know it, but I believe it. I believe science will eventually be able to explain everything —even beauty. Even the so-called religious realm. The way a thing of nature, like a sunset, or a tree, can be so moving, so meaningful, as if something were being communicated. Even intuition. Everything." At this moment I recognize something: just as he wants to believe that, I want not to believe it. I try to figure it out: what is the difference in our way of thinking? Why do we so rarely see eye to eye? These are the conclusions I come to: for him, knowledge is the highest good, along with the rational action that stems from it; for me, it is beauty, and the emotion of love it engenders. To attack beauty with the tools of knowledge is, to me, to destroy it. But to him, mystery is just an unconquered foe.

Later I recall a statement by Einstein, I think it accompanies a photograph of a spiral nebula in *The Family of Man*: something to the effect that what is impenetrable to the understanding can be known to really exist, and that it manifests itself to us as beauty. I tell Bodo what Einstein said (a half hour or so has passed since he last talked), and very surprisingly, he has no reply and just looks deeply touched, or impressed—I don't know whether by the passion with which I spoke or by the authority of Einstein, or by the statement; and then he mumbles, "I'll have to think about that." For a little while I feel proud, as if I had won a debate with him; and then I feel stupid being proud.

The train moves slowly into Ostbahnhof. A loud throng fills the station. Exchange booths have been set up there, guarded by policemen, and people are rushing to find a good spot in the queues that have formed. Many are angry at the government for disrupting their Sunday, but it's obvious they're also enjoying the excitement, just as people will curse foul weather while relishing an invigorating tussle with the elements.

We rush home by taxi to fetch Bodo's money, and hurry on to the bank. The driver is convinced the government is playing a practical joke on the populace. Or is he making subtle fun of Bodo? Bodo sincerely defends the official explanation as the most plausible motive: the idea is to deal a blow to the flourishing business of currency speculation in West Germany and on the black market in the DDR. Now the driver is calling it a "*Schweinerei*," while at first he was calling it a "*Spielerei.*"* Maybe he thinks Bodo's one of the people responsible, since we live in Niederschönhausen.

The new bills are larger and more colorful than the old. Bodo's pleased to see Goethe's face on the new money, but I think it's a mistake to have made his face green. The bill, yes, but not the face. We go to the Rathskeller to eat. The place is jammed, we have to wait for an hour before we get a seat at a table together with a young woman. She has serious, clear-eyed, intelligent, friendly, and also pretty features. Bodo talks to her. (I wish I could do that.) She says she is drawn to all the arts, but especially to literature. She used to work in the Karl Marx bookstore, she says. But then she quit, and now she's studying medicine. She's an intern in the Charité. "Despite your attraction to literature?" Bodo asks. "No, precisely *because* of it," she says. "In the bookstore, I was always limited to a department specializing in something like cookbooks or military books—so I hardly had any contact with real readers. But even if I'd worked in the literature section, I don't think I would have liked it." "And now, as a doctor?" "Oh, yes, I really like what I'm doing now." "And the patients—I suppose at this point they're still experimental subjects for you?" "No, not at all" (she says that emphatically). "If we lost sight of the fact that we're dealing with human beings, the work would become cold and ugly."

There was a story told later, about an old woman who regularly padded to the open market in felt slippers or wooden clogs, wearing threadbare clothes, and who, on the day the money was changed, was observed hauling a fortune in bills to the bank, two suitcases full, or three

---

* "*Spielerei*" means "fun and games." "*Schweinerei*" is a pejorative term, derivative of "*Schwein*," or "pig."

bulging shopping bags full—the accounts varied. Either there were many old women like her, or else she was an archetype, because everyone seemed to have heard about her or knew someone who had seen her, in various parts of the city.

A very different kind of story was told to Bodo by Erwin Strittmatter, the novelist. Strittmatter had a neighbor, Herr N., a retired gentleman, honest and decent, a dedicated Communist and a humble admirer of everything cultural. He was also afraid of agents and spies from the West, and of Western influence in general, to such a degree that, for example, he would never, never listen to a Western radio station—not just because it was forbidden, but because he feared being infected, in a quite literal sense, by bourgeois thought.

As an expression of his interest in culture, Herr N. went to a conference that was attended by many well-known writers from the DDR, and kept a stenographic record of every word that was spoken. Shortly afterward, Strittmatter urgently needed a copy of the minutes of that conference. Knowing that Herr N. had been present, and knowing of his friend's mania for stenographic notation, Strittmatter asked to see what records he had kept, rather than turn to the organizers of the conference and risk having to wait for the slow uncoiling of red tape. Herr N. gladly obliged; he had just finished preparing a neatly handwritten transcript for his own files.

Strittmatter found the information he needed. He also found a wealth of amusing marginalia, consisting of things the famous writers had said off the record. Kurt Bartel, the poet, for example, was reported to have walked out of the room saying, *"Ihr könnt mir alle den Buckel runterrutschen,"* which is, roughly, the equivalent of an invitation to go jump in the lake. Obviously, anything issuing from a poet's mouth might be of cultural value, and Herr N. didn't feel authorized to separate the wheat from the chaff. Eventually Strittmatter came across the following note, written in pencil between the lines of the transcript (which were written in ink): "Sunday, October 13. I lost 200 DM today. Found an official-looking leaflet in my mailbox telling me to exchange all my cash for new currency by the end of the day. I ignored it. Thought it was the handiwork of agents."

([My journal slows down around Christmas of 1957—weeks pass without any entry. Possibly I was too busy studying my lines and rehearsing for *The School for Wives* to reflect on the day's events. It was quite a happy time, that much I remember. My grades were respectable, and I was popular in class. Occasionally I played hooky, without ever getting into serious trouble. I was compliant with Frau Kohl's direction of the play, and that more than made up for my ill-considered objections to her interpretation of *Macbeth*; we grew to like or at least respect one another. Whatever had been the source of my parents' quarreling during the summer had vanished. They went out for walks together, gave parties, and didn't fight. Stefan and I abandoned our drama about the turkey farm and collaborated on a book for children—the story of a restless swarm of phosphorescent plankton (metaphorical spermatozoa?) and their search for the great whale whom they regard as their god; I wrote and he illustrated. Peter and Ralle came over to play badminton; or else we'd go out and steal books, reviving the good old days.

There was only one fly in the ointment, and that was my virginity, or rather my desire to get rid of it. I was seventeen and hadn't experienced the most rudimentary intimacy with a woman's body. It was high time. Peter was having an affair with a married woman. How I regretted those missed opportunities in Thuringia and Ahrenshoop and Münchehofe!

This urgent need to establish my manhood elbowed its way into the center of my life, took root, and grew there until it reached obsessive proportions, disturbing, though not completely upsetting, the peace of those otherwise tranquil months.

I planned and schemed, coldly, seriously. Romantic abductions were unthinkable in the Democratic Sector of Greater Berlin, but a casual pickup or a seduction à la Casanova seemed in order. Once again, I drew inspiration from Eduard Fuchs's inexhaustible *Sittengeschichte*, and lost it whenever I looked into the blankly unseducible eyes of any attractive girl—Anita B., for instance, who lived nearby and who seemed to like me, and who was beautiful as well as sweet-natured and gentle, and charmingly simple and unaffected. That was the problem: she was angelic. What did she know of lustful desire? Once we were walking together on a narrow path that led through a wheatfield. She was eating ice cream. We had spent the day at the beach, where my heart had danced with pride at being in her statuesque company.

"Anita," I said, "let's go into the field, we'd be all alone there."

She stopped to consider it. "I don't think the farmers would like it," she said then, and started walking again. "We're alone anyway," she added.

"It's not the same," I said.

Suddenly a glob of ice cream fell off the cone and into her dress. She shrieked, and then she laughed, and shrieked again as the stuff slid farther down. She bent over to scoop it out with her hands. We were both laughing.

"Come, I'll help you," I said, nearly choking at my own temerity. I hesitated, with my hand hovering near the neckline of her dress, hoping for an invitation to reach in.

"Thanks," she said, and put the cone in my hand. "You can eat the rest if you want."

"Thanks."

She pulled a towel out of her shoulder bag and wiped her breasts. My ears were on fire. "That was really funny," she said, with such warm candor in her blue eyes that I knew she hadn't rejected me at all; she just hadn't noticed anything.

Where were those voluptuous females depicted in the *Sittengeschichte?* Where was there an island such as the one I had seen in a movie in West Berlin, populated only by goats and three sex-starved women? If such women and such priapic places didn't exist, I would have to invent them. The deeper recesses of my desk began to fill up with pornographic stories I had written, and with drawings I made to illustrate them—a lot of masked figures, I remember. One of my favorite themes was an orgiastic costume party where the most unlikely bedfellows happily copulate in the anonymity of their masks.

The following February, at carnival time (here is an instance of the unsatisfactory ways in which life imitates art), Anita's parents gave their annual *Fasching* celebration, a costume party. The music was American—old New Orleans jazz from my mother's collection, new rock-'n'-roll taped from forbidden radio stations. The lights were dim, the drinks were strong. Some people were dancing "open," others stood rocking in each other's arms. A great actor, the pride of the Berliner Ensemble, stood declaiming inspired gibberish next to the punch bowl. Another man, dressed as a pirate, was caressing a woman's face with long, generous laps of the tongue, like a dog. Anita had on a black leotard that splendidly set off the gold of her hair. A black line traced the edge of each eyelid. Another black line ran down the center of her forehead, her nose, her mouth, her chin, dividing her face in half. Alma, who was always more or less in costume by East German standards, looked stunning: her hair was pinned up more tightly than usual above the temples, and this, with the help of eye-shadow and rouge, gave her face an enigmatic, dreamily feline expression, which was strikingly complemented by a large, dark, richly embroidered Mexican shawl, a long peasant dress, and bare feet with brightly painted toenails. Bodo had restricted his costuming to a sombrero and a red paper nose, a combination that lent him an oddly rugged appearance, despite his tweed jacket with the spectacle case sticking out of the breast pocket.

I danced with a tall official of the International Federation of Women. She was wearing a belly dancer's outfit; I was a Mexican bandit: genuine orange charro pants with a white fringe. I danced in the manner prescribed by Fräulein von N. of Potsdam—head high, in elegant formal rounds, a persistent erection the only feature unbefitting a gentleman. My partner had the round pneumatic-looking breasts and even the heavy (if false) lashes of my fantasy women, and she smelled very nicely of talcum powder and musk. Her husband (I don't remember his outfit) was necking with a charming little tigress with fluffy ears and a long tail that lay draped over one of his legs. I knew he was my partner's husband, because each time we passed by, he'd glance at her with a look of ironic caution and a complicated insecure smile that seemed to say: "I'm allowed, am I not?"—to which she responded with a reptilian stare that was only slightly softened by a smile.

During a break while the record was being changed, we stood at ease, so to speak, facing but not looking at each other or conversing. What could we have had to say to one another? Then something astonishing happened. Her hand, which had gone up to adjust a comb in her hair, came down in a smooth semicircular arc and gave the protuberance on my orange bandit trousers an encouraging little bump. Or was it a reprimand? It couldn't have been accidental—there was too much mirth struggling against suppression in her smile and averted eyes.

The music began again: "Basin Street Blues." My

partner put her arms around my neck and her cheek against mine; I embraced her; she mumbled something in my ear. In no time at all, I was groveling among her breasts and kissing her mouth and trying at the same time to dodge the embarrassed and disapproving glances Alma was shooting in my direction. My belly dancer began to breathe heavily, and even softly moaned once or twice. At the next break, she murmured a moist "Thank you" into my ear, asked me to wait, and went to visit her husband, while I rehearsed over and over in my mind the words and gestures with which I was going to propose to her that we make love— perhaps at our house, which was just a little way down the block—until the music resumed, and she came walking back to me, languidly swinging her hips and batting her enormous lashes. Again we danced, again I kissed her and squeezed her breasts. "Careful," she whispered, "don't get too excited." But with her body she said: "Don't stop." Again there was a break, again she returned to her husband, and again I resolved to make my proposition during the next dance, and searched for the right words. Until, during a sudden hush, I heard enough of what she was saying to her husband to understand what was really happening: she was *amused* by me, and was amusing her husband and his pretty companion with running reports about me. I felt the blood leave my face. Just in time, Anita's mother came to my rescue—perhaps deliberately, per- ceiving the situation I was in. "Anita has gone to bed," she said. "She seems very sad. I think she's unhappy because you didn't pay attention to her all evening. Would you please go and talk to her?" I had heard that Anita was in love with me—Peter had said so; my mother had hinted at it. So it was true! I fled upstairs and into her room. She was in bed, her makeup streaked with traces of tears. I knelt down by the bed and began kissing her urgently. "You're out of your mind," she said, shaking her head. I redoubled my efforts. My reading had taught me that the skillful manipulation of so-called erogenous zones would melt even the most stubborn female resistance. A hand up a dress—presto, her head falls back in a swoon. But not Anita. She looked distressed. She held my wrists in an iron grip. "You're completely crazy!" she said. "Please go away!" She finally persuaded me.

So the frontal attack didn't work—at least not for me. Evidently the sensible path to sexual fullfillment was to scrap both the idea of seduction (for which I was temperamentally unsuited) and that of a divinely appointed "falling in love" of souls destined for one another (who could wait that long?), and to do one of two things: (a) find a whorehouse in West Berlin; (b) make friends with a girl and hope for favorable developments. But who could that be? There was no one I liked as much as Anita—and surely I'd botched all my chances with her. It was embarrassing for both of us to meet in the street.

⟨[Frau Kohl once told me, peering over the edge of a letter from Bodo excusing my absence from her class the previous day, that she had never missed a day or so much as *five minutes* of work in the past *five years*. But one morning she was absent from school, without any prior announcement; nor did she call in to excuse herself. She didn't come the next day either, or the day after that. The principal called her home, but no one answered the telephone. The police were alerted; they broke down her door and found a note on the kitchen table explaining that Frau Kohl had gone to live in the West. Maybe she said other things as well, but that was the extent of the information we were able to ferret out. The principal came into our classroom to tell us that Herr Gellert would be replacing Frau Kohl for a while, until a qualified German teacher could be found; and he asked us to please not make life too difficult for poor Herr Gellert, since he had a double workload now. Someone asked what had happened to Frau Kohl. Sadly, much the way a devout Catholic might speak of one who has fallen into sin, the principal said: "She has become *republikflüchtig*."

Because Herr Gellert was trained as an English teacher, not a German teacher, he was forced to improvise his first lessons with us—not an easy task for such a methodical man. No doubt he was cramming the curriculum at home and acquainting himself with the sociopolitical corollaries every progressive person must draw from a reading of Goethe's *Egmont*; but in the meantime we were simply reading it together, and trying to help one another understand it—no more than that, since Herr Gellert didn't know the play any better than we did. One morning, the entire class, including Herr Gellert, found itself galvanized to attention by a mysterious thrill that was being generated, it seemed, by stuffy old Johann Wolfgang himself. Amazing! We were all pleasantly, and some of us, I think, profoundly surprised. Herr Gellert was moved—perhaps by the play as much as by our uncommon responsiveness. We listened while he recited the grand final monologue with ever more tremulous emotion ("I die for Liberty, for whose sake I did live and fight, and to whom now I yield myself in sacrifice"), until he was quite overcome and felt he had to apologize for reading so badly. "Not at all," we protested, "please read on!" We said that in complete sincerity. When the bell rang, no one made the usual impatient motions to get the hell out of the classroom. There was even talk about *Egmont* and Goethe during recess—as if we had just been to a movie together. A few days later, Herr Gellert had us write a two-hour composition for which he supplied the title, a line from *Egmont*: "Freedom? A lovely word, if rightly understood."

There was a multivocal exclamation of protest and

anxiety. "I don't know what to do, Herr Gellert! Do you want us to write about *Egmont*? We don't understand!"

Herr Gellert said: "You may write about whatever you want, so long as the content corresponds to the title."

More groans, more foreheads clutched in bewilderment. "Do you want us to *define* freedom, Herr Gellert? Why don't we just get a dictionary? We're not philosophers, Herr Gellert!"

Herr Gellert turned sideways in his chair and opened a book, his profile a mask of unmercy. My neighbor looked at me with a worried frown and tapped his forehead, as if to say, "We all know he's incompetent, but this is crazy." It certainly was unorthodox. It was hard to imagine that the curriculum didn't require of all teachers of German that they instruct us in the right understanding of that lovely word, "freedom," before giving us such an ambiguous assignment. It would, in any case, have been simple enough for Herr Gellert to provide us with some guidelines—an explication of Engels's famous dictum, for example, according to which freedom resides in the recognition of necessity. Then our compositions would have taken on a more or less uniform ideological design, and Herr Gellert would have had the easy and conventional task of applying his red pen to problems of rhetoric and orthography, instead of having to trace the paths of thirty-two solitary and panicked excursions into uncharted land. He must have wanted it that way, in sly and quiet defiance of the established rule. Pedantic, impeccably proper Herr Gellert, a secret rebel—the improbability of it made me smile. Behind me, a pen started scratching on paper—a confidently flowing sentence—but then it was violently struck out and cursed. A girl in the front row raised her hand and snapped her fingers to catch Herr Gellert's attention. "Can I write about a personal experience? If I stick to the subject?"

"Anything," he said.

"You didn't prepare us for this," muttered a petulant voice.

"Life has prepared you," said Herr Gellert. "But you must stop complaining, your time's running out." And he returned to his book. He didn't seem at all embarrassed. I noticed, then, that I had been doodling labyrinths for a while, and one large window. I drew two tall bookcases on either side of the window. Then I made the bookcases dark, so that the window appeared bright. Outside the window were sunlit trees, clouds . . . the world. My neighbor tapped his forehead again (in reference to Herr Gellert). I smiled. Suddenly the idea for a poem appeared, full-fledged, like some bright glorious creature stepped forth from the sea—its central image, its essential shape and movement, its voice. The voice was big and declamatory, a little like Whitman's in *Leaves of Grass*, which I had recently read. Icarus standing at the cliff's edge could not have felt a more fearful joy than I did with my pen raised over a fresh sheet of paper. There was a moment of reflection, necessary to cast off all ballast of doubt, fear of ridicule, considerations of etiquette and propriety. Then I took off in a blaze of inspiration:

> *Nun endlich, endlich*
> *will ich die trägen Lider aufreissen*
> *und sehen*
> *das Wunderbare*
> *und Schreckliche, überall*
> *vor mir und um mich,*
> *aber jenseits dieser geschlossenen*
> *Fenster . . .*

"At last, at last now I want to force open wide these lethargic lids and see the Marvelous and the Terrible, everywhere before me and around me but beyond these closed windows . . ." Not only did I force open my lethar-

gic lids, I ran naked into the night, leaving behind my
room, my books, my unclean secrets (that's what I
called them) tangled in bedsheets and hidden in
drawers; I threw myself naked into the snow; I sat
down on a bar stool (clothed, I assume) somewhere in
the city, threw my glass against the wall, laughed until
tears ran, cried out in pain, cried out in compassion, fell
in love, sang a glorious song "for myself and for others."
I met my enemy in a narrow lane beneath the moon and
beat him to a pulp and killed him. I met the girl whom I
loved and who loved me ("the incomparable one") in
another narrow lane and touched her and kissed her
and pressed her unto me on the earth beneath the
moon. An orgy of touching followed: I touched trees,
rocks, earth, water, the silver- and amber-colored in-
struments of some tired musicians (again in a bar), the
bodies of sleeping horses and birds, ruins, automobiles,
infants, corpses, and even "unknown and unimagined
surfaces and bodies." Having done all these things in a
single night, what to do with the morning? I left that
open: the morning, I wrote, might find me standing
barefoot in a river, drunk in a gutter, kneeling among
flowers in a field, sleepless in a prison or on a wooden
bench, making love with a girl in a soft perfumed bed,
singing and dancing my head off at a late party, dead
with a cracked skull and broken neck, or any number of
other intense possibilities—anything except to wake up
in my room behind the above-mentioned closed windows,
tangled in bedsheets and musty fantasies, surrounded
by paper and books and the dust of knowledge. *Finis
Operis.*

As I made a clean copy of the violently scribbled
draft, second thoughts came rushing in with a ven-
geance: You stupid fool, you're making a monumental
ass of yourself, who the hell do you think you are, at
least leave out that stuff about unclean secrets, you'll be
laughed out of school . . . I pushed these thoughts away.
It was too late to make revisions, in any case. My life, my

soul, all that I was worth was inscribed on the four large pages of lined paper I handed to Herr Gellert, blushing, moments before the bell rang. Days later, I still blushed and cringed, this time at the thought of those same pages—containing what I now perceived as an embarrassingly naked, farcically rhapsodic, and, worst of all, bad, simply bad, self-portrait—lying exposed to Herr Gellert's red pen. Weeks passed, and Herr Gellert did not return our compositions to us. Was he so embarrassed by what I had written that he'd rather avoid having to comment on it? Or, worse, did he pity me? Or had my classmates written similarly puerile stuff (I hoped so), and the less said about that assignment, the better?

One evening, at a memorable class party held in the school's recreation center, Herr Gellert (who was there to supply the obligatory pedagogic presence) finally did broach the awful topic, discreetly, in a moment of privacy.

"I read your composition, Joel. Your poem."

"Yes."

"I wonder—were you reading Whitman at the time?"

"Yes."

"I thought so. It does resemble Whitman." Then he nodded and smiled, and somehow, without his having to say another word, I knew that he respected the impulse to write what I had written but found the product itself wanting; and also that he felt the whole business was just too delicate—for me, if not for him—to talk about in any detail.

The party, as I said, was memorable. A guest from the twelfth grade spiked the punch with some high-proof stuff, and either Herr Gellert didn't notice or else he chose not to interfere. He sat in a corner of the room, looking sleepy and lonely, and watched while we progressed from charades and musical chairs through kissing games to making party balloons out of condoms, at which point, reluctantly, almost meekly, he called us to order. The offensive balloons were removed, but the hint of debauchery lingered. There was cheek-to-cheek dancing, some couples even stepped out to neck in the hallway. I must have been quite drunk, for the next day I couldn't remember how it had come about that, when Herr Gellert called an end to the party, I found myself having to choose between two girls, each of whom was begging me to walk her home. One was Ilse Jäger, a husky, melon-breasted girl whom I liked very much for her wit and warmth of heart, but not so much for her body; the other was Monika R., nicknamed "Mona," who was very short, very handsomely proportioned, and somewhat irritatingly affected (she aspired to the stage). I chose Mona. Ilse was hurt. "Let's go somewhere, the three of us," I suggested. Ilse declined (there was nowhere to go anyway), turned up the collar of her coat, and left. There was a blizzard outside. It would have been sensible for Mona and me to take a streetcar, but instead we walked, pushing against the wind, shielding our eyes against punishing flurries of fine stinging sleet, and stopping every few minutes to exchange furious kisses. Very late, we arrived at her building, a large brown narrowly windowed cube with puddles in the hallway, and there, in a dark niche beneath the staircase, Mona did her best to accommodate me without seeming too wanton ("I'm seventeen!" she kept whispering, "Seventeen! Seventeen! Seventeen!" as if that word were the most erogenous zone of all), while I burrowed and wedged my way, grimly, with a numb sort of passion, through multiple layers of clothes to the final, impenetrable, and irremovable rampart of a tight girdle. Since Mona was playing the role of seduced innocence, she couldn't very well lend me outright assistance. After a long fruitless struggle, I gave up.

When we met again the following Monday, not a trace was left of Saturday night's carnality. I asked her how she felt about it. "You were just using me," she said. "You were looking for experience." It was true. (It

didn't occur to me that it might be true of her also.) I
was ashamed. But that did not stifle my hunger. It only
made its satisfaction seem more remote.

⟨In the spring of 1958, Ralle decided to retire from the
Helmholtz school ("for health reasons," as he put it)
and become a bricklayer's apprentice. As soon as I
heard about it, I resolved to do the same thing. If I did
well in the apprenticeship and in trade school, Ralle
told me, I could become an architect without finishing
high school. Not that I wanted to be an architect, but at
least it was *some* kind of future. There was only one
minor hitch: the apprenticeship wouldn't start till
September. Shouldn't I wait till the end of the school
year before making my decision? No. I was in danger of
failing the eleventh grade for the second time: better to
walk out with a show of self-determination.

There was little resistance from my parents and from
my teachers; in fact, they seemed relieved. Maybe the
teachers were glad they didn't have to make the decision
for me. Everyone agreed it was probably for the better,
in the long run, and that I could always go back to school
if I needed to.

With this kind of encouragement, cutting the cords
wasn't difficult. One day it was done: no more school! I
could barely comprehend my good fortune. Complete
freedom until September!

Bodo took me to his favorite neighborhood bar, and
made a touching effort to have a talk with me, man
to man, without didactic cards up his sleeve. He had
read some of my writing, he said, and felt that it was
promising. "But I don't think you will be the naïve sort
of writer—I think you will eventually feel the need for
a higher education. However, perhaps it's all right if
you simply live and gather experience for a while. I
have been thinking about your failing in school. Maybe

you are grappling with problems that school cannot prepare you for, and instinctively you want to enroll in the universities of life—to do by choice what Gorky did by bitter necessity." He sipped at his beer and gazed into space for a while, stroking the bristles on his cheek. "Whatever road you travel, I hope you will learn what it is to be a good Communist. Unfortunately, that is something I cannot teach you."

I wondered, and still wonder, what he meant by that ambiguous statement. That true integrity cannot be taught? That he was an unworthy example of what he wanted me to be? That he may have intended to say the latter is suggested by a rather veiled confession he made to me later, on the way home, of something I had been suspecting for quite a while: he was in political disfavor. During the Hungarian uprising, he had published, in *Aufbau*, an ill-advised defense of a dissident Hungarian writer. Not long afterward, *Aufbau* was discontinued, supposedly because another journal, *Sinn und Form*, had effectively replaced it. The Party, he now told me, had been making impatient queries concerning the second volume of *Die Patrioten*, Bodo's projected trilogy about the anti-Nazi underground in Germany. "They have a right to demand that I finish the book," he said. "After all, I've been paid for it, and it's a promise I've made to my readers. For all they know, I'm either lazy or else I've got political problems, in which case I ought to discuss them with the Party. But it's not so easy. There are problems that can't be resolved by talking. The novel—it will just have to wait. Like so many things. But it hurts. I can't tell you how hard it is."

¶[Bodo's tolerance was put to the test by my prolonged fascination with Robert Musil, whose *The Man Without Qualities*, in the posthumous, postwar edition, is nearly

endless: I was rereading and annotating it for the third
time. "This is poison," Bodo said. "Read Stendhal. Read
Tolstoy. Read Balzac." But it was Musil who spoke to
my condition:

> He had trained himself to attend to minutiae: the slightest
> sounds in the walls, the conversations of furniture contracting
> in the cold of night, the heavy rugs of dusk and the delicate
> gray veils of dawn. And he longed for the woman who would
> transform these things into happiness and beauty—for that they
> were not.

He had written these words when he was my age.

Eavesdropping through the door of my room once, I
heard Valentin Birkelbach, the poet, defend me and
Musil against Bodo's vituperations. "Probably he's attracted to the style more than anything. You have to
admit he wrote some splendid prose." "Splendid, brilliant, yes," said Bodo, "the way things that rot start to
shine. It's all brilliance without healthy substance." "I
think there's some substance," Valentin said, "and a
healthy spirit of revolt as well. Certainly in *The Man
Without Qualities*. It's really an adventure book—philosophical adventure, but still—" "Yes, in the best Nietz-
schean tradition," Bodo interjected. "True," Valentin
said. "But young people are drawn to adventure, you
know that. When we were his age or maybe a little
older, we became revolutionaries. Adventure had something to do with that—along with more serious motives,
of course. Surely, Joel could be doing worse things than
reading Robert Musil." "It's poison," Bodo mumbled,
"pure poison." I could tell by his voice that he was
drunk. I burned with scorn. Bodo couldn't hold a candle
to Musil. Why couldn't he admit it? What the hell was
this poison he talked about? I thought about it for days.
Maybe what he really hated and perhaps envied was
Musil's explicit contempt for politics. "*It is moré difficult to write a novel than it is to govern an empire. It is*

also more important." Would Bodo ever have written anything so audaciously self-assertive? And hadn't his commitment to Communism become something of a trap for him as an artist? Ever since the Party had slapped his wrist, he had written nothing but prefaces, articles, reminiscences about dead friends, appreciations of the work of others.

There is a German proverb that likens a good conscience to a soft pillow. Ulrich, Musil's immoralist hero, inverted it: "*Schlechtes Gewissen ist ein sanftes Ruhekissen.*" A bad conscience is an easy pillow—I liked that. Ulrich was a useful alter ego. I liked to feel that I, too, was a Man Without Qualities, an enigma and a threat to right-thinking, civic-minded people. Like Ulrich, I was taking a vacation from life. Unlike him (though I chose not to dwell on the dissimilarities), I was no philosopher, no moral or mental superman; nor was there anything mystical in my withdrawal; nor was I a lover of beautiful, spectacularly articulate women. But I was free to do what I liked, and hence to like what I was doing. What luxury! Somewhere beneath that easy pillow, though, was a pea—the irritating knowledge that such ease could not go on forever, or even till next September, without some rude awakening.

The expected disturbance was not rude at all, and it came from a totally unexpected quarter. I was introduced to a girl. Her name was Michèle. I thought it suited her perfectly. She had long black hair, dark-brown, rather sad eyes with timid little glints of humor in them, pale, luminous skin, and a Viennese accent. She had just arrived from Vienna with her mother, who had recently married an old friend of Bodo's, a sculptor. I was asked to help her find her bearings in this new country, show her the sights of the city, keep her company, introduce her to other young people.

One of these was Wolfgang, a drama student with whom I had recently struck up a rather excessively intellectual friendship. Wolfgang liked Michèle as much as I did, so the three of us spent a lot of time together; and Wolfgang and I, hoping to impress Michèle, exchanged more witticisms and engaged in more abstruse polemics than ever. I don't think she understood much of this constant cerebration, or was even interested. But she felt flattered that we should be competing for her attention, and spurred us on by withholding or graciously supplying the appreciative smile we craved, according to her whim.

I fell in love with her, platonically; i.e., in a spirit so chaste and delicate as to be virtually disembodied. What enchanted me about her was an ineffable loveliness and goodness of which her slight and graceful figure seemed but a sign. There was something melancholy about her, and that made you want to make her smile. At times she even looked hurt, without there being any apparent cause; some trouble came over her like a shadow from within. I kept trying to think up ways to amuse her. There was a baker on Vinetastrasse who made cakes shaped like perfect little swans, filled with whipped cream and sprinkled with fine confectioners' sugar. These swans floated in decorous groups on top of a long pane of mirror glass on the counter, reflected as if on a lake. I took Michèle there. For a moment, her whole being seemed to light up with pleasure. Those swans were more successful than all the movies, museums, and theaters Wolfgang and I took her to.

One day it dawned on me: I was in love. I confided my feelings to Wolfgang. "You must tell *her*," he advised me earnestly. "There's no use telling *me*!" I couldn't do that. A declaration of love! She'd probably find it ridiculous, or embarrassing. And anyway, I loved her—what need was there to claim her affection as well? Let her love whom she pleased, it didn't concern me.

But when Wolfgang began seeing Michèle without me, this platonism vanished. My pride was wounded. I imagined the agreement they must have made: "Let's leave Joel out of this." "Yes, I'd much rather see you alone." "I hope the poor fellow doesn't take it too hard." "He'll survive it." I considered murdering Wolfgang. Peter told me they had spent a week in the country together. With a shock I recognized the important fact I had been ignoring: Michèle had a body! She had slept with him! It was almost inconceivable. I wasn't in the least attracted to her in a sensual way. My God, wasn't that why I had lost her? What kind of man was I? And what woman not sprung from the pages of the *Sittengeschichte* would want me?

In my journal, shortly after that, I underlined a quotation from a collection of American Indian poetry: "*Above my head I can hear the terrible sound of the wings of failure.*" I might have pinned this dreary motto to the wall above my desk, had I been able to count on complete privacy in my room. There was nothing I wished to avoid more than having to endure "serious talks" and concerned questions about my plans for the future. The future was a void, it made me dizzy to think about it. With last-chance desperation, I threw myself into work and study: poems, attempts at short stories, reams of pages covered with notes on physics and chemistry, anatomical sketches, exercises in literary description. I even kept my room neat. Now or never I would have to prove myself. Some of twelve-year-old Stefan's satirical sketches were circulating among Bodo's colleagues, and there was talk of publishing them. That would be unendurable! Peter was about to finish the twelfth grade, and had already secured a tentative acceptance at the film school in Babelsberg on the strength of a sketch for a scenario he had submitted to them; also, his affair with a married woman had made him the enviable object of rumors among our parents and their friends. Wolfgang would be co-directing a play at a major theater soon, and he hadn't even been required to finish high school—that's how superlatively gifted he was. Even Ralle had a job now. He was load-

ing trucks in a warehouse depot. Not that I envied him
that—but I seemed to have nothing with which to justify
my existence. And though, for the first time in my life, I
worked at my writing with something approaching professional dedication, the results were so shameful I
didn't even discard them in the wastebasket, for fear of
being judged by such drivel; every day I went down to
the cellar and burned my misbegotten brain children in
the furnace that fed our central heating system.

Several months later, on New Year's Eve, my parents
went to a party and I stayed home, fearing I might run
into Wolfgang and Michèle somewhere. Stefan was asleep.
I could hear our maid making love with her boyfriend
upstairs. I went outside, vaguely contemplating several
ways of killing myself. I lay down behind a bush by the
side of a field where some ruins had recently been cleared,
and stared at the moon. The city was celebrating, and I
felt immensely sorry for myself; but then I seemed to feel
nothing at all. Thinking of Michèle, I felt hatred for
her; but after nurturing that for a while, I felt numb
again. "You're just empty," I said to myself, "like a character in a book, full of words and make-believe emotions." And that rang true. Someone was running down
the street. I peeped through the leaves. It was a young
woman with her head tied up in a kerchief, running as
fast as she could and crying loudly. After she disappeared I went home to sleep.

On May 8, 1958, I received a long telegram from Jack
Burling, a friend of my father's:

LT-JOEL AGEE UHSE CARE REDACTEUR BODO UHSE KUCKHOFFSTRASSE
39B NIEDERSCHÖNHAUSEN BEI PANKOW BERLIN-
EVERY AMERICAN PAPER TODAY ANNOUNCES YOUR FATHER
POSTHUMOUSLY AWARDED PULITZER PRIZE THIS IS AMERICA'S MOST
ESTEEMED LITERARY PRIZE STOP I REMEMBER MY PERSONAL DEEP
EMOTION WHEN JIM READ SOME PASSAGES TO YOUR MOTHER AND
ME AND REMEMBER DOUBLE JUDGMENT COLON AS ALWAYS COMMA

YOUR FATHERS READINGS INCREDIBLY BEAUTIFUL SEMICOLON
PASSAGE ENTITLED KNOXVILLE ONE OF MASTERPIECES OUR MOTHER
TONGUE STOP AS ONE WHO KNEW AND LOVED JIM AND REGARDED
HIM AS A TRUE GENIUS AND WHO KNEW YOU BEFORE YOUR
RECOLLECTION COMMENCES FEEL WITH SON WHOSE DEAD FATHER HAS
WON PRIZE FOR LITERATURE HIGHEST POSSIBLE WITHIN AMERICA'S
GIFT BUT ALSO ASK YOU TO SYMPATHIZE WITH ME BOTTOMLESS SENSE
GRIEF JIM NOT HERE STOP BY PURE COINCIDENCE HAVE FOUND
NEGATIVES SEVERAL PHOTOGRAPHS I TOOK OF JIM PLUS ONE OR TWO
OF MOTHER AND OF HOUSE WHEREIN YOU WERE PERHAPS CONCEIVED
STOP SENDING YOU SAME IN ANY SOCIAL SYSTEM COMMA NATION
COMMA OR CULTURE A SON MAY BE PROUD OF HIS OWN FATHER
PERIOD SURELY YOU ARE TODAY ENTITLED BE PROUD OF FACT YOU
COMMA JOEL COMMA ARE FIRST BORN SON ONLY MAN EVER RECEIVED
AMERICAS HIGHEST LITERARY AWARD POSTHUMOUSLY PERIOD REPEAT
AM PROUD JIM MY FRIEND HOPE YOU PROUD JIM YOUR FATHER-
JACK BURLING 24 GRAMERCY PARK NEW YORK+24+

No, I didn't feel proud. I couldn't even conceive of what it meant to be proud of someone else's achievement. Glad for them, yes—but proud? Why did he call me Joel Agee Uhse and not Joel Uhse, the name he surely knew I had adopted since coming to Germany, and which was printed in my identity papers? What was he implying when he spoke of the "double judgment" of my father's reading of "Knoxville," "one of masterpieces our mother tongue"? Did he mean that Alma's judgment had been insensitive, stupid, or even perverse? And what was this stuff about "in any social system, nation, or culture a son may be proud of his own father"? If I read between the lines, I thought I could decipher a rather pointed message: "Your father is American, and so are you. You should be proud of him. Your mother should never have left him, but then she didn't know any better. And she certainly shouldn't have taken you to a Communist country. Your name is Agee. Your roots are in America."

I told Alma and Bodo I didn't intend to answer the

telegram. She said that would be very unkind of me; it had obviously been sent in good faith and with an open heart, and deserved an answer.

"What should I tell him?"

"Tell him you're happy and proud."

"But I'm not."

"Sometimes it's best to lie," Bodo said. "And who knows, maybe someday today's lie will be the truth."

I went to the telegraph office and sent off the following message:

JACK BURLING 24 GRAMERCY PARK NEW YORK
VERY HAPPY VERY PROUD MY FATHER GRATEFUL TO YOU STOP
LETTER FOLLOWS JOEL

⟨[I felt ashamed of myself as I walked home from the telegraph office. Not for lying so much as for betraying my own feelings. Wasn't Bodo my father in a much more real sense than Jim ever was? Hadn't I hurt him? It was hard to tell, he so rarely showed what he felt. He had even encouraged me to answer the telegram. Maybe he really didn't care whether I thought of him as my father or not. Maybe he didn't really love me. It was hard to tell.

As if he had read my thoughts—maybe he read my journal—Bodo asked me, just two weeks later, if I wanted to accompany him to Hiddensee, a resort on the Baltic Sea where he was planning to write a film script. He requested, flatteringly enough, that I help him, at least with the typing, maybe even in the composition of it. Just he and I would go; Alma and Stefan would stay in Berlin.

We had the place pretty much to ourselves—the empty hotel, the stone beach, the hundreds of vacant beach chairs, the weird windswept trees, the sun, moon, and stars. I still have three photographs I took of Bodo.

In one, he is musing over a glass of beer; in the second, gazing with fondness at a plump, dappled horse cantering across the dunes; in the third, aching over some half-completed sentence while his cigarette smolders in an ashtray before him. We usually spent the morning hours working on the scenario. My contribution turned out to be mostly secretarial; I typed while he dictated, drank, pondered, and occasionally groaned with frustration. I had never realized what an agony writing was for him. By the time we were called for lunch, he looked about ten years older. Maybe his subject matter had something to do with it: old Käthe Kollwitz sketching a portrait of the murdered Karl Liebknecht, surrounded by mourning workers, in a morgue.

After lunch (just the two of us, on a terrace, in the first warmth of the year) we'd go to the beach, I with my camera, he with his writing stuff and several bottles of beer, which he'd bury in wet sand to keep them cool. It was too cold to swim. How peaceful and how remote were those long afternoons.

"I feel we've gotten closer," he said. "I realize how much better Alma understands you, and how distant from you I tend to be. I'm so glad you came here with me."

At times when Bodo was working and did not require my assistance, I sat in my room sketching, or reading *War and Peace* (to Bodo's pleasure, no doubt), or went for walks on the beach, taking photographs and filling my notebook with metaphysical ponderings—for example: Can and will there ever be a "kingdom of heaven on earth," and what would that be like, and what would be the preconditions for it? Any Marxist reading my notebook would have recognized me as a dyed-in-the-wool Subjective Idealist. But I was convinced I had found a link between socialist theory and Messianic prophecy, and dreamed of establishing the possibility and the Necessity (*vide* Herr Bender) of their practical (which is to say, materialist) fusion someday. The flush

of creativity must have shown in my face, for Bodo remarked at breakfast early one morning: "Your eyes have
become brighter, you know? More blue, more bright.
The way they were when you were little." I remember
how moved I was when he said that—as if I were a child
again, living without care and without guilt, knowing
myself the secure possessor of my parents' love, and
thinking myself the very source and object of their greatest pleasure.

A strange pair wafted into our life like a transient
southern breeze: a fat, expansively gesturing, dark-
skinned man with a white Nehru cap, and a beautiful
girl who seemed to have materialized from my most
exotic fantasies—a gold-olive, perfectly oval face, large
black eyes under highly arched brows, a red dot at the
center of her forehead, lips of a bluish shade and
shaped like segments of an orange, high full breasts
gathered up in a sari. I had just recently found consola-
tion for my seemingly irremediable shyness in Tolstoy's
description of the fright that seized Pierre Bezukhov
when he came face to face with a beautiful woman.
Now I felt that I knew what he meant.

Her name was Kamala; her father's, Mahmoud. (I
had thought they were married at first.) Mahmoud was
a poet whom Bodo had met at a PEN conference in
Tokyo. They could only stay for a day, Mahmoud said
regretfully; they had to go on to Karl-Marx-Stadt, where
Kamala would be going to school. The awesome fact
then emerged: this stunning creature was only fifteen
years old. Bodo and I expressed our surprise and, I
think, our admiration as well, for Kamala flashed a gratified smile and lowered her eyes, while her father smiled
down at her warmly with his entire face, including his
several chins. Gradually, as the four of us walked together on the beach, I adjusted to the fact of her age,
but it took some effort, like trying to see past a persistent optical illusion. In the evening, after dinner, Kamala
and I played Parcheesi, and she rolled the dice with a gig-

gling enthusiasm that would not have been at all becoming in a lady. That helped.

By the next day I felt more at ease with her. She still looked beautiful, but she had replaced her sari with slacks and a thick woolen sweater, and maybe that removed the veil of glamour. I liked her very much. I had never known anyone so easy to amuse. The slightest joke and she'd squeal with laughter, clapping her hands together. Bodo and Mahmoud were glad to see us getting along so well (though Mahmoud looked just a bit wary). They walked off discussing some literary topic while Kamala and I sat in a beach chair and talked (in English, since she didn't speak a word of German). I was worried at first that I might have to keep entertaining her all day and would run out of things to say, but she cheerfully took charge of the conversation, chattering almost without pause in her liltingly clipped Indian accent. Eventually she became quite serious. She said she hated India, everything was so backward there and so many people were hypocritical and stuffy, especially if they were well off. Her father used to go to the outskirts of the city where they lived and do the work of the untouchables, cleaning latrines and burning the dead, and he'd have reporters photograph him doing so, not to make himself important, but to destroy the authority of the caste system. Also, he'd arrange for untouchable children to go to school. But he had to stop because the great landlords kept beating him up, and beating the people he wanted to help as well. "My father always says tradition is like the summer monsoon," she said. "It keeps coming back to wash away everything new. Rain is good, but too much rain is destructive. My father says you have to build the new world with machines, use machines against the old world, the old habits and the old beliefs, then the rain does no harm. That's why I'm going to be an engineer. First I'll learn German and finish high school, and then I'll study engineering. That way I can serve my country. What are *you* going to do?"

The innocent aggression in that question unbalanced me. I said the first thing that came to mind: "I'm going to be a poet." I was surprised by my own words. What an insubstantial vocation that was, compared to engineering.

"Really?" She seemed delighted. Of course: it was her father's profession. Now I felt like an impostor.

Later, at the dinner table, Kamala said: "Daddy, you know, Joel is a poet, too." "I thought so," Mahmoud said, and smiled at me. I have never received more generous recognition from anyone.

I was impressed by Kamala. I thought she was very intelligent and sensitive, and so much more mature than I had been at fifteen. And at the same time so beautiful. I imagined us falling in love and eventually marrying, maybe after a few years of pre-conjugal bliss. I would be twenty-one, a pipe-smoking poet widely regarded as "promising," and she would be eighteen, learning to build bridges or irrigation dams by day and making passionate love with me at night. Wolfgang and Michèle would be separating when we got married. She would be sorry and he would be envious. Every man in Berlin would be envious.

After dinner, we all drank hot punch and played Parcheesi at the card table in the lounge near a crackling wood stove. Kamala was losing and started to yawn. There was a storm outside. The rafters creaked and the wind flew howling around the hotel. Once in a while there was a distant roll of thunder. Kamala and I went to the window to watch the spectacle. Her breath fogged the glass. She wrote on it with her finger, in small letters: "You and I, I and you." Then she wiped away the words. I spent the next five minutes considering that extraordinary statement. Was it addressed to me, or to no one in particular, like the arrow-pierced hearts

young girls like to draw, containing their initials, a plus
sign, and a question mark representing an unknown future lover? After a while she turned around and I followed her back to where Bodo and Mahmoud were
engaged in an animated and rather silly argument about
how long a book should be. Mahmoud's opinion was
that the novels of old were written for people of the
leisure class, and hence could afford to be long; but the
contemporary novel, particularly the contemporary *socialist* novel, written for people who work at least eight
hours a day five or six days a week, ought to be short,
short, short. I personally thought he was full of beans
on this subject and had to restrain myself from hotly
championing the irreducible merits of mammoth books
like *War and Peace*. (I wouldn't have mentioned *The
Man Without Qualities*.) Bodo wagged his head amica-
bly and conceded that maybe Mahmoud had a point.
"However," he said, raising a finger, "once technology
shortens the workday . . ." "Absolutely!" Mahmoud interjected with enthusiasm. "Once we have Communism,
we will sit down and write vast entertainments for the
masses. You will write ten-volume epics like Roger Mar-
tin du Gard. I will write endless sagas like the Rama-
yana. And then we will get together with friends from
all over the world and write a whole series of *enormous*
bibles, the holy writ of liberated humanity." "Unless the
filmmakers steal our audience," Bodo mumbled. Kamala
tugged at my sleeve: "Let's go to the veranda and look
at the sea." As we started to walk out of the room,
Mahmoud said: "Kamala. Don't stay up too late. We're
leaving early in the morning." She smiled her most radiant smile and raised her palm—as a sign of fealty, I
suppose. Mahmoud had that wary look in his eyes again.

It was quite dark outside now, and the lights were out
on the veranda. Through the rain-streaked windows we
could barely distinguish the dunes, and beyond them
the beach and the sea. The wind had toppled several
beach chairs; we could see their hunched shapes in the

light of the moon whenever it rolled out through a hole in the wildly churning clouds.

Kamala displayed a fear of thunder that hadn't been evident when we were standing by the window in the lounge. Each time a distant flash of lightning lit up the sky, she would grip my arm in anticipation of the clap of thunder that would follow. She said there were terrible storms where she had grown up, several thunderclaps a minute sometimes, and she used to think God was angry at the world when it happened. I told her I used to think God was moving heavy furniture in the sky. She laughed. Suddenly a magnificent branch of lightning ripped open the darkness, holding the dunes and the crooked pines in its fantastical glare for several seconds, and then there was darkness again, and then something happened that isn't supposed to happen in life because it has happened so often in movies and books: a violent crash of thunder sent Kamala flying into my arms with a shriek. There she stood with her head pressed against my chest and her arms clasped tightly around me. I stroked her hair in a "there, there" sort of fashion, powerfully aroused and gulping with anxiety. As the thunder withdrew with a long diminishing grumble, she loosened her embrace and looked up at me with a face that, if I was not completely self-deceived, was asking to be kissed. Once again, a series of inhibiting considerations paralyzed the impulse to respond: what if I was mistaken and Kamala shrank back in surprise? Maybe she was simply frightened and clung to me for protection—just that? She was only a child, despite her exquisite mouth. "It's all right," I said, woodenly patting her back, "there's no real danger." "I know," she said, and leaned her head against my chest. The thought of Mahmoud floated in, a straw to clutch at: what if he walked in now with that suspicious look in his eyes and all the kindness draining out of his face, leaving only disappointment and anger? "I think we should go back," I said, gently disengaging her arms, which were still wrapped around me. I tried to feel virtuous and mature as I escorted her back to the lounge, where Bodo and Mahmoud sat chatting and drinking. Mahmoud looked up and stroked Kamala's cheek with the back of his hand. "You look tired, dear," he said. To me she looked sad. After we had all gone to bed, I lay awake in my room conducting a merciless trial. I was a coward, no question about that. I didn't deserve to be given another opportunity like that one. Shoot him, drive a lance through his stupid face. Squash him. Throw him away.

A small thin voice intervened in my defense. There's still time, it said, all is not lost, her room's just a flight of stairs away, you can make love to her before the night's over. I leaped up and paced the room with clenched fists. *All is not lost*—I kept muttering that, trying to silence the chorus of mocking and dooming voices; and: *I'll do it . . . I'll do it . . . I'll do it . . .* Mercifully, the prosecution fell silent. I, too, became quiet. The trial was adjourned. I sat down. I planned, I prepared myself. Two o'clock, I decided, would be the most propitious time. A shower seemed called for. A change of pajamas could do no harm. I lit a candle, sat and observed the minute hand of my watch, listened to the withdrawing thunderstorm, the stiff rain, the whiplash flurries rattling the windows. Promptly at two o'clock I left my room and climbed the winding staircase, so quietly I could hear my ankles crack like snapping twigs. There were Mahmoud's casually splayed, boatlike shoes in front of his door, and there were Kamala's much smaller, parallel shoes facing his from across the hallway. Other people had put out their shoes, too: men's shoes, women's shoes, matrimonial shoe-couples with small lacquered offspring, all waiting to be cleaned by an early-rising maid. I put my ear to Kamala's door: not a sound, only the drumming of rain on the roof and the distant patient breathing of the surf. I don't know how long I stood there with my heart in my throat and my red pajamas pyramidally distended. Eventually I pushed

down the handle. The door was warped and opened with
a blunt scrape.

There she lay with her face turned toward me, one
naked arm and shoulder dark against the white featherbed. An alarm clock ticked on the night table. I shut
the door. The room was almost dark now, but as I
slowly approached the bed, my eyes began to distinguish again the glow of the featherbed, and the darker
glow of Kamala's long arm and round shoulder, and the
two thick brushstrokes of ink-black hair framing her
face. Very cautiously, I sat down on the bed and put a
hand on her shoulder. Her skin was cool. My heart was
pounding like a fist on a door, so loudly it seemed she
must hear it. I shook her. She didn't move. I shook
again. She worked her jaws, making sucking sounds,
like a baby. I shook harder now, insistingly, urgently.
Her eyes opened, blinked, and, to my dismay, shut
again. Then she opened them very wide. She sat up
with a start, pulling up the blanket to cover herself. My
heart fell. Then her arms were around my neck. I kissed
her with the passion of desperation, her mouth, neck,
breasts, while she pulled at the hair on my head with
both hands. We sank back into the pillows. I pulled off
the blanket. She was naked. I tried to reach between
her legs. She gripped my wrist, breathing in deep gasps.
We struggled. Remembering Anita, I relented. She put
my hand to her breast. I forced my tongue into her
mouth, tried to pry open her locked thighs with a knee.
She shook her head. She looked frightened and hurt. I
rolled off her and lay on my back, eyes shut, mentally
murdering myself with half a dozen devices at once.
Tenderly, kindly, Kamala stroked my cheek with her
fingers; and then she brushed several figure eights on my
chest with her palm, and touched her lips down upon
mine—whether to console me or to apologize or to make
sure I didn't turn cold I don't know, but the instantaneous
effect was to fan the diminishing flame to such vehement
ardor that she felt constrained to bite me, and threatened

to scream. Again we fell apart, and again she recalled me, this time with the most carefully chaste inducements. And then the whole struggle started again—more gently, though, now, on my part, and more yieldingly on hers. Hours later, in the first rosy glimmer of dawn (a maid was suppressing a cough in the hallway and picking up shoes), my hand, still fettered tightly at the wrist, was permitted a briefly lingering fingertip touch of the warm, soft, moist goal of all my striving, and was exiled again. And then (why hadn't I thought of this before?) she let me guide *her* hand to cautiously grasp and uphold my penis, like a scepter, like a magic wand; and thus we sat for a brief eternity, mouth to mouth, in trance-like communion, already torn by time, which was announcing itself in the muted din of kitchen sounds and of a creaking dumbwaiter. Mahmoud would be getting up any moment, would perhaps knock on her door . . . come into her room? We were almost immobile, except for a fine rapid tremor that shook both our bodies. "I have to go," I said. She nodded, and let go of me, again cautiously, as if releasing a bird. I reached my room undetected. Very shortly after, Bodo knocked on my door to wake me.

A taxi took the four of us to the station. Bodo sat in front with the driver. Kamala and I sat in the back, with Mahmoud between us. The train was already in the station. Mahmoud and Kamala took their bags into their compartments and came back out onto the platform to say goodbye. The stationmaster ordered the passengers to board the train. Mahmoud and Bodo embraced, clapping each other's back. Then Mahmoud shook my hand and told me to keep making good poetry. Then Bodo took Kamala's hand and patted it. Then Kamala stepped up to me, put her palms together before her breast, and made a small bow, looking into my eyes. It felt as if she had offered me her heart. Impulsively, I put a hand on my heart as I said goodbye. Then they got into the train, and were moving into the distance a few moments later, leaning out the window and waving. Bodo and I waved, too. Soundlessly, I called after her, hoping there really was such a thing as telepathy: *Kamala! Don't forget me! I love you!* For days after, I drifted about in a kind of delirium, like a desert traveler following a mirage. Having discovered her scent on my fingers, I treasured it, taking care not to wash it away, until it faded. Bodo impatiently urged me to return to work on the scenario—he needed my help, he said. Old age, martyrdom, bereavement, the gray light of the morgue, the scratching sound of charcoal paying homage to a corpse—what a dreary movie this was going to be! But it helped keep my mind off Kamala, and gave me a sense of importance. Several times I made suggestions which Bodo found valuable. Maybe I could even get my name into the credits. That would be a step in the direction of a profession, a beginning at least.

¶[And then Frau Meissner arrived, and Bodo began to lose interest in Käthe Kollwitz and the morgue. Though tired and evidently in need of a vacation, Frau Meissner was a good-looking woman. She and Bodo began taking long walks together, and I did my best to entertain myself. Bodo apologized to me: "I hope you understand this. Luise and I have grown fond of each other. She's been having a very difficult time with her husband, you know—and she loves me, and I feel much love for her also. I am very happy." I nodded. Through the window we could see the dappled horse scaring up some gulls. When I looked at Bodo again, I could see that he really was happy. I had never seen him look so serene and content. "You must be wondering about Alma," he said. "Don't worry about it. Alma and I are very good friends, *old* friends. We understand one another well. Don't trouble your mind with it, she'll understand." He stroked

my forehead, as if to wipe the worry off it. But I knew
that he wasn't being honest, with me or with himself,
and I suspected that Alma would not "understand."

More convincing than Bodo's words was the brevity
of Frau Meissner's stay—a mere week's episode against
sixteen years of marriage. Also, I thought I noticed that
Bodo was relieved when she left (to confer with a law-
yer about her divorce). Or was it some kind of afterglow? He talked more gaily and lightly than usual,
about all kinds of things, and didn't hedge his opinions
so much. Once, at dinnertime, between a gulp of sauer-
braten and a sip of beer, he cheerfully informed me of
something that concerned me deeply, and that, for reasons I couldn't even guess at, he had chosen to withhold
until then: "Incidentally, there's something I forgot to
tell you. Mahmoud told me Kamala liked you very much.
So did Mahmoud. Actually, I believe Kamala developed
a crush on you. Anyway, we made a tentative agreement
that she will spend her Christmas vacation at our house. I
hope that's all right with you."

"Oh, of course, of course." All was not lost! Next time,
I swore, I would seize the moment, or die!

I had the good sense to divulge nothing to Alma of
Frau Meissner's presence in Hiddensee; but, by whatever channel—an informer, an accidental or deliberate
confession on Bodo's part, a revealing encounter with
the fatal lady herself—the news did reach her.

Probably it happened during the summer, while we
were in Ahrenshoop, because that's where Alma and
Bodo started fighting again—grief, rage, accusations,
impotent rejoinders, cold intervals of silent hatred. I
tried to regard it as simply a revival of similar fights
they'd had in recent years, or of that night long ago, in
Mexico, when they came home late from a party and
Bodo sat down on my bed, waking me up, and took off
his shoes and threw them angrily against the wall, and

Alma stood watching him with that same fierce look of unforgiving scorn; then he'd broken a window and cut his hand, and Alma, seeing that I was sorry for him and afraid, stopped hating him, and told me, crying, and wiping away my tears with the blanket, that everything was all right and that Bodo had had too much to drink and that they loved each other even though she was mad at him for something he'd done; and then Bodo lurched in our direction with his hair hanging in his face, and put his arms around both of us clumsily and kissed my forehead and then walked out; and the next day they were friends again, and Bodo told me he was sorry. But this time was different. Alma had never been angry at Bodo for so long or with such intensity.

Bodo didn't fight back, mainly because he was in the wrong, but from time to time he'd remonstrate in a tone of strained reasonableness, objecting to some exaggeration or bringing up some small point in his defense, and invariably this would set off an intensified wave of recriminations. Once, in the beginning, he made the mistake of trying to console and pacify her, but this he never repeated, at least not while I was within earshot.

During the day, for Stefan's sake, Alma would do her best to throttle at least the vocal expression of her feelings; but at night, when Stefan was asleep and I lay awake in a room separated from Alma and Bodo's by just a thin wall, the fight would resume—always the same revolving pattern: brief hot bursts of fury followed by long spells of cold sullen scorn, on and on, a relentless ebb and flow which Bodo tried to weather with endurance and patience, like one of those wind-buffeted trees on the beach. This attitude of stoic suffering made her more angry, since the injury under discussion was hers and not his. Her attacks, as a consequence, became swifter, more accurate and terrible. After several days of this punishment, Bodo began to look punch-drunk (though maybe he was just drunk), and Alma's nerves were worn down to a state of hair-trigger irritability. Just how brittle she was, none of us knew until Sunday, August 24. I began to record that day's turbulent events the same evening, with the scrupulous fidelity of a plaintiff submitting his grievance to a fair-minded court of the future. A second installment followed the next day, a third and fourth the week after. And then a revision to make sure I wasn't loading the dice with resentment. Little by little, in the steady spotlight of objectivity, the first person singular became a character, my feelings and actions those of another; and what began as a report came to resemble a one-act play, divided into two scenes.

I

[*Bodo is the first to climb the dune. He sees storm clouds piling up on the horizon,* and a gray sheet of slanting rain in the west. He turns to say something to Alma (with a characteristic expression of doubt and worry on his face), but she trudges past him with long steps and lowered head. Joel and Stefan follow her without speaking. Because she is walking in thick dry sand, her progress is slow, and her sons, who are keeping to the hard-packed wet sand near the water, eventually pass her and walk ahead. There is some distance between them, but not as great as that between Alma and Bodo. Alma is carrying a large towel and Stefan another; Bodo is carrying his briefcase and a red-and-white ball; Joel is carrying a large beach bag and a folded inflatable rubber raft.*

They arrive at their burg, spread towels on the sand and settle down. It is too cold to get undressed, so they keep their bathrobes on.]

ALMA. Does anyone want a pear?

[*No answer. Alma sighs for the six-hundred-and-forty-third time since she got up this morning. Joel is irritated because he*

---

* I ask the critical reader's indulgence for the repeated intrusion of thunder and lightning at dramatically significant moments in this book. Since I invented neither these moments nor the dubious effects that accompanied them, I plead innocence.

_has the impression that Alma wants to remind everyone with
her sighs that she is "low" and not to be consoled._]

ALMA. Does anyone feel like blowing the raft up for me?

JOEL. I will.

[_The rubber raft is made of three parts, each of which must be
inflated and stoppled. Somebody—not Joel—has knotted together
the strings that keep the three stopples attached to the raft.
Joel sets about disentangling them._]

STEFAN [_possibly envious of Joel's healthy lungs_]. Don't stick
the stopples in too far, they're always so hard to pull out.

JOEL [_irritated_]. Yes, yes.

[_Conscious of his tendency to be careless and unobservant of
practical matters, he reacts with exaggerated sensitivity to criticism and instructions, and even to well-intentioned advice._

_He blows up one section of the rubber raft and pushes the
stopple in._]

STEFAN. Don't push it in too far!

JOEL [_angrily_]. All right!

ALMA. Why are you so irritable?

JOEL. Why am _I_ so irritable?

ALMA. Yes.

JOEL. Because everyone's _hacking_ at me!

[_He immediately regrets this reply, for the reason that it is
inaccurate and ridiculous and because it fails to express what
he actually wanted to say: namely, that he knows very well how
to inflate the rubber raft, much better, in fact, than Alma and
Bodo, and that therefore remarks such as Stefan's are super-
fluous._]

ALMA [_shaking her head_]. Nobody's _hacking_ at you.

JOEL [_with passionate conviction_]. Well, _you_ most of _all!_

[_Who is this addressed to? Not Alma, or not the Alma of
present-time, surface reality—she doesn't comprehend it any
more than Joel does. Someone else responds in her place and in
her body, with a face that is not hers and with a gesture that
appears to be moving slowly through time as if through a thick
fluid, even though the physical motion is swift; a gesture that
is the repetition of several instances, separated by years, of this
same gesture begun and held back, begun and aborted again._

This time it is completed. Her upper lip is raised to reveal the incisors. Her eyes bulge and stare. She rises to her knees. She throws back her arm in the clumsy manner of an unathletic girl throwing a ball, and strikes. Joel pulls back his head and throws up his hands for protection. Her fist—not the flat open palm he expected—hits him in the mouth. In a moment of blinding rage, he knows he will hit back with all the strength he has, but unable to aim at her face, he closes his eyes and, with a moan, strikes against her retreating body. Bodo comes lunging toward him with contorted features. Joel, thinking he is about to be punished for striking his mother, turns his face away and, overwhelmed with loneliness and self-pity, begins to cry. Bodo sits down next to him, embraces him tightly. Joel buries his face in Bodo's lap and cries loudly, like a child, and with such abandon that a pleasant sense of release is mingling with his sorrow. The tears running across his nose and cheeks exude a consoling warmth, as does Bodo's hand stroking the back of his head. Now Alma, too, is weeping, and Joel notices that he is glad; that he is hoping that each sob and sigh shuddering out of his breast will stab her right through the heart and repay the blow she dealt him at least threefold. He notices this, feels ashamed of it, condemns himself for it, tells himself that she is suffering a hundred times more than he is; yet he feels powerless to control this craving for revenge that is finding such a convenient weapon in the mechanisms of grief, guilt, and pity.]

ALMA [*sobbing*]. I didn't . . . I didn't want to . . . hit in the face . . . I *swear* I didn't.

BODO [*very quietly*]. I know. I know. It's all right. I know.

    [*With a great effort of will, Joel suppresses a new upwelling of sobs. Alma continues to weep quietly. Joel's nose is stuffed. Bodo pulls a handkerchief from the pocket of his bathrobe and hands it to him. Without raising his head from Bodo's lap or opening his wet eyes, Joel blows his nose, and it feels as if he is expelling the pain, the confusion, the hate, the shame. Sadness remains, and a warm childish feeling of safety in Bodo's arms, and shyness of the moment when he will have to open*

*his eyes. Then it is very still. Alma is no longer crying. Bodo
is breathing quietly, evenly, as if in sleep.*]

BODO [*squeezing Joel's shoulder and leaning over to speak
into his ear*]. Come on; let's take a walk.

[*Joel opens his eyes and gets up. It's not so bad. Alma is
sitting on her towel, tightly hugging her knees, her head bent
low so that her face is hidden behind them. Stefan sits next to
her with averted face, serious and silent, and very lightly strokes
the sand with his fingers. Bodo and Joel walk off together.*

*It is windy. The tide is running far beyond the narrow strip
of seaweed and stones that ordinarily marks its limit. Joel is
glad the beach is almost empty; he is ashamed of his red, tear-
stained face. From time to time he is shaken by deep shuddering
sighs. Bodo lays an arm across his shoulders. Near the edge
of the water stands a small group of people: three gentlemen
dressed in their Sunday best—their hair, neckties, and jackets
flapping in the wind—and a naked, thickset girl with curly blond
hair. One of the gentlemen holds a Contax to his eye, and the
girl, who is shivering in the cold, smiles and lifts a triangular
piece of cloth high above her head. The cloth makes a vigorous
attempt to fly away, but is held in place by her fleshy, grace-
fully bent hand. The two gentlemen standing next to the photo-
grapher squint in mystical participation with the index finger
that is about to release the shutter; and as soon as the picture is
taken, they burst into exuberant and vocal applause.*]

BODO [*shaking his head and laughing*]. Awful!

[*Joel laughs briefly. It hurts. They keep walking. Occasionally
a large breaker crashes and casts a wide net of cold swirling
water around their naked feet. They pass a muscle-packed young
man in an outsized bathing suit who is about to perform the
shotput in Olympic style. A large, heavy-looking round stone,
cupped in his right palm, lies pressed against his cheek. The
elbow juts out at a 45-degree angle. The torso turns and twists
to the right. The left knee swings up and to the right like a
baseball pitcher's. Now the whole body is tensed for the light-
ning-swift thrust that will propel the rock—how far? The mighty
spring uncoils, accompanied by an intense grunt. A leap and a*

push—and it is astonishing to behold the flight of the stone, for it drops with a soft thud almost immediately after leaving his hand, no more than five meters from where he stands.]

BODO [*laughing*]. He's no champion.

[*Joel, too, laughs, but unwillingly this time. He laughs so as not to be rude, and again it hurts to hear and feel himself laughing. Moreover, it sounds false. Perhaps Bodo notices that, for they walk on for a long time without talking.*]

II

[*Apologies have been made, and words of forgiveness have been spoken, and the words have received the consent of the inmost heart; grudgingly at first, but then with complete generosity. Joel has forgiven Alma, she has forgiven him. They have embraced and wept together. Between Stefan and Joel, no healing words or gestures were needed, their little altercation is long forgotten.*

But Alma and Bodo remain unreconciled, and as they all drive home—Alma at the wheel, Bodo beside her, Stefan and Joel in the back—there is an almost tangible feeling of cold coming from that separateness, that chasm that has opened up where just a short while ago there was trust and friendship. It is only five o'clock, but the sky is so overcast it looks like nightfall. The wind is flattening the dune grass by the side of the road. The car stops at the place where it usually slows down before cautiously bumping across the railroad tracks that traverse the dirt road. A chain of boxcars is blocking the way. Nothing to do except leave the road and cross the tracks somewhere else. But they are not passable anywhere. In one place, there's a depression filled with thick sand; in another, a fence stands in the way; in a third, the tracks are too high off the ground.

Alma tries driving through the sand. The wheels whirl, the car slides and swivels. They are stuck. What now? Bodo points out a pile of boards next to a wooden shack at some distance from the tracks. Alma sends Joel to fetch a board. An elderly man steps out of the shack as Joel approaches.]

JOEL. Excuse me. May I borrow a board to help us get out of the sand?

OLD MAN [*shaking his head*]. No. This is *Volkseigentum*, the people's property.

JOEL. I'll bring it back right away.

OLD MAN. You can't have it. It's forbidden.

[*Joel returns to the car and reports what the man said.*]

ALMA. Did you tell him we're stuck?

JOEL. I told him. He says he can't help us. He must be a guard.

BODO. I'll talk to him.

[*He gets out of the car and walks up to the watchman and the pile of boards. It is beginning to rain. Alma starts the motor and sets the windshield wipers in motion. Through the window, Joel, Stefan, and Alma watch Bodo trying to persuade the guard and the guard shaking his head. Bodo reaches for his wallet; the guard vigorously shakes his head and thrusts his palm out vertically, in a forbidding gesture.*]

STEFAN [*fascinated*]. He won't budge!

ALMA. Why not? He *knows* we need it!

JOEL. He's got his instructions. He's a man of honor.

[*Alma is abruptly shaken by sobs. She covers her face with her hands. Then she sits up very straight and resolutely wipes her eyes with the sleeve of her bathrobe. Bodo continues to reason with the watchman, who is obviously discomfited by the rain and wants to go back inside the shack.*]

ALMA [*shaking her head slowly*]. Oh, how I hate this country.

[*Now the watchman, with a shrug and a final shaking of the head, turns around and enters the shack and closes the door, and Bodo comes back toward us. The rain comes down hard now. Alma leaps out of the car, slamming the door, and starts walking swiftly toward the boards. Bodo tries to stop her. She pushes him aside, stumbles, catches her balance, keeps walking, reaches the stack, and is about to pull off a board when the watchman dashes out of the shack shouting and waving his hands as if trying to scare away a flock of birds. Alma starts dragging away the board by one end. The man seizes the other end, yanks the board out of Alma's hands, and turns back to put it neatly in place on the pile. Meanwhile, Alma has grabbed*]

*another board and is hurrying off with it. The man again
hastens to take it away from her. A tug-of-war ensues; Alma
wins it. The old man staggers backward, waving his arms for
balance. Bodo is hurrying in their direction. There is a thunderclap at some distance, followed by a flash. Joel steps out of the
car, hoping he won't have to intervene in a physical fight
between his parents and the old man, who has again seized
hold of the board. He looks frightened. Alma yanks the board
out of his hand and swings it around, trying to hit him with the
flat side of it. She misses him. His cap falls off. He has short-
cropped white hair. Alma stalks past Bodo, dragging the board
behind her, her hair and the hem of her robe flying in the wind.
The old man no longer tries to stop her, he just shouts, more
imploringly than angrily.*]

OLD MAN. Stop! Don't do this! Give it back! It's Volkseigentum! This is forbidden!

[*Alma throws the board under the car, bends down to push
it against the back wheels, gets in the car, slams the door, starts
the car. The back wheels grip the board, the car rolls out of
the sand pit, bumps roughly over the tracks, and stops next to
Bodo, who is standing next to the old man. Alma throws open
the door for him, and he gets in, dripping wet. As they drive
home, the thunderstorm breaks out in earnest.*]

JOEL. I think we should have put the board back on the pile.

ALMA. I don't think that man deserves the slightest consideration
from us.

BODO. He meant us no harm. He was only trying to do his job.
Don't you see, he was under orders—

ALMA [*whirling her head around at him*]. That's right! Just like
those obedient butchers who built the concentration camps and
trampled down half of Europe! "*Arbeit macht frei!*"

[*In splendid and uncanny synchronicity with Alma's fury,
there is an ear-rending thunderclap. Alma jams her foot down
on the gas pedal. The windshield wipers are fighting a losing
battle against thick sheets of rain thrown against the window
as if from buckets. Blurred forms of fences, trees, cows, straw-
thatched peasant houses fly past. The storm points a wild*

*uncertain finger of light at some nearby target, and another
at a more distant place.*]

After we returned to Berlin, Bodo broke off all contact with Frau Meissner, definitively—and, it seemed,
to Alma's satisfaction. Alma told me that she was too
hurt to be able to forgive Bodo fully, just yet—though
she wanted to. It would take time. But at least there
were no more eruptions, either by day or by night. Possibly Stefan's aggravated asthma helped induce our
parents to make peace; they couldn't have failed to realize that there was a connection between his suffering and
the emotional climate at home.

[On September 1, 1958, I arrived a prudent half hour
early at the Ernst Thaelmann trade school for masons.
Some fifteen other boys and one girl made up the rest of
the class. One of these boys was Ralle (who came a half
hour late). Herr Jadrzewski, the master, introduced
himself to his new apprentices. He had been working at
this craft for more than thirty years, he said. It was a
good craft, an honorable profession ("as are all profes-
sions," he added), and one for which there would continue to be a need, even though prefabricated construction units were being used ever more frequently. "We
have a housing shortage," he said, "and fast construction is necessary. We are in a period of transition, as
you all know, and to build a house brick by brick is not
the fastest way. But the beauty of expert masonry—not
to mention its structural advantages—can never be replaced by mass production." Then he led us to a room
where, on a long shelf, lay dozens of white mason's out-
fits—square-shouldered white jackets, baggy white
pants, white caps with large visors, and wooden clogs.
"Pick out an outfit that looks like your size and change

in the locker room across the hall. Please—don't try for
a perfect fit. You'll be working in these clothes, not
dancing. Young lady, you may change in the bathroom."
When Ralle and I confronted one another in our ma-
sonic disguise, we burst out laughing.

There was pleasure in learning the rudiments of
bricklaying: feeling the brick's solid weight, its dry
granular texture against the palm; the trick of slicing a
brick in half with a sharp chop of the trowel's edge;
mixing mortar and water in a wheelbarrow and churning the gray mass about with a shovel until it had just
the right texture; slapping a trowel-tipful on top of
what was beginning to look like a wall; sliding the new
brick into place; scraping off the excess mortar—there
was even a certain thrill to it. And the twelve hours a
week of classroom theory (mechanics, some chemistry,
technical drawing, mathematics, and, almost completely unrelated, literature) were tolerable, if not exactly interesting. Nevertheless, as the dulling effects of
routine began to set in, both Ralle and I discovered that
we really didn't particularly want to be bricklayers. And
so accustomed were we to not doing what we didn't
particularly want to do that the Thaelmann trade
school soon developed disciplinary problems very similar to those of the Helmholtz high school.

It began with our playing hooky. After warning us
two or three times, Herr Jadrzewski took it upon himself to visit our parents after work. Poor Bodo! He had
just returned from an important banquet in honor of
some foreign guests, and hadn't had time to get out of
his elegant black suit and into his everyday clothes. I
discovered this when I peeked through the dining-room
window. Apparently Bodo had thought it best not to
widen the social distance between himself and Herr
Jadrzewski by asking him into the wealthy-bohemian
clutter of our living room, with its thick cream-colored
Chinese rug, its sun-flooded studio windows, the bronze

nude by Fritz Cremer, the grand piano, the Chinese
scroll and Alma's paintings on the walls, the hundreds
of books, the extravagantly colorful Mexican papier-
mâché devils hanging by strings from the ceiling. But
even in the dining room, Herr Jadrzewski sat stiffly upright on the edge of his chair (which was not an ordinary chair but an antique with bowed legs and an oval
back), holding his cap on his lap and talking, and taking careful sips from the drink Bodo had offered him,
while Bodo sat sunk in the couch in a slouched position,
quaffing beer, sucking on his cigarette, nodding and
looking worried. As soon as Herr Jadrzewski left, I went
inside and promised Bodo, blushing and with sincere
contrition, that I would never cause him this kind of
embarrassment again. "I am getting too old for this kind
of foolishness," I declared, in a bizarre imitation of formal Selbstkritik. "I, too, am getting too old for it," Bodo
said.

I didn't play hooky after that. But Ralle did. In fact,
Ralle managed to produce as ludicrous a caricature of a
mason as he had of a student. Under his hands, the
simple constructions assigned to us took on a weird,
surreal quality—misplaced curves and corners, walls
with arched backs—that could hardly be ascribed to in-
efficiency. Once, he left out a brick in the middle of a
solid eight-by-four-foot wall. "It's for ventilation," he
said. "I thought of it as a bathroom wall." The master
(who already suspected Ralle—unjustly—of having
bumped him off a scaffold into a pile of sand) threw
down his trowel in a rage. Our fellow apprentices
wanted to learn how to build good walls, and were more
embarrassed than amused. At a meeting of the school's
faculty, it was decided that Ralle would have to leave,
and soon after that I, too, dropped out; learning to lay
bricks was no fun without him.

I expected Alma to be angry over my new betrayal of
her hopes for me. But since she had never hoped I'd

become a bricklayer, this failure did not disappoint her. She just felt sorry for me. Once or twice she apologized for all the fighting that had gone on over the summer— as if that were the cause of my floundering. Once again, I had an opportunity to take a "vacation from life," like the Man Without Qualities. This time I found fault with Musil's formula: a bad conscience was *not* an easy pillow. Alma frequently criticized me for "lounging" while the rest of the world worked. What's more, it was *unattractive*, she said; no woman worth her salt would be drawn to a man who spent his time at play. How could I deny it? There certainly weren't any adoring women to prove her wrong. And it was a fact that all my reading, writing, painting, and piano playing had, for the most part, no purpose beyond the immediate pleasure they gave me, while everyone I knew (except Ralle) was productively employed: Bodo at preparing a collection of his stories; Alma at writing articles for an English-language publication and practicing the viola; Stefan, bedridden with asthma for weeks at a time, at keeping up with his curriculum; Peter at learning how to make movies (he'd given up on painting); Wolfgang in the theater; Michèle in school (they were still seeing each other); Kamala in Karl-Marx-Stadt, learning to be an engineer.

(Kamala . . . my hope, my fate. Throughout the summer, I had been looking forward to her Christmas visit, had imagined her suddenly standing before me at the door, gift-wrapped, as it were, in her sari, had even written her a discreetly affectionate letter—but now I was beginning to worry. If my mother thought my purposelessness unattractive, why should Kamala think differently? True, I had passed myself off as a poet-in-the-making, and that was, I supposed, some sort of alibi. But what if she asked to see my work—all those patently juvenile romantic exclamations? I'd have to lie, as I had to Alma when I was eight, and palm off someone else's writing as my own. Otherwise, how could I face her with any self-respect, let alone manly assurance?)

Once, after listening to me practice the piano for a good part of the afternoon, Alma asked whether I had ever thought about a career in music. Well . . . I did daydream about it. But now that I considered the idea seriously, it didn't seem too farfetched. I didn't work hard enough at the piano to really test my potential, but I sang well, and had composed a few pieces that, though technically primitive, were pretty and communicated some feeling. And music had tremendous power over me, eliciting the world-transcending confidence and good will that religion can engender in believing souls. Alma's suggestion, therefore, that I apply for admission to the composition class of the State Conservatory, and her offer to arrange for an interview with the director of that school (a friend of our family), seemed to promise, against all doubts and cynicism, the beginning of a new life, devoted simply and purely to Beauty. Yes, I said, I think about it a lot. Yes, I want to study music. Oh, how I would work and make up for the years wasted in idleness! And when I was ready, what glorious harmonies would pour from my pen! A new classical era would dawn in Germany. Bach, Mozart, and Schubert would find their resurrection in me. With such unbounded hopes and the concomitant trepidations, I went to my interview, scrubbed, groomed, and dressed up as if for a wedding.

The director of the conservatory and I were utterly unprepared for one another. When he asked me to improvise on the piano, I explained as best I could that my improvisational powers were almost entirely imaginative and emotional, since my fingers hadn't received adequate training. "What makes you think you could compose music, then?" Mozart, Beethoven, I thought to myself, but I didn't say that. I shrugged. "I'm afraid that without some impression of your ability I can't accept you as a student—especially since, aside from your mother's kind words about you, I have only your unfortunate school record by which to evaluate you." There was nothing more to say. I accepted his offer of a second interview any time I felt ready for an audition, and went home, full of self-contempt, and slammed shut the great door that gave entrance to the vaulted halls of musical creation.

Kamala sent a postcard, addressed to "Bodo Uhse and family"—one of Canaletto's paintings of eighteenth-century Dresden. Had she even read my letter? She would not be coming for Christmas, she wrote, because some "very dear friends" had invited her to spend the holidays with them in the Harz mountains, and she had never skied and didn't want to miss that opportunity. But she'd be sure to visit us around Easter, "if you will have me" . . . No, that was just a polite British phrase. No message for me, not even a hint of an intimation of any thought of me. Why? Those dear friends . . . I pictured a family group, several round featureless faces and bulky bodies, all snapshot-gray, but in their midst, in color and in odiously sharp focus, was a fellow about my age equipped with pressed slacks, polished shoes, a broad chest in a blue FDJ shirt, a Medal for Good Knowledge, a handsome self-satisfied smile, and a dunce's forehead. Never mind, I told myself then, I can wait. I can wait till Easter.

❨[Among the colorfully wrapped presents opened on Christmas Eve that year was one marked "From Grandpa—for Stefan and Joel." He had sent it quite a while ago, but ideological scruples had prevented Alma and Bodo from giving it to us right away. What made them change their minds? They must have tested it. I know that Bodo had never heard of it before. I can picture them rolling the dice, secretly, after our bedtime, advancing the little silver thimble or boot or racing car, investing in real estate on Park Place and Boardwalk, exacting fees for water and electricity, grudgingly dishing out luxury taxes.

News of the Uhses' hilarious *Gesellschaftsspiel* from America spread quickly, and some of the visits we got during the days that followed were not your ordinary cordial Christmas-week stopovers. Monopoly capitalism, shorn of its bloody mechanical might and reduced to a contest over play money and miniature property, was exerting an irresistible attraction upon some half dozen dedicated Marxists. Fortunes changed hands, passions rose, laughter and clattering dice resounded until the wee hours of the morning. Stefan made an interesting observation: Certain people had a knack for the game—not only were they always winning, but they evinced a ruthlessness and greed that unpleasantly surprised their friends and spouses; others took pity on the losers and offered gifts and loans (arrangements which the first group either opposed or sought to amend, in keeping with the spirit of the game, with complicated notions like interest and collateral).

My own ambition was to lose most of my assets and land on the property of a pretty and kindhearted young guest, the wife of a neighbor, thus becoming the object of her charitable impulses. This was especially gratifying when other players objected. My benefactress would passionately uphold my rights as a poor person victimized by a cutthroat economic system: "Some socialists you are! You should change these stupid rules instead of defending them!"

"He's getting what he deserves! When he was rich he was just as bad a capitalist as we are!"

"Well, I don't care! These are *my* hotels, and he can live there for free!" Then she'd bail me out of jail, too, just to spite them.

Joel, ca. 1960

1959-1960

In February 1959 I left home to work in the Warnow-Werft, a shipyard in Warnemünde. I didn't particularly want to go—especially since I might miss Kamala's Easter visit if I did—but I felt I couldn't refuse a job when it was offered. There was not only other people's opinion, there were laws obliging me to either work or go to school. Better to *choose* to become a real worker than be exiled "into the Production." And conceivably, just a few months of patient self-transformation—I pictured it as a kind of psychic sculpting, with shipyard workers for live models—might put me one up on the Party, the teachers, the Intelligenz, the whole set of Bonzen and big shots, of which I was promising to become such a sorry representative. It would be they, the cultural and political servants of the First German Workers and Peasants State, whose efforts would have to measure up to my, the class-conscious worker's, standards.

Bodo had made all the arrangements. I was to live a few miles away from my place of work, in the apartment of an admirer of Bodo's novels, an architect named Lothar P., who had paid us several visits during the previous year together with his wife, Irma, and their little girl, Trini. When I arrived at their house, Irma was five or six months pregnant; she seemed happy about it, and Lothar proud. They both spared no pains to make me feel at home. This wasn't so difficult, for their place didn't differ greatly from home.

It was the Warnow-Werft that took some getting used to. This was the genuine article, a *Schwerindustriezentrum*, not a little halfway house between school and Production, like the Ernst Thaelmann school for masons. Of course I'd seen places like it before, in countless newsreels and photographs—all those masked welders hulking over their fireworks, the incandescent bars of steel sliding soundlessly along steel floors at the behest of responsible-looking women wearing visored caps and moving little levers with their hands; and then the dance of products and machines, the soldierly processions of bottles, cars, noodles, tubs, the interlocking cogs conjoined more perfectly than lovers' hands, the hundred-ton load floating into the hold of a ship . . . Somehow all these images hadn't prepared me for the experience of being part of the picture, so to speak. Unlike the camera world, the Warnow-Werft appeared boundless. You, the worker, were small, chipping or shoveling or welding away in the midst of a sprawling tumult and clangor of steel. It wasn't bad or unpleasant, being small, but it was laughably unlike the brawny, sleeves-rolled-up, chest-out, heave-ho sort of self-image I had hoped for.

Every morning around eight the handshaking ritual was performed. (This, incidentally, is a traditional German, not a socialist, ritual.) The day-shift brigade would arrive and the night-shift brigade would leave (these shifts alternated each week), and since each brigade was made up of nine persons, that would amount to seventeen handshakes. And you had to keep track of them all, so as not to omit someone or, just as bad, shake his hand a second time. Alma had converted her friends in Berlin to the American casually raised palm and "Hi" sort of greeting—such a time-saving approach, someone said, and with no loss in friendliness ("and essentially collectivistic!" someone else quipped); but the last thing I wanted to do was introduce foreign customs to the Warnow-Werft and provoke questions about my identity. It actually felt very comforting to shake all those hands and feel affirmed with each one: "You're one of us." (But I wasn't really one of them—*I* knew it, even if they didn't guess from the clumsiness with which, in the beginning, I handled even the simplest tools.) My job consisted of attaching the heavy grasping hooks of a crane to steel plates that were anywhere between one and several inches thick and about the width and length of a small room, and of releasing them again, once the load was deposited, with the help of a crowbar. My job title was *Anschläger*—literally, "on-hitter" (it doesn't make sense in either language). Two Anschläger were assigned to each crane, and there were six Anschläger and three crane operators in each Anschläger brigade. Many of the crane operators in the Warnow-Werft were women, but all the Anschläger, so far as I remember, were men, probably because the work was deemed too physically taxing for women. There must have been dozens of such brigades in the shipyard, and each bore the name of some hero: Anschlägerbrigade Walter Ulbricht, Anschlägerbrigade Rosa Luxemburg; ours was named after Stakhanov, the Soviet steelworker who had distinguished himself as a maniacal pacemaker during Stalin's race for increased productivity before the war. No brigade could have been less inclined to exert themselves unnecessarily. We did what had to be done and no more. Since the volume of work varied from day to day, no norms could be imposed by the management, and our foreman, a mild pipe-smoking man, moved at a leisurely pace. During the night shift, we took turns sleeping, and day or night, a good deal of time was spent quietly sipping a cup of coffee, or talking. It was hard for me to follow a lot of this conversation, because my colleagues kept lapsing into Plattdeutsch, which, despite its occasional similarity to English, and of course to German, might as well have been Finnish or Serbo-Croatian.

The only time I remember being worked to exhaustion was on a day when I was teamed up with Otto, an athletic, dashingly handsome man three or four years my senior, who was wooing Lieselotte, one of the crane operators, and wanted to show her how strong, agile, and tireless he was. She encouraged him, too, rolling the crane along at twice its normal speed (the little warning bell tinkling madly), hoisting high the steel plate we'd just hooked up, and swinging it at the same time toward the open-topped railroad car into which Otto had already leapt, and lowering the plate swiftly, almost dropping it, and throttling the speed of its descent just before it reached his upstretched hands. I guess she was showing off, too. They waltzed around like this for several hours, laughing and calling out to each other, with me an only half-willing and eventually dog-tired third party.

Usually, though, I preferred working with Otto, and he, too, liked to have me as a partner, since the other men tended to get annoyed at his playful attitude and especially at his unnecessary athleticism. He was a good worker, no one would deny it, but was that a reason to make a circus out of the job, complete with handsprings and cartwheels? "He treats it like a sport," muttered Gustav, the old man of our brigade, on one of the rare occasions when he said anything at all. But that was just why I liked working with Otto, and with Otto and Lieselotte, once their romance had simmered down a little. Quick reflexes were needed, strength (on the part of the Anschläger), good coordination of eyes and hands, and, especially, teamwork. Sometimes, under the eyes of visiting schoolchildren or foreign delegations, we spurred one another on to efforts even Stakhanov might have found excessive, had they not been so brief. But usually we didn't rush. It was style that mattered.

My home life with Lothar and Irma proceeded happily enough for the first few weeks. But Lothar annoyed me sometimes with his opinions and patronizing advice. The sea air, he said, the discipline of hard physical work, the company of "real workers"—all this would make a man out of me, and a Communist, too. Once or twice he advised me on matters of the heart. Young girls, he declared, with a chuckle and a chummy wink at Irma—watch out for young girls, they're false, they'll tease and deceive you, especially the pretty ones. Another time he asked to read my father's novel, *A Death in the Family*, which I had brought with me from Berlin, but returned it to me after reading fifty pages or so, with the explanation that it was poorly written. "What's wrong with it?" I asked. "All that 'he said,' 'she said,' 'he said,' 'she said' "—he said—"it's amateurish." "Well, how should he have put it?" " 'He exclaimed'? 'He interjected'? 'He remarked'? 'He disagreed'?" I disagreed, and Lothar said: "*De gustibus non est disputandum.*" I felt a hot rush of contempt for him then.

I liked Irma better. Unlike Lothar, she didn't pride herself on her opinions, and where he was nervous and edgy and forever preoccupied with unfinished business, she ambled about doing her household chores with serene thoroughness, gently smiling and sometimes humming to herself and, amazingly, never getting annoyed, even when Trini ate her way into a chocolate cake and smeared the rest of it on the floor—that incident provoked a moment of shock and then laughter. Once, I walked in on the end of a conversation between her and Lothar. He was saying, "Look, dear, such things simply can't be explained." Irma quietly and sincerely replied: "But they can be understood." Lothar looked confused, and covered it up with a sage puff on his pipe. That moment seemed to encapsulate the difference between them. Could two people in fact be any more different? Yet she seemed happy with him.

I think Irma had fantasies of adopting me as a younger brother. On weekends, when Lothar welcomed some quiet time by himself, she and I often went out for a walk, and took turns pushing Trini along in her stroller. One day we went to a park not far from the house. Trini was unstrapped and let loose to crawl and scrabble among the dry leaves, and Irma and I walked up and down a hard-trodden dirt path beneath stout rough oaks and slender smooth-skinned plane trees, talking. Irma laughed about something I said, then took my head between her hands and planted a kiss on my cheek and said, "Oh, I like you so much." Then she took my hand and gaily swung my arm. We continued walking together like that, hand in hand, arms swinging, like Hansel and Gretel. At least that's how I imagine Irma thought of it. At the time I wasn't quite sure what to make of it, especially after she reached for my hand the next time we went walking in the park, and the time after that; and when I reflected that, on the street, she never wanted to hold hands, maybe because some acquaintance might see us and start spreading dangerous rumors.

Among the books in the living room was a fat collection of Sigmund Freud. Reading in it led me to wonder whether I might not be in danger of getting caught up in an Oedipal triangle, with Lothar and Irma standing proxy for my parents. The Freudian seed, once planted, immediately sprouted a series of questions that weren't so easy to simply uproot and discard:

"Why does Lothar irritate you so?"

Because he's overbearing, that's why.

"But why do certain gestures of his that don't even involve you annoy you especially? Like the way he spreads the fingers of one hand across her belly as if to gauge the growth of his offspring?"

It's the proud smile that bothers me, not the gesture —he obviously thinks her pregnancy proves him more of a man.

"Ah, I bet you envy that pride. Why else would it bother you? And what about his pipe smoking—why do you get so worked up whenever he lights a pipe? Hmmm?"

Because he's so smug and fastidious, that's why. If Stefan were here, he'd understand; he'd draw a picture of it, he'd see it the same way, and *he* certainly has no designs on Irma, he's only twelve and he doesn't even know her. *This is all nonsense.*

And to prove that, I wrote a letter to Stefan in which I described Lothar's lighting-up ritual in all its obnoxious detail: "First, into the bowl of his pipe, which is carved to resemble an old man's head with bushy eyebrows, he stuffs tobacco by means of a spatulate thumb, lips pressed shut, breathing hissingly through his nose. Then he strikes a match and proceeds to phase two, the sucking phase, which is always accompanied by a beetling frown. Phase three is the *aaaah* phase, the most repulsive of all. He leans back with an expression of blissful deflation and sensually exhales the first of the evening's aromatic puffs. Sooner or later, the worldly pronouncements follow."

These lines, far from settling the matter, only strengthened the Freudian prosecution's case:

"Pipe = Penis. Assuming the validity of this premise, ask yourself: Why such *fascinated* disgust? *Why the involvement?*"

Paralyzing question. And what a ghastly-fascinating answer it suggested: floating and wiggling right beneath the placid surface of everyday life—*my* everyday life, the life of a timid young man with vague aesthetic yearnings—there swam all sorts of blind lurid monsters —murder, rape, homosexuality, castration, incest! You had to watch your every move and thought if one of them wasn't to stick up its snout for everyone to see. Lothar, especially, must have a trained eye for psychopathology. The volume of Freud had his *Ex Libris* on the endleaf, and the pages were copiously underlined and annotated in his handwriting.

One day—it was a Sunday, but Lothar had to go to

a meeting that took all afternoon—Irma avoided talking to me or even looking at me. I imagined it was a sudden mood unrelated to me, maybe something to do with her pregnancy. I could understand the need to be alone, whatever the reason, and kept out of her way. That evening, Lothar approached me with a tight frown, pinched lips, and a hard look in his eyes, and curtly informed me that he and Irma thought it best that I move out of their apartment right away. He had already made inquiries at the Warnow-Werft, and they said there was room for me in a workers' domicile just a half hour's walk from the shipyard; so I could leave the very next day. I didn't ask what had happened. I couldn't imagine what I might have done to deserve this dismissal, but I felt guilty nonetheless. I must have done *something*. So why ask questions and add humiliation to injury? Lothar was probably being charitable by not throwing his accusation at me. Maybe it was all a misunderstanding? No, I didn't believe that. The very persistence of the dull, melancholy sensation of guilt seemed to justify my condemnation.

Early the next morning Lothar summoned a taxi by phone, gave me carfare to pay for the expensive ride, and helped me carry my bags out of the house. Irma did not emerge from the bedroom. "Good luck!" Lothar said, holding out his hand. I shook it and, in complete bewilderment, thanked him for his hospitality and asked him to say goodbye to Irma and Trini for me. Then I drove to the Wohnheim Gross-Klein.

❲I can't even guess why it was called that: "Living Home Great-Small." It consisted of several wooden barracks. I shared a room with three young men, two of whom were married, though their wives lived many kilometers away. Once in a while, one wife or the other would visit, and everyone but the fortunate couple would vacate the room for a number of hours. The whole place reeked of sexual frustration. The walls were plastered with pinups. Talk of women, or of parts of women, was almost always going on whenever two or more men were awake in the same room; and there was one guy who occasionally continued talking about sex in his sleep. Two other popular topics were money and personal animosities, but sooner or later the conversation would veer back to the subject of women. Yet, for all the bold talk, no females ever entered our room, or anyone else's, so far as I know, except for two elderly cleaning women and the above-mentioned wives. On weekends we went bar-hopping: beer after beer after beer after beer after beer, interspersed with bockwurst and sauerkraut so we could hold the alcohol better, until someone got sick or fell off his chair. I remember being driven home in a taxi one Saturday night and being carried into the barracks and dumped on my bed, and groaning forth a rich froth of vomit, and waking up in it the next day, and sitting up and asking some skat players at the table near my bed—not my roommates—whether I owed them any money from last night. They looked at me and at each other and broke into hysterical laughter. I could still remember the sound of my words: I had spoken English. But the men—fortunately—had heard only thick-tongued gibberish. I didn't want anyone to suspect me of being anything other than a German Anschläger.

I was pleased that I'd managed to pass undetected for as long as I had. No one here had ever heard of Bodo Uhse. My foreign-sounding first name, too, was obliterated by the nickname *"Langer"* (Long One). To all outward appearances I was a worker among workers; given a little time, I might actually come to *feel* that way. In the meantime, I'd continue playing my appointed part, even if that meant getting drunk every weekend.

I did wish I'd fallen in with a more congenial bunch, though. Surely not all workers were alcoholics and skat addicts. On the other hand, what could anyone do in this town *except* drink and play cards? The place was a desert. A meagerly stocked library or two, an FDJ club-house with a warped Ping-Pong table, two or three movie theaters—these were the handful of half-desic-cated oases sprinkled among vast gray wastes of commerce and Schwerindustrie. What the hell did my colleagues in the brigade do with their free time? They had families, all of them except Otto and Lieselotte, who were now lovers—that's what took up their free time, love and family. And Waltraudt, our "progressive" brigade member, a quiet, very serious young woman with a bad case of acne, probably went to meetings in addition to spending time with her husband and her little boy. Once Waltraudt asked all the members of the brigade if they'd like to join the Society for German-Soviet Friendship; there'd be cultural programs, meetings with Soviet citizens living in the area, things like that. It wasn't something I really wanted to do, but Waltraudt looked so isolated in her progressivism, and some of the others grumbled so unthinkingly about how they'd gotten their fill of Soviet-German friendship in 1945—as if the Soviets hadn't had *their* fill of German barbarity—that I offered to join. Waltraudt was of course pleased. But then it turned out her chapter needed at least five more members, and until these five were found, no cultural programs and meetings with Russians would take place. She hadn't been able to get those five together by the time I left Warnemünde.

One weekend, during an hour of solitude, I was sorting through a pile of notes and drafts for poems, and came across the description of Lothar's pipe smoking in my letter to Stefan, which I had never sent off, and a rather heartless account of Irma's repeatedly taking hold of my hand, followed by the conjecture, in icily psychoanalytic terms, that perhaps Irma was sexually unsatisfied and that therefore the friendship she showed me might be strongly charged with libido. So that was it!

How embarrassing! Lothar or, more probably, Irma must have read this! What a pity, though, to have hurt her feelings like that. And why? Just for the sake of a little exercise in self-aggrandizement. What would Dr. Freud have to say about *that?* Well, his book was at Lothar and Irma's house, and the local library said I would need a special study permit to read Sigmund Freud. Just as well. Peering into yourself was like diving down into Glienicker See with your eyes open, into the cold and the dark. Better to forget.

Sometimes I went walking alone in the city after sundown and, in passing, watched people through their windows, putting their children to bed, heating their tile or metal ovens, talking on the phone, laughing together at the dinner table . . . Whenever I did that, I felt homesick. Wouldn't it be better to quit working here and get a job in Berlin? Everyone would criticize me for it, but so what? I'd be home. I'd see my friends, especially Ralle and Peter. I could see Fellini and Bergman movies in West Berlin. Peter had written me about a wonderful movie called *The 400 Blows.* And I could go to the theater and concerts in the East. Also, Kamala would be staying with us during her Easter vacation— that alone was reason enough to at least take a week off from work. On the other hand, she had never once written to me; maybe she wouldn't come after all. And if she did, would she sleep with me? Probably not. Maybe I should wait till after Easter to go home. The more I deliberated, the less capable of decision I felt.

⟮One day a group of foreign visitors paused briefly during their tour of the plant to watch the Anschläger- brigade Stakhanov at work. Among them was a young woman with blue-black hair and a red dot on her forehead. She wasn't anywhere near as pretty as Kamala, but it was a week before Easter—it had to be an omen. I contrived an excuse to take the Easter week off, and took the train to Berlin.

I found both Alma and Bodo in terrible shape. Frau Meissner was pregnant, and refused to have an abortion. She wanted Bodo to marry her. Bodo declared he had no intention of leaving Alma; and he professed to be angry with this woman, who, he said, was using emotional blackmail on him. But he obviously cared for her, too. He couldn't hurt her. And he felt responsible for the child in her womb. Alma was even more violently scornful than she had been during the previous summer in Ahrenshoop. She kept accusing Bodo of weakness. The very word seemed to cause him pain. He anesthetized himself with alcohol, one double vodka after another, each one chased by a glass of beer. He sat for hours, disheveled and unshaven, his jaw hanging open, exactly as if he were trying to bite through some invisible obstacle. From time to time he'd make repulsively sentimental efforts to reclaim the love of his children, which, at least in my case, he hadn't lost. With Stefan it may have been different. Sometimes the sight of his father nauseated him—particularly at the breakfast table, where, Stefan told me (trying to convey the specifically *visceral* noxiousness of this perception), Bodo's checked brown-and-yellow bathrobe and pale bristly face closely resembled the patterns and hues of spilled egg yolk and fried potatoes on the plate before him. Alma, like Bodo, was unkempt, and haggard, her eyes puffed from crying (always in his absence—she never cried when he was around). She looked suddenly old. Sometimes both she and Bodo seemed practically crazed by the intensity and persistence of their emotions. I had been reading Spinoza in Warnemünde (keeping the book wrapped in brown paper and hidden in the drawer of my night table) and couldn't help reflecting, in long, pedantically analytical journal entries, that here was a doleful example of passion divorced from reason. But my efforts to

mediate, to advise, and to understand felt uncomfort-
ably dispassionate. Here was my mother talking of suicide and of taking off for America with me and Stefan,
yet I was acting as if all this in no way concerned me.
Kamala's visit was called off—by Alma and Bodo, not
by her; she had been planning to come. It was just as
well, I concluded philosophically; this was no atmosphere for love.

Stefan and I both felt glad of each other's presence.
Together we shook our heads at the sound of the miser-
able drama in our parents' bedroom, and passed the
time as best we could, listening to music, playing Parcheesi, joking, talking about books and movies.

I met with Ralle and Peter a few times. Ralle had just
quit work at the post office, where he had been lugging
mail sacks for a few weeks. He said he couldn't take the
routine, the boredom, the stupid regularity of work—
any kind of work. "What about anthropology?" I asked
him. "Why don't you finish school and get into that?
Eventually you could travel, maybe live somewhere interesting for a while. That's what you've always wanted,
isn't it?" "It's too much of a long shot," he said. "I'm not
cut out for schoolwork, and even if I managed to get top
grades, chances are I'd end up in some office. Can you
see yourself doing that? Forty years in an office?" "No."
"One of these days," he said, "you'll get a letter from
me, from Mexico or Brazil. Don't ask how I'll do it. I'll
tell you then." "Do you have plans, or are you dreaming?" "I'm working on it."

Peter spent a lot of time looking at movies at the Film
Institute, of which he was now a member. He really was
serious about becoming a filmmaker. He seemed altogether more sober, more mature, and also more modest
than he used to be. For instance, he said he had given up
his dreams of becoming an artist, on canvas or on cellu-
loid or in any other medium. I was shocked to hear him
talk like that. "No, it's true," he said. "Real talent is given
to very few people, and I know I'm not one of them. That

doesn't mean I can't make good films. It just means I'll never be a Jean Renoir or an Eisenstein." "But what's the good of making movies if they're not works of art?" "They can be good without being great—don't you understand? They can be minor works of art, if you will." "I understand that, but what I don't understand is how you can resign yourself to it." "The difference between you and me," Peter said, after thinking for a while, "is that you want at all costs to go your own way, even though you don't know what that way is. I want my own way too, but I'm more willing to take direction from others. Look—the state offers us real opportunities to learn a profession and be of some service. Why did we resist that for so long? Have you ever asked yourself that?" "No, actually not." "Don't you think it's selfishness? All that talk about art and genius—when the really important thing is to be of some use. And the way I see it, that's the only way to be happy." We were walking home from the Film Institute, where we'd just seen Bresson's *Pickpocket*, the story of a young man's apprenticeship to two thieves with long, thin hands and sad, beautiful faces, the faces of fallen angels. At the very end, the young man's neighbor, a lovely and gentle girl to whom he has paid only passing and unfriendly attention, visits him in prison. They kiss through the bars of his cell and he says: "How far I had to travel in order to find you." Reflecting on what Peter had said, and remembering at the same time the deep reverberation of feeling the film had stirred in me, it suddenly occurred to me that if there seemed to be a big difference between Peter and me, it might be that I hadn't received the kiss of grace and he had, whatever its source might have been— maybe literally the love of a girl. After all, I, too, wanted to do something that would be useful and helpful to others. I just didn't know yet what that something might be. "I'm sorry I said that," Peter said then, as if he'd been reading my thoughts. "I was wrong to criticize you. I was really talking about myself. Everyone has to find his own way." "His own way to what?" I asked. "To society," he said. "To community," he added. Dear Peter—praised be your good heart, honorable old friend!

❨[Wolfgang and Michèle, I learned from a neighbor, had married. Married! Like parents, like mature and responsible citizens! At first, instead of being jealous, I felt abandoned by them, left behind to wander aimlessly through years of adolescent murk. Then the thought of them living together just five subway stops away became intolerable. What a relief to get back to my barracks, back to work, back to Spinoza! Never mind that the management, without explanation, moved me and old Gustav to the brigade that alternated shifts with ours, composed for the most part of middle-aged men and women who were conscientious about work and not at all sporting. Any place was an improvement on living at home. And besides, one of my new colleagues, August Larisch, told stories during our breaks, and that was enough to lure me to work each day.

Larisch said he was a disabled seaman. Why his disability (a fractured spine) would incapacitate him for work on a ship and not for work in a shipyard was never made clear. He bore a remarkable likeness to Popeye, mainly because of the humplike curvature of his back, a pair of knotty biceps, and a corncob pipe that perpetually jutted at a right angle to his wizened face, the lower part of which was prematurely toothless and concave. All that was lacking was the little sailor's cap. I asked Ralle to do me the favor of going to West Berlin and finding a Popeye comic and sending it to me. Larisch was delighted with the resemblance. He asked me to send for more pictures of Popeye, so he could paste them on his windows and send them to friends. He didn't even mind people calling him *Knallauge* for a while, the literal translation of Popeye's name. In fact, I suspect he toyed with the idea that he really *was* Popeye, or that the cartoon character was his double, or some such notion. All the stories he told us were in that sort of crazy-fantastical vein. Actually, it was one endless picaresque tale that continued in daily installments. His voyages had taken him to lands where muscular women carried out raids on the helpless male population, raping everyone in sight ("And since you women don't believe me, why don't you come to my place after work, I'll show you how it's done"); he'd been to the Mariposa Islands, where the natives have transparent skin, so you can watch the digestive process in operation ("And they think *we're* ugly! But you get used to it"); and he'd been to America, where the women no longer know how to cook and many people are unable to walk for more than half a kilometer, so atrophied are their legs by the excessive use of automobiles. He had encountered pirates and had become friends with cannibals ("It's not bad, human meat, kind of like turkey, but sweeter, more like eagle—but I suppose you've never tasted eagle"); he had been through the gates of death and returned with enough memories to put Emanuel Swedenborg to shame. What was most extraordinary about these stories was that no one objected with any force to their absurdly fabulous character. We were all gladly willing to be lied to, so long as we could find out what happened next.

Often, when I arrived at work, I found a small package of food—a sandwich, a piece of wurst, or a jar of pickled herring—waiting for me on the table in the canteen with a note attached, scrawled in a round, feminine script: *"Für den Langen."* Someone in the Anschläger-brigade Stakhanov was concerned that I wasn't eating enough.

On September 21 I got a telegram from Bodo asking me to call him immediately at a number in Stralsund:

Vitte 48. I hurried into town, placed my call, and was
told by a hotel clerk in Stralsund that Bodo had just
checked out, without leaving a forwarding address. I
then called Alma in Berlin. She said that Bodo had gone
on a business trip to Leipzig several days ago—at least
that's what he had said. But Stralsund—that was hundreds of kilometers away from Leipzig, wasn't it? Now
she was worried.

The next day a letter arrived, posted in Stralsund, and
written in English:

Dearest, beloved Joel—I could not go on drinking at day and
crying at night—I have been in Leipzig, now I am in Stralsund.
I drank very little, and—though always, or at least sometimes,
being on the edge of a crying-fit—have not shed any tears.

I have been playing around with the outline of the movie,
wrote some parts of it and hope to finish it maybe tonight or
maybe tomorrow. You get a copy when it is typed.

You would like to know what is going on with me.

I still don't know.

I was afraid of going crazy.

I have to get hold of myself. That does not necessarily mean
what Alma means by it.

Let me have a few days of rest, work, loneliness. I am going
from here to Hiddensee—Alma should not be afraid—I am going
alone.

I would love to see you.

When I think of you and Stefan I see you in your youthful
beauty, glorious, shining, archangels with flaming swords.

Have, both of you, mercy with me.

                                                    Bodo

P.S. Call me up: Vitte 48.

It saddens me that it didn't occur to me then that
there might be a special meaning in the unusual fact of
his writing to me in English. It was Alma's language,
just as the language of open-hearted feeling was Alma's,
not his. Perhaps, by writing in English, he was hoping

to magically lay claim—virtually at the close of our life together—to a spontaneous empathy that had always existed between my mother and me, and from which he felt excluded by his own diffidence.

The day after, another letter came, also from Stralsund, and again in English:

Joel dear, I had so much hoped for a call from you, but very likely you got my telegram too late and I am afraid I shall not hear from you before I leave.

As I told you, I am going to Hiddensee, but I am going alone and shall stay alone. Do call me if you can.

What is going to happen—forgive me, I still don't know. I would be grateful if Alma still could be patient, as terribly hard as it might be for her.

I shall write to her in a few days. Still fussing with the last third of the movie story.

Please do call Vitte 48.

Yesterday's letter, I hope, didn't shock you too much.

Love,
Bodo

There was no point in calling Vitte 48 again. Nor could I remember the name of the hotel where he and I had stayed together. I was half glad about that. I felt disturbed, even slightly repelled by the desperate tone of his letters. It was almost as if he were asking *me* to be *his* parent, to hold his hand, guide and comfort him.

As it turned out, these unanswerable letters were the last straightforward communications I received from Bodo before I left for the States.

⟨Spinoza had convinced me that one must seek to associate with people who share one's values and shun intimacy with those who don't. In this spirit I turned away from my roommates and applied for membership in the shipyard's amateur theater group, which until recently I hadn't even known existed. I was just in time: they needed someone tall and strong for the part of the Third Sailor in a play about the sailors' revolt in 1918. I was tall. The breadth of my shoulders could be augmented by padding. No memorizing, no talent was needed, just a convincing physical presence. I was to appear on the stage three times. The first time I would be carrying a tray laden with champagne glasses, follow some officers into a room, subserviently hand them their drinks, and exit upon command. Some time later, I would appear, heavily armed, together with two other men; a nasty officer would tell me to fetch a rope with which to tie up an innocent man. I would exit and return, given a certain cue, and hand over the rope with disgust. A few minutes later, the mutiny would erupt, and I would prevent the nasty officer from running out of the room. That's where the convincing physical presence came in.

Curious: for eight months I'd been playing the role of a worker; at first with an uneasy feeling of illegitimacy, a clumsy secret agent from the land of the Bonzen; eventually with growing confidence, wielding my crowbar with ever more expert assurance, signaling to the crane operator, by means of cheerful circular motions of an upward-pointing arm, that the load was securely attached and ready for lifting—earning my living, in short, like any other Anschläger; until the actor was very nearly one with the act, and I was, in my own eyes, a worker. I remember the day I discovered in the fine print on the back of my work papers that Anschläger were classified as *Schwerarbeiter*—manual laborers or, literally, hardworkers; I stomped the wooden planks of my barracks with secret pride. When Aubrey Pankey, a black American singer of German lieder and Negro spirituals, a refugee from McCarthyism and a close friend of our family, came to sing for us during the lunch hour, I stood among my peers, the workers of the Warnow-

Werft, incognito at last, not to them but to Aubrey, the
classy and exotic guest from Berlin, whose artful inter-
pretations of Schubert, amplified by loudspeakers,
sounded so alien in the temporarily silenced shipyard,
and whose rendition of "Let My People Go" elicited
widespread amusement, since this plea, to anyone who
speaks Plattdeutsch and no English, translates exactly
to "Let go of my penis." Now, suddenly, having joined
this theater club, I was being asked to *make believe* I
was a worker; or rather, to clothe my alleged prole-
tarian self in an unaccustomed but nevertheless prole-
tarian outfit—that of a sailor. I felt exposed in the glare
of the stagelight, like a suspect in a line-up. I knew I
was no working-class hero, even if nobody else did.
Working-class heroes don't read Spinoza, and they
aren't virgins either. And my sailor's cap was too large
and kept slipping over my ears. Nevertheless, I managed, and was found acceptable for the part. During
rehearsals, the actor representing the leader of the revolt played his role with such intensity that my three
brief appearances on the stage went practically unno-
ticed. But the director attributed this stage absence to
some carefully thought-out conception; it just didn't
occur to him, since he was short, that someone large
could feel small. "You're right," he said, "the man you're
playing is so used to serving drinks and taking orders
that he doesn't have any class-consciousness. That
makes his turnabout at the end all the more dramatic.
But please be a little more forceful there, when you stop
the officer. Square your shoulders!" He was fond of violent contrasts, in speech even more than in action.
Whenever one of the characters had cause to speak with
difficulty—embarrassment, for example—the director
would ask the actor to first sigh very deeply and then,
with a subdued tone of voice, blinking rapidly, push out
the unavoidable confession as haltingly as possible. At
other times he would demand that the voice swell passionately until glasses and ashtrays rattled on the tables

and then, as suddenly as if someone had thrown a switch, lapse into a tone of lamb-like goodliness. These variations in tone, he said, were necessary in order to bring some movement into the dialogue.

After a few rehearsals, I began to look forward to the paid vacation I would get when we went on tour. A trip to Poland might be in the offing! But a week before opening night a telegram from Alma called me home to Berlin.

She had decided to go back to America, and asked me to come along with her and Stefan. Unsolvable complications had sprung up. Frau Meissner had given birth to a boy, and was now begging—no longer just asking—Bodo to live with her and the baby. Bodo was torn, and was spending half his time with them and half with Alma and Stefan. Stefan's asthma was worse than ever. There was nothing to do but leave, Alma said.

I acknowledged this bit of news with a stoic nod, but actually I was extremely happy about it. To leave everything, just like that! To start a new life unencumbered by my long string of failures—in America, where no one would know me! This was nothing less than a complete reprieve. (Trading a socialist for a capitalist country didn't trouble me in the least: what bearing did that have on my personal happiness? But if someone had persuaded me that only in the Soviet Union or China, or in the DDR, for that matter, and never in any capitalist country, could I find a woman to love, or accomplish something worthwhile in the eyes of the world —then I would have felt obliged to let Alma and Stefan go to the States without me.)

We weren't sure how soon we would be able to leave. Letters had to travel to and from the United States, and we had to make numerous visits to the American Consulate in West Berlin, where our passports were to be issued. Alma seemed to feel more at ease with her countrymen—whose politics certainly clashed with hers—than she would have with any similar set of East German officials. I, too, appreciated their air of relaxed, comfortable, quiet prosperity. Their faces were softer, their smiles more genial than those I was used to. Everything in that building seemed to shine with the same pleasant gloss that distinguished American magazines from their East German counterparts. In the lavatory, above the sink, was an extra faucet that would squirt liquid soap into your palm if you pushed a little button on the top; and there was another contraption that dried your hands with hot air. This, a small plaque explained, was more hygienic than drying your hands with a towel.

The American consul always looked as if he had recently taken a shower. His face was floridly clean, his short white hair lay flat on his scalp and was perfectly parted in the middle and—Alma pointed this out to me —tapered. No East German barber was capable of such fine work. One thing was certain: once we got to America, I would be able to get the "decent haircut" Alma had been trying to procure for me for the past twelve years.

The consul was friendly, but he also seemed a little wary of us. I felt this especially when he questioned me about my "indoctrination." I had never heard the word. "Propaganda," he said. "Weren't you taught to believe various things about the United States?"

"Oh, of course, yes." The consul made a note.

"Well, what sorts of things did they teach you?"

I squirmed. I didn't want to spoil our chances of leaving by telling him something he shouldn't know; but it would be just as bad to be caught, or suspected of, lying. I decided to tell him the truth.

"Basically," I said, "I was taught that America is a capitalist country. That there are extremely rich and extremely poor people there, and that the poor don't have much of a chance to get rich. That people are exploited. Especially the Indians and the Negroes. That it's a racist country."

"What else?"

"That capitalist economy involves a lot of waste."

"What sort of waste?"

"Waste of people, in the form of unemployment and war, and waste of raw materials and food and things like that. Like destroying milk or crops to raise the prices. I don't know if all that's true," I said, somewhat mendaciously, since I was fairly certain that all of it was true.

"Well, it's not," said the consul. "There are some half truths in what you've said, and a whole lot of exaggerations, and some outright lies. But you'll be able to see for yourself, you don't have to take my word for it. I'm sure that in a few years you'll agree with me that you're a citizen of a mighty fine country. That you can be proud of being an American."

"I never taught him otherwise," Alma interjected.

"That's true," I said. The consul didn't seem to believe us. But it *was* true: no one had ever made me feel there was anything to apologize for in being American.

"One more thing," the consul said. "Did either of you ever belong to a Communist organization?"

Alma shook her head.

I said: "Yes. The Young Pioneers and the Free German Youth."

"Do you still belong to these groups?"

"Well, to the FDJ, yes. Unless they've struck me off their list for defaulting or something. I haven't been involved with them for years. The Pioneers—you stop being a Pioneer when you're fifteen."

The consul took notes on everything I said.

"Oh, and I belonged to the FDGB—the Free German Labor Union. That's automatic when you're employed by the state."

"You work for the state?" He looked alarmed.

"Well, I worked in a shipyard, it's state-owned. If I

worked for someone private, I wouldn't belong to the FDGB."

"I see." He looked relieved. "Well, everything should be clear in a week or two," he said then.

¶[We would be sailing in April. Because Stefan was so unwell, he was sent ahead a few weeks before to stay with friends until we arrived. Bodo begged Alma to stay and have Stefan brought back. She said she would if he stopped seeing Frau Meissner. He wasn't able to do that, he said; he just couldn't, not yet, at any rate. Couldn't she wait for a while, postpone the trip, settle for a temporary separation . . . Alma couldn't bear to listen anymore. "*How can you be so weak!*" He stood pinned to the wall and roared two, three times. I used to be afraid of his shouting when he got mad, but these were the cries of a man who no longer believed in his own strength. Alma refused to pity him, glared at him with her arms crossed. I left the room.

Bodo and I hardly ever talked to one another, even though he was home much of the time now. There seemed to be nothing to say. "I wish you didn't drink so much" . . . "I'm sorry" . . . "I wish you could stop seeing Luise" . . . All that was self-evident, so why say it? But it would have been better to say something. He, too, should have talked. "I do love you"—either of us could have said that. And then other things could have been said. Bodo must have felt guilty beyond any hope of deserving my forgiveness; and his continual avoidance of even so much as eye contact with me must have multiplied this guilt every day. I, too, felt guilty for remaining silent so long. I knew it must seem like a judgment. I wasn't angry at him, and wished he could know that. But I couldn't even begin to just tell him so. It always threatened to come out as something like "It's all right." But it wasn't all right. It was appalling, that's

what it was—and that certainly didn't need to be said.
Alma had become haggard and eventually so weak
she had to spend much of the day lying in bed. She was
scarcely eating. She couldn't read or do much of anything except count the days until we would leave. She
did listen to music. I sat by her bedside a lot, listening
to her talk. We grew very close during that time. All her
talking was of the distant past; memories of her childhood in Utica, of her mother, who had died of cancer, of
her pets; of her first boyfriend and how they had lain
together in the woods with their heads touching, and
how, when she missed her period soon after, she
thought she was pregnant from lying with him like that.
And she talked a lot about Jim, especially about the
year they lived in Frenchtown, New Jersey, together
with two goats and a lot of mice; how she cut Jim's hair
a few days after they moved in, and tied a blue ribbon
around a bunch of hair on top of his head, without his
knowing it, and just at that moment the doorbell rang
and Jim went to see who it was, and it was some ladies
from the church come to invite them to join the congre-
gation, and Jim stood nodding before their astonished
faces with that ribbon bouncing on his head; how they
took in an old tramp named Walter Clark, who sat rocking on the front porch all day with such an awesome
look of peace or completeness or wonder, it was hard to
find a word for it; how, when they had to leave Frenchtown, Alma was afraid for the mice, who had become
tame and would surely be killed by the next person to
live there; so she got a special "catch-'em-alive" trap
and she and Jim helped the somewhat overfed mice
squeeze through the door into the cage, and then Alma
sat next to the incredulous driver in the moving van,
holding that cage full of mice on her lap; and as soon as
the furniture was set up in the new place, she let the
mice loose . . . Talking like this was a drug that helped
her drift into the past, to the happiest days of her life.
There were moments when she seemed so far removed,

the smile on her face so wan and placid, her hand in my hand so dry, cool, and tensionless, that I was afraid she might be dying.

Alma and I had agreed not to discuss our plans with anyone until we were ready to leave, but I couldn't restrain myself. One day at Peter's house I popped out with the news: "I probably won't be able to stay here much longer." "Why not? Where are you going?" "To America." Then I told him the whole story in detail.

He was upset and said he was very sorry I was leaving. He didn't blame Alma, nor did Bodo's behavior surprise him. "The whole generation is like that," he said. "All the old Communists are turning into petits bourgeois. Look at my father, it's really a very similar case. He and my mother were Comrades before the war, and had to separate for years because of the political work they had to do. Imagine how dedicated you'd have to be! After the war they got together again. They were Communists! Now he's fifty, and he gets rid of my mother so he can live with someone young and pretty. He was a hero in the French Resistance—you know about that—and in Spain, too—and now he's wrapped himself up in office work and domesticity. His only concerns seem to be his child, his plants, and the latest cultural gossip. And it's not just age that did it. The minute the war was over, the moment our fathers came back from exile, they stopped being artists and fighters and turned into anxious, obsequious little officials."

Most of my parents' friends sided with Alma against Bodo. Frau Meissner had a reputation (whether deserved or not, I don't know) for having affairs, getting pregnant, and putting the babies in an orphanage. Had she been more respected, our friends might have acknowledged her rights as Alma's rival, and Bodo's rights as a lover. It seemed to me, at the time, that there was no one in the German Democratic Republic, excepting Frau Meissner, who didn't disapprove of Bodo; though

since then I've been told that Valentin Birkelbach was
very supportive of him, and that others were, too, in
lesser degree. I'll put it this way; the disapproval was
near-universal. Even the Party, which, one would think,
could have afforded to keep an impersonal distance,
took a critical position. I, too, began to blame him—
partly, I'm afraid, out of opportunism. America was just
around the corner, and a reconciliation would have removed this marvelous escape hatch. It was easy to fall
in with the general consensus; even Bodo seemed to
agree, since he didn't defend himself. He seemed to value
nothing—not Alma, or me, or Stefan, or even his own
dignity—so much as he valued Frau Meissner. He had
surrounded himself with mementos of her. They were
everywhere—in his pockets, on his desk, under his pillow:
feathers from Hiddensee, little knickknacks she had given
him, wilted roses, photographs, a lock of hair . . .

An old school friend of Bodo's named Hans, who
lived in Hamburg, came to Berlin to assist us (probably
at Bodo's bidding) in packing hundreds of household
articles and sending them by rail to Bremen, where they
would be loaded on the ship that would take us to New
York. He was a thin, red-haired man with a dour busi-
ness-like air about him. I think he was a clerk in a ship-
ping office, or perhaps one of the managers. He was not
an intellectual. I had the feeling Bodo looked less unhappy, soberer, not so stooped and disheveled when he
was with Hans. They walked together in the garden,
gravely talking in subdued voices, holding their hands
behind their backs.

The day before we left, Bodo received a phone call
from Luise Meissner. She said she needed to see him
immediately—she was just two blocks away, in the Café
für Dich. He started to put on his coat. Alma said: "You
have to see her *now?* It can't wait till after we leave?"

"She told me it's urgent," Bodo said. "I have to go. I'll
be back soon."

"Don't you have any decency? This is my last day

here. You can see her all you want after tomorrow."
"I can't just leave her standing there. She came all the
way out here . . . *Oh, I can't bear it any longer!*" And he
left the room, slamming the door. Alma and I could
hear the bedroom door slamming, too. After a few minutes, Alma followed him. Bodo was sitting on the bed
shaking sleeping pills out of a bottle into his hand. He
gave her a wild challenging stare.

"You don't have the courage," Alma said, and turned
her back on him and left the room, and rejoined me
where I was sitting, next to the yellow tile stove in the
living room. A few moments later, the door opened and
Bodo stuck his head in. "Goodbye!" he shouted at both
of us, with a terrible look in his eyes. Then he left the
house.

We got a call from the Charité hospital the next
morning—the morning of the day we left. Bodo had
walked to the Café für Dich and collapsed on the street
in front of Luise. She called an ambulance. The doctors
at the hospital pumped his stomach. The nurse on the
phone said he had taken a large dose of sleeping pills,
but he was all right now. He had a message to convey.
He wanted Joel to visit him.

Everyone advised me not to go. Things were hard
enough for me, they said. No, no, it was best I stay
away from him. And it might complicate everything if I
went. What if he asked me to stay? "He'll be all right.
Hans is with him." It was easy not to go, much easier
than to obey the prompting of my troubled conscience:
he needed me, he had said so: I would hurt him by
staying away. I pushed these thoughts aside. As I said,
it was easy, with so much support. But ever since Bodo
died, not quite two years later, the memory of that decision grieves me; for I never saw him again.

Later that same morning, Frau Meissner called. She
urged Alma not to leave the country, and begged to
have a meeting with her. She promised to separate from
Bodo, and declared herself willing to consider any con-

ditions Alma might make. But it was too late. Not that
our steamship tickets couldn't be reclaimed or the lug-
gage shipped back from Bremen or Stefan returned
from the States; but something more compelling than
Frau Meissner's assurances was needed to brake the
momentum of Alma's decision, sprung as it was from
months of unremitting discord.

I don't remember feeling much during the hour or
two of our final departure. Instead, I remember pictures. By riffling through them quickly, one after the
other, I get a semblance of motion. The first picture is
of Alma and me in the train at Bahnhof Friedrichstrasse.
We are leaning out the window, arms touching. Everything is gray outside: the long platform, the high walls
of the station, the clocks, the stationmaster's little
house. Even the billboards are gray. Maybe this monot-
ony is a trick of memory, because, just as improbably,
the only people on the platform seem to be those who
have come to see us off, about twenty people. One of
them is Ralle; the rest are either friends of Alma's or
prominent members of the Intelligenz who have come
to register the Party's position on Bodo's behavior.
Being highly educated, they know how to blunt the
edge of sorrow with a little irony, a little philosophical
humor. They skip and flap their arms, ostensibly to
keep themselves warm. Ralle stands a little apart, with
his hands buried in the pockets of a black trenchcoat he
has recently stolen. What time of day is it? It can't be
morning, but there's something dawn-like in the atmosphere. Maybe the sky is overcast. A pigeon has strayed
into the station, sails about in the big hall, frightened by
sudden clanks and hisses and jets of steam. Alma has
rouged her cheeks more brightly than usual. She's smiling, nodding, saying a few words. Her friends take turns
keeping the talk flowing. Ralle and I hardly talk at all—
just some promises to keep in touch, good-luck wishes.
Peter Vogel's mother says to me: "Joel, I hope you real-

ize what an enviable opportunity this is for you." I nod and smile in full agreement. "In a few years," she adds, "you will have gotten to know capitalism at first hand, not just theoretically. And with your experience of life in a socialist country, you'll be in a position to become a very fine Marxist indeed." I mumblingly thank her for this undeserved vote of confidence. Now the whistle blows, the stationmaster holds up his baton, the train jerks into motion, and a moment later the little group of waving figures is abruptly yanked around a curve and into the past.